HUMAN RESOURCES
MANAGEMENT

HUMAN RESOURCES MANAGEMENT

THE COMPLETE GUIDEBOOK FOR DESIGN FIRMS

Mark C. Zweig

Mark Zweig & Associates
Natick, Massachusetts

A WILEY-INTERSCIENCE PUBLICATION

JOHN WILEY & SONS, INC.

New York / Chichester / Brisbane / Toronto / Singapore

Library of Congress Cataloging in Publication Data:
Zweig, Mark C.
    Human Resources Management: The Complete Guidebook for Design Firms
    Mark C. Zweig.
        "A Wiley-Interscience publication."
        Includes bibliographical references.
        1. Personnel management–United States. 2. Architectural firms–
United States–Personnel management. 3. Engineering firms–Unites States–
Personnel management. 4. Design services–Unites States–Personnel
management. I. Title.
        Title and series added entries

| HF5549.5.U5z87 1991 | 720'.68'3–dc20 | 90-47917 |
| ISBN 0-471-63374-7 | CIP | |

Printed in the United States of America

10 9 8 7 6 5 4 3 2 1

CONTENTS

FOREWORD

The importance of human resource management in an A/E/P firm has come to be appreciated as being of enormous consequence. The reason is very simple and straightforward: A/E/P firms produce advice that can be given only by people. These people must be properly motivated, feel they are being dealt with fairly, and have a sense that they are achieving all that can be achieved as measured by their own high expectations.

Most managers of A/E/P firms have unfortunately tried to emulate the type of management that has dominated American industry, that being the vertical organization with authoritative as opposed to participative management. The emergence of the Japanese in the American marketplace over the last decade, however, has made A/E/P firms in this country aware of the necessity to employ proven human resource development and management practices to achieve company goals.

Mark Zweig, in his background of recruitment specifically for the A/E/P industry, followed by his years of involvement in human resources management and consulting, is a leader in advancing the human resources management and development practices so necessary in today's business environment.

IRVING N. WEISS, P.E.

President
The Pickering Firm, Inc.
Memphis, Tennessee

PREFACE

A key in itself isn't worth anything—but the knowledge of where it fits might be worth a great deal.

—Frederick D. White

I have been fortunate enough to work my entire postgraduate career as either employee of or consultant to design (A/E/P) firms, and I have learned a great deal from that experience. I consider myself extremely lucky to have worked with people who, by and large, are the most honest, ethical, and well-intentioned souls imaginable.

There's no other industry that offers a greater opportunity for intellectual and creative stimulation and personal development. Design firms perform a truly worthwhile function in our society. Yet design firms across the country have always had problems attracting, developing, and retaining staff with the same values and work ethic as their founding principals.

With this mountain of good intentions, and with all of that brain power, it's easy to wonder why we, as an industry, have such a problem. People should be clamoring to come to work for us. In theory, our work is intrinsically so satisfying that there should never be any shortage of people, and certainly no discontent.

That is why I am writing this book. The whole subject of human resources management probably offers more opportunity to improve our firms' productivity and performance than any other area. Yet, when compared to the multitude of books available on quality control, project management, financial management, and marketing management for the design professions, very little information exists on the subject of human resources management aimed specifically at design firms. I want to impart what I have learned in my years of experience dealing with a diverse cross section of design firms about the mystery of how to get the best people, turn them on, and keep them working for us.

And, although there are many mysteries left to be solved in the areas of managing organizations and predicting human behavior, there *is* a body of knowledge on these subjects just as there is on how to design an HVAC system, size a sewer line, or plan a hotel.

It is precisely this fact that most architects, planners, engineers, and interior designers have such difficulty understanding. Too often we regard the disciplines we have been educated in as the only *real* science, and we simply "fly by the seat of our pants" in all other areas. Even though there's more to be learned on the subject of human resources management, I don't want to discount the value of common sense or deliberately shroud the subject in mystery and needless complexity. Too many so-called experts on management subjects for design firms today use that technique to bolster their own poor self-images.

People frequently ask me, why is the design business any different from other businesses? Every firm employs people. The best answer I can give is twofold.

First, it's a well-accepted notion that design professionals consider themselves different from other people. They feel that what works in other settings may fail in design firms because the people and demands of the profession are "different."

Second, because a design firm sells time, expertise, and advice, human resources management may, in fact, be more critical than in other organizations. Because the people who staff design firms are by and large an educated and intelligent group, they may be more in tune with their work and less likely to remain in an unsatisfactory environment. But more on that in the book.

My travels and experiences lead me to believe that too many people running design firms today have the wrong priorities. Managers spend too much time solving problems that would take care of themselves if higher-order issues were dealt with first. Instead of defining the firm's mission, determining strategy, and agreeing on common goals, they worry about complex and futile project management and quality control systems; or they institute marketing programs requiring technical people to function in roles they are completely unequipped to handle; or they hire and fire people on an unplanned basis; or they open new offices and close them; or they purchase, install, and scrap new software systems; or they define new organizational structures that are soon abandoned.

No one would argue that people are the key to solving all our problems. Yet how many firms in this industry will spend the money necessary to get full-time professionals in marketing and financial management roles, but won't hire or appoint anyone to devote full-time attention to human resources management? And how many firms in this industry have spent the time (and money) required to develop a hiring process that delivers a consistent quality of staff? Not nearly enough.

Why is that the case? Are we simply following what everyone else in our industry does, the established traditions and practices? Isn't human resources management every bit as important as accounting, or administration, or marketing?

If I haven't convinced you by the end of this text that improvements in human resources management may be the last great frontier and opportunity for finding the proverbial "greener pastures," then I've failed in my role as a communicator of the human resources management gospel.

One last thought: human resources management is not a panacea, nor will effective human resources management be a quick fix for all your firm's ills. Most firms don't have just a single problem undermining their human resources management efforts, but instead have a multitude of smaller issues that need resolution. It will take time to institute change and see results. So, when you close this book, don't waste any time getting started.

Read on.

Mark C. Zweig

Natick, Massachusetts
March 1991

ACKNOWLEDGMENTS

I want to thank the many people who helped me formulate my ideas on human resources management and who directly contributed to the effort it took to complete this book.

Irving Weiss of Pickering in Memphis, Tennessee, was the first person I ran into in this industry, who, after he completed the Executive MBA Program at Memphis State, took the whole idea of human resources management seriously and tried out some innovative concepts.

Jerry Allen, president of Carter & Burgess in Fort Worth and a close personal friend, taught me in a mentor's role the importance of how to influence others as well as patience with the process of implementing change in a larger firm.

Michael Latas, President of Michael Latas & Associates in St. Louis, first introduced me to the design profession and gave me an education in recruiting that I will always be thankful for.

Frederick and Evelyn Zweig, my parents, have always encouraged me to follow my heart and do what I was capable of.

Frederick White, my partner in the business and close friend, is a super writer and editor who made many contributions to this text and kept the job-chargeable work going at MZ&A while I was writing.

Susan Zweig, my wife of 8 years and my best friend and supporter for 14 years, pushed me into self-employment and with love and tenderness takes care of me and everything else in my life, including my beautiful daughter Christina, so I can spend whatever time it takes to accomplish my work.

To these individuals I owe many thanks.

HUMAN RESOURCES
MANAGEMENT

1

INTRODUCTION

"A company is known by the people it keeps."

—Anonymous

1.1 WHAT IS HUMAN RESOURCES MANAGEMENT?

Nowhere is the chapter-opening quotation more true than in a design (A/E/P) firm. Because design firms directly sell the individual and collective skills, abilities, and attributes of their staff members, the value of human resources (HR) management would seem to be obvious. One would think that all design firms would have well-tuned HR management programs. Yet anyone who has ever worked in an A/E/P firm could tell you that just isn't the case.

There are four functional areas of management that any business must concern itself with. These are financial management, production management, marketing management, and HR management.

1. Financial management in an A/E/P firm is concerned with such issues as supplying adequate capital to ensure ongoing operations, cash flow maximization, and return on investment for the firm's ownership.

2. Production management deals with issues related to how the firm produces its products or services. Production management in an A/E/P firm is concerned with design processes, utilization rates, quality control, work scheduling, and so on.

3. Marketing management determines what is sold to whom, at what price, and where. Marketing management in a design firm deals with issues such as making the go/no-go decision on any particular project, marketing materials, or presentation strategies.

4. HR management in a design firm has three primary functions: acquiring human resources, developing human resources, and maintaining human resources—in other words, staff recruitment, retention, and development. A fourth function has recently been added to these: minimization of employment-related liability issues. Liability issues are becoming a greater and greater concern to design firms, as all management activities today have potential liability implications.

Now to look more closely at the specific human resource management functions in the four primary classifications. But first beware: the following summary isn't a comprehensive laundry list of HR management concerns; rather, it is intended to serve as an overview of the topic. Every one of these points will be discussed in later chapters.

Recruitment

1. Developing a method for determining whether or not the company needs to recruit additional staff

2. Developing and maintaining the firm's hiring process in an effort to achieve consistent quality in hiring

3. Establishing a clearly articulated recruitment philosophy for the firm, including the company's posture toward recruiting, whether or not the firm adds staff in a shrinking market, what kinds of people and personalities the firm looks for, and so on

4. Establishing interviewing techniques and processes used by the firm when hiring new staff (including packaging and selling the company and the immediate geographic area to prospective employees)

5. Making offers of employment, including setting starting salaries, determining how to extend the offer, what to do for relocation, and closing the deal with an offer acceptance

6. Developing guidelines for college recruitment, including matters such as whether the firm hires new graduates, what the hiring criteria for new grads are, and what schools are recruited from

7. Articulating the firm's posture toward dealing with employment agencies and executive search firms, including determining if and when they are used, at what position levels, what kind of fees are paid, and what firms the company uses

8. Designing and implementing co-op programs for different areas of the firm, including structuring the entire co-op recruitment process, developing co-op assignments, establishing benefits and other policy issues for co-ops, and setting pay

9. Use of contract employees/job shoppers, including development of resources that provide consistent quality in temporary employees at all levels where it is

practical to do so, setting compensation for contract staff, and determining internal pricing policies that don't discourage the use of contract labor by project and department managers when it's in the firm's best interests

Staff Development

1. Designing and administering the firm's orientation program for all new employees
2. Developing the firm's philosophy and practice in the area of promoting people from inside the company to fill management and other more senior level positions as they develop
3. Creating the firm's organizational structure, including reporting relationships, specific job descriptions, and formalized career paths that individuals can follow
4. Providing firm-sponsored training including seminars, in-house courses, on-the-job training, co-op programs, self-instruction programs and materials, and tuition reimbursement programs
5. Developing the firm's performance appraisal system as well as other performance feedback systems and processes for employees
6. Developing the process for establishing mutually acceptable goals and objectives for all employees, and the monitoring and feedback process for tracking the accomplishment of those goals
7. Instituting reward systems and practices that communicate to employees what behavior is valued and what it takes to "get ahead" in the organization

Staff Retention

1. Monitoring and improving the effectiveness of the company's recruitment and development programs in getting people with realistic expectations and a clear understanding of their roles appropriately placed in the organization
2. Streamlining the firm's processes for providing two-way communication between management and all other levels of staff
3. Developing the firm's compensation and benefits programs, policies, and practices, including bonus and incentive compensation plans; frequency and method for determining base salary or hourly rate adjustments and distribution of wage data within the firm; health, welfare, and retirement benefits; and other perquisites granted to employees
4. Eliminating the demotivating factors that drive people out of the company
5. Developing the company's personnel policies and procedures, including both their content and how they are communicated to staff members
6. Establishing, articulating, and regularly reinforcing the firm's mission and the values of its leaders

Minimizing Employment-related Liability Exposure

1. Developing a hiring process that does not illegally discriminate against any member of a protected job group or inadvertently obligate the firm to a longer or different employment obligation than originally intended, including development of the firm's process and practice of maintaining all necessary records to protect the company in a suit alleging either of the above

2. Training managers to minimize employment-related liability exposure in how they conduct their daily activities by sensitizing them to the issues and obligations related to employment law

3. Establishing and maintaining fair, equitable, and nondiscriminatory promotion practices, and keeping of the all necessary documentation to prove it

4. Rewarding real on-the-job performance and value to the firm, and being able to prove differences in the performance levels of any two or more employees

5. Developing good in-house communication networks and channels so that management has early warning of potential employment-related liability problems

6. Developing and administering clear, concise, common-sense policies and procedures, that are consistently adhered to

7. Developing and maintaining sound, written affirmative action plans— one for minorities and women, and one for the handicapped and special disabled/Vietnam-era veterans—both of which should be defendable in a compliance audit from the Department of Labor (DOL), Equal Employment Opportunity Commission (EEOC), Office of Federal Contract Compliance Programs (OFCCP), or various other state or local government agencies who scrutinize them

8. Following all relevant federal, state, and local laws in conducting business and dealing with employees in each of the firm's business locations

9. Developing a sound termination process that does not discriminate against any protected group, and maintaining all necessary records to prove it

10. Designing severance, outplacement, and other terminated-employee benefits to reduce the probability of former employee lawsuits, maintain the firm's image in the community, and reduce the time of unemployment for anyone terminated

11. Developing the firm's reference-checking and reference-providing policies and practices

HR management is indeed a broad and important concern of any company in the A/E/P business. Whether or not an individual or department has been identified to deal with these issues, they exist and cannot be ignored.

1.2 HUMAN RESOURCES OR PERSONNEL?

The terms "human resources" and "personnel" are often used interchangeably, but they shouldn't be. Personnel is a subset of human resources, much the same way as sales is a subset of marketing. Personnel is more concerned with administrative issues such as record keeping and benefits—just a fraction of all that concerns HR management. Further evidence of these important differences is the recent name change of The American Society for Personnel Administration (ASPA) to Society for Human Resource Management (SHRM).

The personnel function in a design firm has traditionally been one component of the finance and administration wing, which structurally limits its prominence. Human resources, however, is more likely to report directly to the company CEO/president and should theoretically have equal importance with the other three functional management heads—marketing, production, and finance. Personnel reports to the HR director in firms that have one.

That's not to say that HR management cannot report through the finance and administration component in a firm and still work well. There are several design firms where such a situation exists and the firm's human resource management efforts are adequately supported and quite successful. However, the reason for these exceptions lies in the fact that the finance and administration director has a major interest in and understanding of HR management, and is simply filling a dual role because the firm lacks other staff resources. It takes a rare person to manage both areas effectively. In one case where an enlightened individual ran both human resources and marketing for a 300-person firm, his performance in both areas suffered.

1.3 HUMAN RELATIONS OR HUMAN RESOURCES?

In spite of some firms' financial success, most managers and owners running design practices today do not understand what HR management is. They tend to see it as "icing on the cake," something that can be trimmed from the firm's operating budget, just like a project's landscaping budget might be cut. Much of this confusion lies in misunderstanding the terms "human relations" and "human resources."

This is a pet peeve of many design firm human resources professionals. They hate being introduced by a firm principal to others outside the organization as the company's "human relations" person. Unfortunately, this misunderstanding is keeping far too many A/E/P firms out of the serious business of HR management.

The human relations approach to management advocates better treatment of subordinates in the belief that it will lead to greater productivity. This is based on the assumption that contented employees with high morale will work harder. And, indeed, common sense dictates that a terribly unhappy staffer won't perform at peak productivity. However, experiments going back as far as the Hawthorne studies in 1927 have time and again refuted the link between contentment and job

Human Relations: High morale means high productivity.

Human Resources: Management's role is to maximize productivity of people.

FIGURE 1.1   Human relations versus human resources

performance. In fact, some experts in motivation maintain that only dissatisfaction motivates people (more on this in Chapter 5).

The human resources approach to management and motivation is completely different. Advocates of this school of management believe it is their obligation to maximize the productivity of their firm's human resources. They pay particular attention to their recruitment and reward strategies, streamline decision making, and demand higher performance. The human resources school does not subordinate the organization's goals to those of the individuals working in the organization.

Human relations advocates are constantly developing more giveaway programs that increase overhead and arouse the insatiable appetite of the firm's workforce. They design compensation and reward systems (such as across-the-board salary adjustments) that bolster the low performers at the expense of the high performers. The human relations advocates do these things in the name of being nice to people and acting in a socially responsible manner. But is it "socially responsible" to contribute to the unrealistic expectations of many employees to get more and more for doing less and less? Or is it "responsible" to erode the firm's competitiveness and productivity in the name of good human relations?

The answer to both questions is an emphatic "no." Human resource maximizers are not afraid to reward performance. They realize that the competitive marketplace is a "zero sum" game (that is, somebody has to lose), that the market for services is only so great, and that they are in a competitive struggle whether they want to be or not. The HR managers emphasize fairness for everyone and high rewards for those most deserving. They foster loyalty in their workforce by refusing to tolerate a double standard for management and employees, and they avoid demotivating their highest performers by clearly recognizing and rewarding their contributions.

This is not to say that human relations is not part of effective HR management—it is. The danger lies in overemphasizing human relations issues to the point where the human relations view compromises HR management.

1.4   WHY GOOD HR MANAGEMENT IS GOOD BUSINESS

There's no better way to sell managers on a new idea than to appeal to them rationally and economically. Although it's not always possible to justify what you propose economically, it could probably be done far more often than most people realize. And there really are some tangible economic benefits to effective HR management in an A/E/P firm. Those economic benefits fall into one of two categories—indirect benefits and immediate benefits.

Indirect benefits to the firm arise from not being punished for some misdeed. These misdeeds and their penalties include firing someone for the wrong reasons and then getting slapped with a lawsuit; violating the Fair Labor Standards Act by not paying people properly, then getting stuck with a back wages and punitive damages judgment; or having one of your managers make unwelcome sexual advances to an employee, thus getting the firm stuck with a million-dollar sexual harassment suit. Good HR management provides tangible economic benefits to the firm by minimizing the likelihood of these events.

Immediate benefits have a direct effect on improving the bottom line of the company. Immediate benefits include fee savings resulting from doing all recruiting with in-house resources instead of using executive search firms and cost savings resulting from restructuring the employee benefit program. The really big immediate benefits are a little tougher to quantify but are nevertheless quite real. These include the benefits of selecting better new staff members each time a position is open and the higher work quality resulting from a low-turnover workforce.

Here are some more justifications for good HR management:

1. Between 1986 and 1988, jury verdicts in wrongful discharge cases averaged $602,000.

2. Design firms are in the business of selling labor and are therefore only as good as their people.

3. About 15 percent of the women in U.S. companies say they've been sexually harassed on the job in the past year.

4. Labor is always an A/E/P firm's greatest single expense.

5. The competition for experienced staff has never been greater than it was in the 1980s, and it will undoubtedly get worse in the 1990s.

6. About 15 percent of workers age 51 and older in Fortune 500 companies say they've been discriminated against because of age.

7. The mean annual turnover rate in A/E/P firms is 22.6 percent, and the average cost to replace just one professional is over $6,000.

8. The average cost to relocate a home-owning employee is over $30,000, and the average to relocate a renter is $9000.

9. Health benefit costs are skyrocketing, with some firm's premiums increasing by 50 percent to 100 percent per year.

10. Half of the companies who fire anyone for any reason at all are sued.

11. Low inflation is resulting in smaller raise budgets (typically 5 to 7 percent) than firms may have had in previous years.

12. Technical skills alone won't cut it any more. Client and liability considerations dictate that technical staffers must have good communication skills.

It should be apparent by now that good HR management both saves and makes money!

1.5 HR MISSION AND STRATEGY

Whatever the pursuit, there won't be much accomplished if no goals are set. But before you can set goals for your HR management program, you need to decide on an HR management mission and get everyone to agree to it. Management staff should not be left wondering why HR management is important because if they don't join it, they're going to try to beat it.

The HR mission should provide a focus, a rallying point, for all HR management programs and processes. Everything you set out to accomplish should support the intent of your mission. Your mission is the first part of the who, what, when, where, and why of the HR management process.

To avoid any misinterpretation, the mission should be short, direct, and clearly stated. Here is a sample mission:

> To ensure that the owners of XYZ Associates get maximum value from their human resources through implementation of effective strategies in the areas of employee recruitment, development, retention, and minimizing liability exposure.

Next, decide on the basic strategies you will follow to accomplish your mission. The strategies should be specific actions you will take or courses you will follow in your day-to-day activities that will further your mission.

Here are some sample strategies. Keep in mind that these are by no means intended to be all-inclusive, nor are they meant to be indicative of your actual priorities.

1. Centralize all hiring activities through the headquarters office to concentrate expertise in hiring and achieve consistency.
2. Hire only candidates with excellent academic records (3.0 or above GPA) and outstanding verbal and written communication skills.
3. Develop a companywide co-op program for ABC Associates that provides a progressive experience and retains the brightest students as full-time employees upon graduation.
4. Eliminate demotivators wherever possible.
5. Minimize employment advertising, agency, and executive search firm expenses by focusing on effective in-house recruitment.
6. Minimize the voluntary turnover rate by effective hiring, development, and reward practices.
7. Make it possible for top performers to earn significantly more than those in comparable positions at other firms.
8. Use effective internal and external public relations campaigns to promote the idea that ABC Associates is the best possible interior design firm in the Pacific Northwest to work for.
9. Treat all employees fairly, following the principles of the "human resources" management as opposed to the "human relations" school of thought.

10. Develop and administer performance appraisal and reward schemes that identify and provide recognition to the firm's highest performers in all job categories.

11. Continually look to upgrade staff capabilities by consistently recruiting for difficult-to-fill position types, even when no formal opening exists.

12. Develop and maintain a meaningful career development process that identifies long-term goals and potential obstacles for each employee in the company.

13. Develop a comprehensive training program for all employees at all levels, with specific training aimed at building the skills necessary to fulfill the duties and responsibilities of each position in the firm.

1.6 GOALS AND STATISTICS

The next step in the process is to set some very specific goals for your HR management efforts. This is tough for many firms because, in most cases, they don't have any historical data to use as benchmarks for how they are currently doing.

As a bare minimum, performance statistics should be maintained in each of the following areas:

Turnover: How often each position in the firm, branch, department, or job category is filled with someone new over the course of the time period specified. Performance statistics should be kept on professional, technical, and support turnover and on department-by-department, office-by-office, and firmwide turnover. They should be reported on a current month, year-to-date, and annual projected basis each month.

Staff Numbers: The number of people who work in the firm, branch, department, or job category. Numbers should be kept on a professional, technical, support, department-by-department, office-by-office, and firm wide basis. They should be reported on a current month, year-to-date, and annual projected basis each month.

Utilization rates: The percentage of staff time charged to billable projects. Utilization rate performance statistics should be kept on a professional, technical, and support, department-by-department, office-by-office, and firmwide basis. They should be reported on a current month, year-to-date, and annual projected basis each month.

Number of positions open: The number and type of positions open in the firm. This list should be updated and posted weekly, with positions open and positions filled reported on a current basis each month.

Agency/search firm fees: The total dollar amount paid out to employment agencies and search firms. This should be reported month and should include data on the current month, year-to-date, and annual projection compared to budget.

1. Turnover
   a. Forced
   b. Voluntary
2. Staff numbers
3. Utilization rates
4. Number of positions open
5. Agency/search firm fees
6. Employment advertising expenditures
7. Relocation expenditures
8. Interview/offer ratio
9. Offer/acceptance ratio

FIGURE 1.2 HR goals

Employment advertising expenditures: The total dollar amount paid out for employment advertising. This should be reported monthly and should include data on the current month, year-to-date, and annual projection compared to budget.

Employee relocation expenditures: The total dollar amount paid out by the firm to relocate new employees. This should be reported monthly and should include data on the current month, year-to-date, and annual projection compared to budget.

	Industry Norms	*What Can Be Achieved*
1. Turnover (total)	20–22%	<10%
Forced	10–15%	5%
Voluntary	5–10%+	5%
2. Utilization rates		
Company (total)	62–65%	70%+
Branch office	70%	75%+
Technical department	75–85%	85%+
3. Number of positions open	N.A.	<than 5% of total staff
4. Agency/search fees	N.A.	$0
5. Employment advertising	N.A.	0.11–0.15% of total revenue
6. Relocation expenses	N.A.	<$2000 per head hired
7. Interview/offer ratio	6–10 : 1	3–4 : 1
8. Offer/hire percentage	<50%	80–90%

Note: These numbers are based on the author's experience and may vary depending on firm type, size, disciplines, and geographical location.

FIGURE 1.3 HR performance statistics

Interview/offer ratio: The number of candidates the firm interviews for a position before extending an offer. This statistic should be kept on a current month and year-to-date basis and reported monthly.

Offer/acceptance ratio: The number of offers for employment the firm formally extends compared with the number of acceptances received.

1.7 THE HR ACTION PLAN

After you've adopted your HR management mission, determined your strategies to accomplish the mission, and set some concrete goals to achieve in the human resources area, you need to develop what is referred to as the HR Action Plan.

The HR Action Plan is where you develop the implementation process for everything you've decided so far. It should very clearly spell out what you plan to do, how it will be done, who will do it, and when they will do it. Each element in the plan should be carefully phrased. Here are sample items from one hypothetical plan:

1. Design and implement a value-based wage and salary review process. John Jones to handle. Submit to executive committee for approval by 10/15/90. Review and approve. Modify and implement by 12/1/90.

2. Design and implement a career development meeting program for all employees. John Jones to handle. Submit to executive committee for review and approval by 12/1/90. Modify and implement by 1/15/91.

3. Design and implement a new performance appraisal system for all employees. John Jones and Paul Smith to handle. Submit to executive committee for review and approval by 1/4/91. Modify and implement by 3/1/91.

4. Explore company health insurance benefit alternatives. John Jones to handle. Submit to insurance committee for review and approval by 3/1/91. Implement changes, if any, and communicate to all employees in all offices by 5/1/91.

5. Develop job descriptions for all positions in the firm. John Jones to handle. Submit to branch/department managers for comments by 4/1/91. Submit modified/updated descriptions to executive committee for review and approval by 6/1/91. Distribute semi-final job descriptions to all employees by 8/1/91. Gather employee comments and feedback by 8/15/91. Resolve differences through executive committee by 9/15/91. Distribute final job descriptions to all employees by 10/1/91.

6. Establish a company wide co-op program for civil engineers. John Jones to handle with participation from survey, structural engineering, construction services, and civil engineering department heads. Submit to executive committee for approval by 7/1/91. Implement by 8/15/91.

7. Update company policy manual to reflect current personnel policies and procedures and minimize potential employment-related liability. John Jones to handle. Submit to CEO by 7/15/91. Submit amended version to legal

Monthly Human Resources Report (December 1989)

I. Employment

	Boston	New Hampshire	Rhode Island	Florida	Overall
Professional	55	45	48	5	153
Technical	30	20	18	2	70
Administrative	15	10	8	2	35
Total	100	75	74	9	258

II. Turnover

	Current Month		Year-to-Date		Annualized Projection	
	Forced	Voluntary	Forced	Voluntary	Forced	Voluntary
Professional	–	0.5%	4.2%	5.9%	4.6%	6.4%
Technical	–	0.5%	5.9%	7.5%	6.4%	8.2%
Administrative	–	–	4.1%	9.9%	4.5%	10.8%
Boston	–	1.0%	3.2%	8.2%	3.5%	8.9%
New Hampshire	–	0.6%	5.9%	7.2%	6.4%	7.9%
Rhode Island	–	0.2%	6.3%	7.8%	6.9%	8.5%
Florida	–	–	10.1%	12.8%	11.0%	14.0%
Overall	–	0.6%	4.8%	8.4%	5.2%	9.2%

III. Positions Open

	Boston	New Hampshire	Rhode Island	Florida	Overall
Positions open	12	3	0	2	17
Utilization rate	72%	75%	68%	84%	75%

IV. Hiring Process

	Month	Year-to-Date
# of interviews/# of offers ratio	5:1	2.5:1
# offer acceptances/# offers ratio	3:4	3:4
Employment agency or search fees paid	–	$20,000
Relocation $ paid	$6,000	$31,883
Recruitment/signing bonuses paid to employees	–	$10,000
Employment advertising paid	$ 550	$16,000

FIGURE 1.4   Monthly HR report

Applicant Flow Log

OFFICE: _____

NAME	POSITION APPLIED FOR	SEX (M/F)	RACE/ORIGIN (W, B, A, AI, H)	HANDICAP (Y or N)	VEV (Y or N)

FIGURE 1.5 Applicant flow log

counsel by 8/15/91. Submit amended version to executive committee by 10/1/91. Formally adopt and provide copy to each employee by 1/1/92.

8. Develop a 5–10 minute corporate recruitment video. Sally Smith to handle with participation from John Jones. Submit concepts to executive committee by 9/1/91. Executive committee to provide feedback by 9/15/91. Complete video by 12/1/91.

1.8 MONITORING THE PERFORMANCE OF HR MANAGEMENT EFFORTS

There are four main vehicles for monitoring the performance of your HR management efforts:

1. The HR statistics that you have been keeping monthly and reporting via some version of the monthly HR report
2. The number of employment-related lawsuits, investigations, or audits you are going through (hopefully, none!)
3. The number and significance of complaints coming in from managers regarding company policy issues, morale, staffing, and so on
4. The number and significance of complaints coming in from staff members regarding policies, compensation, management, and so on, as identified through formal suggestion box or career-development interview reporting (more on that in Chapter 8)

All these things should be tracked and reviewed by the company CEO on a regular schedule, with adjustments being made in the systems and processes as dictated by the feedback. Like anything else important to a firm's success, rigorous self-scrutiny of the area's performance measures leads to higher overall performance.

1.9 THE HR MANAGER IN TODAY'S A/E/P FIRM

In the mid to late 1980s, everybody in the A/E/P business started to think about their firms' HR management. Today, most companies of 75 or more employees have someone in the role of HR manager or HR director.

The development of the HR management function in most design firms has followed the same evolutionary pattern as the other management functions. Starting as a part-time role for one of the firm's staff members performing only the most rudimentary tasks, it eventually grew into a full-time position filled by an experienced, educated HR management professional.

Although the generally published rule of thumb is to have one HR staff member for each 75 to 100 people in the firm, some design firms get by with very little in the way of full-time human resources management staff. One 250-person, multidiscipline firm has only one person in the HR role, someone who is primarily concerned with personnel administration matters. They do, however, have a chief executive officer who has a sincere interest in the human resources management function. *He* effectively functions as the top human resources manager in the firm. And when he doesn't have the time or expertise to tackle a human resources management problem, the company has a specialized A/E/P industry HR consultant on annual retainer to help out. This set-up works quite well for them.

The role of the HR manager in a design firm is to guide the company's activities in the four functions of HR management—staff recruitment, staff development, staff retention, and minimizing employment-related liability exposure. The HR manager or director is a staff manager (not directly involved in the production, sale, or delivery of design services) with the primary role of assisting the company's line managers.

The role varies greatly from company to company. In some cases, the role is filled by one person, a jack-of-all-trades type with a generalist background. In the industry's largest companies, the HR manager or director manages a staff of specialized experts in the fields of compensation, EEO, benefits, recruitment, training, and so on.

However the role is filled, it's important that the HR manager be involved in planning at the highest level and participate in development of the company's strategic business plan. He or she should also play a major part in all hiring, promotion, and termination decisions. And finally, he or she should be fully capable of serving as an internal management consultant, something of an impartial advisor.

In any case, human resources management is not a stand-alone function that can be delegated to just one person in the company. *All* of a firm's top managers have to be concerned with it. The human resources manager cannot operate in a vacuum. The responsibility for effectively handling the function has to be shared. Not everyone in the company will understand what the HR role is from day one; these people will have to be influenced by the human resources manager.

What's really important in an HR manager is probably completely different from most people's thoughts. The critical qualities for a HR manager to have are, in order of significance, as follows:

1. *Selling skills.* These are needed for two reasons: (1) to be able to sell human resource management ideas to company management, and (2) to be able to convince both new and existing employees that the firm is a great place to work.
2. *Knowledge of the overall design "business."* It's common knowledge that architects, engineers and other design professionals don't believe anyone from outside this industry has much credibility when it comes to management advice. Right or wrong, a good knowledge of the overall A/E/P business will, at the least, make for a more efficient and effective recruiter. At best,

it makes for someone who has more sensitivity to management's big picture agenda and to staff issues and concerns.

3. *A willingness to work hard.* Not much ever gets done without a committed and hard working person pushing it. Being willing to work is also useful when it's 6:30 P.M., your spouse expected you home a half-hour ago, your dinner is getting cold, and you're still talking with a senior designer who can't figure out why he was once again passed over for a project management position.

4. *A broad-based knowledge of HR management and personnel law.* The HR manager doesn't need to know everything—but he or she does need to know just enough to know when the firm needs outside help.

Other qualities that help significantly in the HR management role are good listening skills, the ability to form relationships with a wide variety of different people, and superior verbal and written communication abilities.

This list may reflect the exact opposite of the priorities of your current HR manager (if you have one), or what you might have thought. Typically, technical knowledge is sought above all else, and sales ability rarely makes it to any list of formal selection criteria for an HR position.

On the critical qualities list, selling skills come first. Anyone wanting to initiate an HR management program will need the ability to sell the firm's principals on the economic benefits of HR management. Anything worth doing will have to be sold. Selling skills do not often arise in discussions of qualities necessary to the success of someone in a staff advisory role. They are, however, required for anyone wanting to challenge the status quo. And, in most design firm settings, good HR management practices *will* challenge the status quo.

What doesn't work well, and what far too many firms are saddled with, is an HR manager or director with a "reporting" mentality as opposed to a "results-affecting" mentality. These people view themselves as helpless. They may, in fact, be overloaded. Their idea is to get through the day with the least amount of trouble. They rarely initiate a new idea because any change represents more work for them in the short term. They are not boat-rockers. And, perhaps most importantly, they have serious difficulty when forced into a position where they need to defend management to someone in the rank and file. The reason for this is that they don't consider themselves anything but another employee who is "getting screwed by the company."

With this kind of negative attitude, your HR person has already lost every battle, not to mention given up on the war. If you have to make a change, consider keeping this person on in a role that is commensurate with his or her skills and personality. Some can be completely turned around with proper leadership and example. Perhaps they can function effectively as a personnel administrator. Most, however, need to be traded in for someone who feels that he or she, as an individual, can make a difference in the company.

HUMAN RESOURCES MANAGER

Reports to: President   Status: Exempt   Date: 7/31/86

Job Group No.:   1E   EEO-1:   Officials & Managers

I. General Description of Duties, Responsibilities, and Work Performed

Responsible for all human resources management functions for the firm, including recruiting, EEO compliance, career development, training, wage & salary administration, performance appraisal, and complaint resolution. Produces in-house company newsletter. Maintains all interviewing/off/hiring/termination records. Conducts career development meetings and produces written reports. Functions as in-house consultant on any organization/management issued where top management needs assistance. Sits on executive committee and wage and salary review committee. Develops and maintains written job descriptions for each position in the company. Develops recommendations for personnel policies and procedures. Supervises personnel manager and any administrative support staff assigned. Develops and administers budget for human resources management activities. Responsible for budget compliance. Maintains inventory of all positions open in the firm. Performs all other duties as assigned.

II. Qualification Requirements

A. *Experience:* Five years of broad-based experience in recruitment and other human resource functions, plus five years concurrent/other A/E/P industry experience.
B. *Education:* B.S. degree in business or psychology required. MBA highly desirable.
C. *Registration:* Not applicable.
D. *Knowledge, skills, abilities, and attributes:* Must have and outstanding ability to recruit and sell the company, excellent communication skills, and an ability to interact with different types of people. Must be able to listen well and take good notes. Must keep up with state-of-the-art in the human resources management field. Must have outstanding communications skills, both verbal and written. Must have an internal service orientation. Should be well-versed in A/E/P business.

III. Degree of Decision-Making Latitude

A. *Spending authority:* Can make expenditures within confines of human resources department budget.
B. *Contracting authority:* $150,000 for senior officers and $75,000 for officers. Human resources manager may or may not be an officer.
C. Can make employment commitments if approved by company president. Complies with company policies and acts in company's best interests at all times.

FIGURE 1.6   Sample human resources manager job description

1.10 THE PROBABILITIES INVOLVED IN EFFECTIVE HR MANAGEMENT

One necessity for truly effective human resources management is a clear understanding of certain probabilities and how they apply to the HR function. Effective human resources managers use their knowledge of probabilities every day. To do so, they must understand the following:

1. The probability that if someone is coming out of a similar role in a similar firm, he or she will likely have the basic technical competence to do the job.
2. The probabilities associated with hiring people who will have to be relocated, that the risk they won't last on the job is much higher than it is for those who won't have to be relocated.
3. The probability that if someone made poor grades in college, he or she will be more likely to fail in the job than another person who made good grades, all other factors being equal.
4. The probabilities associated with keeping inadequate personnel records—that you'll be likely to need them some day when you are under the scrutiny of the EEOC in an audit, or at the mercy of a judge and jury in an employee lawsuit.
5. The probabilities associated with making salary offers to currently employed people that aren't significantly better than they have now—that there is a greater likelihood the person won't accept your offer than if at least a 10 percent base pay increase is offered.
6. The probability that if you spend money training managers in managerial skills, you will have more effective managers.
7. The probability that if you actively solicit your employees' career concerns and aspirations, you will be more likely to be able to meet their needs and retain them over time.
8. The probability that if you restrict access to who makes how much in your firm, you'll be rewarded by having fewer employee complaints centered on the issue of pay.
9. The probability that if you reward performance and sanction non-performance, you'll have a more profitable company.

1.11 THIRTEEN RULES OF HR MANAGEMENT

If you don't get anything else out of this book, the following 13 rules of effective HR management may help guide your daily management decision making.

Rule No. 1 Develop a consistent hiring process and then stick with it religiously.

Rule No. 2   Wait until exactly what you want comes along before you extend an offer of employment. If the right person can't be found to fill a position, leave it open. Save your "bullets" for your ideal candidate.

Rule No. 3   Employment candidates with mediocre track records are unlikely to change. Look at a person's past accomplishments to predict what he or she will accomplish in the future.

Rule No. 4   Don't waste time and money training people and getting them acclimated to your firm who will never be able to move ahead to the next level. You can't afford to hire people who don't have the potential to advance to a higher level position beyond the one which they are entering. Either you'll end up firing them, or they'll be devastated and demoralized by being repeatedly passed over for promotion.

Rule No. 5   Listen 80 percent more than you talk when hearing out an employee with a problem. Nothing is worse than the supposed ombudsman who can't stop defending the company long enough to at least serve as a catharsis for a frustrated employee.

Rule No. 6   Don't wait for your formal performance appraisal or pay review time to deal with a problem employee. Do it now instead of later.

Rule No. 7   Promote from within whenever possible. Passing over existing staffers for a promotion almost always causes discontent. Hire and train the right people in the feeder positions so you don't have to go outside. Also, people who know the company and have established relationships with others are productive sooner than outsiders.

Rule No. 8   If you don't know the answer to a human resources problem, get help from a qualified outside expert. Not doing so can create major liability problems.

Rule No. 9   Don't have a double standard for yourself and your staff. Leadership by example is the most powerful kind. To advocate a new program and then not follow it yourself is a sure-fire way to ensure that no one else will, either.

Rule No. 10   Keep your management structure as flat as possible. The fewer layers communication has to flow through, the less distorted it will become. Also, the fewer stages employees have to advance to, the less concerned they will be with moving up in the hierarchy.

Rule No. 11   Immediately adopt a "no nepotism" policy if you don't already have one. Nepotism will demotivate the rest of your staff and may cause problems for the relatives who work in the organization.

Rule No. 12   Pay top performers substantially more than those whose performance is just adequate. Your best people will always have other options. Don't treat them poorly because everyone else hasn't performed as well as they have.

Rule No. 13   Don't concentrate on pay at the expense of the other critical human resource variables. This may seem to conflict with Rule No. 12, but it doesn't have to.

1.12 CONCLUSION

HR management can and should be an important function in any design firm, equal in prominence to marketing, production, or financial management. Yet rarely is that the case.

There is a great deal of confusion in most A/E/P firms as to what is meant by HR management. HR management is concerned with recruitment, development, and retention of staff, along with minimization of employment-related liability exposure. Proper development and management of the function pays for itself in the generation of short-term cost savings and longer-term opportunities for the firm.

2

RECRUITMENT

87 percent of all people in all professions are incompetent.

—John Gardner

2.1 INTRODUCTION

Every firm in the A/E/P industry complains about the difficulty of finding good people. There is a serious shortage of talent for most positions. It is estimated that firms spend an average of $6000 and 22 man-hours of labor for every person hired. When it comes to the long-term survival and prosperity of a design firm, there is no more important activity than recruitment. Design firms not systematically recruiting for their historically hardest-to-fill positions will be left behind by their more progressive competitors in the 1990s and beyond.

In simplest terms, *recruitment* is the set of activities a design firm uses to attract job candidates possessing the abilities and attitudes necessary for the enterprise to achieve its objectives. The recruitment process is a systematic, ongoing attempt to find qualified prospects for existing or potential openings in the organization.

2.2 RECRUITMENT PHILOSOPHY

There is one CEO of a 275-person, five-office, E/A/P firm who believes nothing is more important than recruiting. He puts his money where his mouth is by keeping a specialized, design-industry executive search firm on annual retainer just to look for certain types of staff. He drops whatever he is doing to meet with an employment prospect and interviews all applicants for each position personally.

A large international A/E firm had an unpublished practice of laying off the bottom-ranked 10 percent of its staff every year regardless of workload, forcing itself to improve. Interestingly enough, this firm has an HR manager in each of its offices and a corporate HR staff that includes someone responsible for company-wide training. This continued emphasis on recruiting and human resources has helped the firm to grow phenomenally over the last 10 years.

These forward-looking firms don't wait for somebody to turn in his or her notice to start recruiting for new staff. And this contrast between *strategic recruiting* and *ad hoc* recruiting illustrates differences in what is referred to as *recruitment philosophy*. Ad hoc recruiting is recruitment by crisis to fill an unplanned opening. It is not a consistent way to produce the best candidates. It is, however, the preferred method of most design practices today. Strategic recruiting is keeping an eye open at all times for people who would fit into each level or position in the organization, so that if a need does develop, it can be filled quickly with the best-qualified candidate. This type of recruiting produces the most consistent results.

How often have you learned of a highly desirable, experienced professional, only to have your competitor hire the person before you get off the dime? The best people have a habit of making themselves available when you're not looking, so you must be ready—even if existing staff members have to be cut in order to add someone better. For a firm to build a top quality staff, it must have feelers that allow it to learn about the best people as they become available, and then it must be prepared to act when the time is right.

This is what is meant by *recruitment philosophy*. The establishment of a recruit-ment philosophy for your firm is the first step in attracting the best job candidates. There has to be consensus at the top management level of the firm that recruitment is a priority activity that deserves constant attention—not just when there is a par-ticular position to fill. The firm should always be on the lookout for quality people and should always strive to upgrade its staff resources, regardless of whether there is a specific position to fill.

The recruitment philosophy extends well beyond merely placing importance on the recruiting process and having a continual interest in improving a firm's staff quality. It crosses over into sales and marketing. The firm's key principals and managers should constantly sell people on the idea that the company is a great place to work. There's an added benefit to this kind of enthusiasm for the company. When your owners and managers feel their firm is a great place to be, they become more effective ambassadors in the marketplace, translating into new business opportunities.

Giving recruitment the priority it is due, making ongoing efforts to find the best people and upgrade existing staff, and selling the firm to new and existing empioyees are all parts of a recruitment philosophy. And this recruitment philosophy may be the only competitive edge you have over other design firms as we enter the 1990s.

2.3 IS THERE A NEED TO HIRE?

Although the time to hire an outstanding candidate is always *now*, that doesn't mean that firms should hire at will, without any consideration of the alternatives.

For routine recruiting and hiring decisions, it's important to have a decision-making process to ensure that the key recruiting resources go to the most pressing needs. This cautiousness may seem to contradict the previous advocacy of aggressive recruitment philosophy, but the concept is simple. Outstanding people are the exception, not the rule; you'll know them when you see them. All too often, firms go out to look for a particular kind of specialist who, as a little reflection would show, isn't really needed. And hiring to fill a slot when there are other ways to address the need can be a costly mistake.

When a branch manager, department manager, project manager, or studio head comes to you and says he or she needs to hire someone, how do you know if the need is real? You should start by looking at a number of different factors, including but not limited to:

1. *Utilization rates*: Do you have established utilization rate (percentage of time worked that is job-chargeable) targets for all organizational units? If not, why not? If utilization rates (see Figure 2.1) have fallen below targeted levels in the recent past, why do you need to hire someone else?

2. *Duration of the need*: How long will you need this person? If it is only for a short time, you may be able to fill the need with overtime, part-time staff, or personnel who aren't fully utilized in some other office or department of the company. If there is resistance to using staff from internal sources, is it because your labor-transfer–pricing policies penalize either the users or providers? Do you have established transfer-pricing policies that encourage inter/intraoffice personnel swaps?

3. *Use of temporary/subcontract help*: If it's only a short-term crisis, have you fully considered the possibility of using temporary employees/subcontractors?

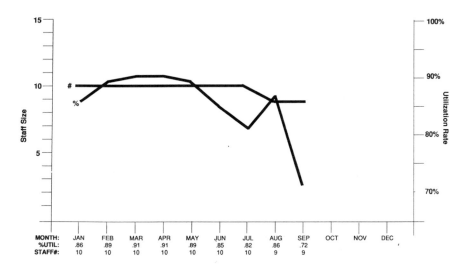

FIGURE 2.1 Staff number vs. utilization rate graph

If not, why not? More and more temporary employment, technical service, and job shop firms are catering to the A/E/P marketplace than did as little as five years ago.

4. *Dropping marginal projects and/or raising prices*: Rarely considered by a design firm is the possibility that all work cannot be taken on. Are there any clients who won't pay fair fees or who don't pay their bills promptly? Are your prices too low? Perhaps that's why there is so much demand for your services? Elasticity of demand is a reality in the design business, and all services are to some extent price sensitive. Higher profits and better work could be the result of being more selective about whom you work for and charging more for your services.

5. *The "create a job for friend or family member" syndrome*: Does your manager have someone he or she wants to see hired? Is that the reason for the sudden interest in hiring a new staffer? Do you have a no-nepotism policy? If not, why not?

6. *Working overtime*: How much overtime is the group or department working on a regular basis? Is it possible for the existing staffers to work more hours? Have they been asked, or is it assumed what their response will be?

These are some of the most important factors to consider before embarking on a recruitment assignment to fill a specific position with someone on a full-time, regular employment basis. Your HR director should value his or her time and fight adding jobs to the company's "positions open" list unless really needed and management is committed to filling it. The important thing is not to react too quickly, mobilizing firm resources and spending time and money chasing down "rabbit trails" until you're absolutely sure the need is valid. However, once you've determined that the need is real, pull out all the stops and fill the job as quickly as possible.

There is a good way to ensure that this deliberation process is followed regularly. Before going out to hire anyone, see to it that a "Request for Authorization to Hire" form (see Figure 2.2) has been filled out and signed off on by all required parties. This formal authorization to hire is a critical element in any firm's hiring process. It is one more step to help the firm keep down unnecessary recruitment expenses. For whatever reason, when something has to be "signed off" on, people think about the implications of what they are authorizing. And, in the case of our example form, three people will have the opportunity to ask whether the need is real and whether alternatives to hiring have been considered.

However, don't let this hiring form turn into a bureaucratic obstacle for the firm's front line managers. If a manager expects recruitment efforts to be made on his or her behalf, then it is his or her responsibility to get the form signed. But if a manager is so overloaded that he or she has not taken the time or refuses to follow the established procedure to get the form signed, it would be a mistake for the HR manager to do nothing. For managers who need special treatment, the HR manager/director should hand carry the form to all those who need to sign it, and either get the authorization to begin recruiting or tell the manager that his or

Request for Authorization to Hire

Title of Position: _____   Date: _____

Branch/Department: _____   Initiator: _____

Job Description Attached: ☐

Description of Ideal Candidate for Position: _____

_____

_____

_____

_____

_____

_____

Expected Salary Range: _____   Date Needed on Board: _____

I authorize Mark Zweig & Associates to move ahead with this recruitment effort:

_____   _____
Department Manager   **Date**

_____   _____
Division Director/Branch Manager   **Date**

_____   _____
President   **Date**

After all three signatures are present, please forward to Fred White for action.

FIGURE 2.2   "Request for Authorization to Hire" form

her higher-ups won't approve it. It is important for the firm's HR department to avoid a reputation of being a less than cooperative team member; it is critical if HR management is to be fully embraced by the firm.

To summarize, you should be actively recruiting all the time; that's the key to the recruitment philosophy. But you also need to make the best use of your recruitment dollars and time. Effort spent recruiting someone that you don't need now and are unlikely to need in the future is money down the drain.

2.4 INTERNAL POSTING

There are a number of sources for potential employees. Most firms *should* first attempt to fill a position from within the organization. Promoting from within not only contributes to high morale, but holds down recruitment and training costs. Yet, far too often the first thing A/E/P firms do when an opening develops is place an advertisement and wait to see who responds.

After the authorization-to-hire form has been processed, see to it that the position is listed on the firm's "positions open" inventory and posted conspicuously in all office locations immediately. There are three good reasons for doing this:

1. It boosts morale. Employees won't get the impression that they are being overlooked—provided that every so often an internal candidate is actually hired.
2. It may generate referrals from outside the firm. Existing staff are your best recruiters, especially if they like working for the firm. Most employees worked somewhere else before starting at your company. Even if they haven't, they are bound to know people in other firms and government agencies who could be prospects.
3. It reduces the firm's potential employment-related liabilities.

This last reason needs some further explanation. Here's an example of how the internal posting process paid off big for one A/E/P firm. They laid off their varitypist, a 14-year employee in her mid-fifties, after years of trying her out in other positions, such as secretarial, drafting, deed research, and so on. Although the position of varitypist was formally eliminated, the woman filed an age discrimination complaint against the firm through the local office of the EEOC. In her complaint, she claimed that she had applied for several openings in the company in recent years, and was never given any consideration. Because the firm had a rigorous practice of posting all position openings along with spelling out the process for consideration and because they kept good records that could prove the woman never came forward, the potentially costly complaint against the firm was dropped.

This example also illustrates two critical points with respect to internal posting:

1. The process should be followed religiously. All positions open should be posted, and the list should be kept up to date on either a weekly or biweekly basis.
2. The process interested parties need to follow should be clearly communicated to everyone and spelled out right on the *Positions Open* list itself (see Figure 2.3).

Frequently, in concert with a firm's internal posting routine, a recruitment referral fee policy or program is instituted. Recruitment referral fees are paid to employees who refer applicants for various openings in the firm who get hired. Typically, there are different levels of fees paid, based on the history of difficulty encountered in

Memo to: All ZN56C, Inc. Employees
From: Marshall Zebowitz, Director of Human Resources
Date: June 4, 1989
Subject: Position Vacancies

Attention all employees—the following positions are now open:

(1) Design Architect (Orlando): 4–10 yrs.' exp. in health care facilities reqd.

(1) HVAC Engineer (Dallas): 3–6 yrs.' exp. reqd.

(2) Electrical Engineers (Peoria): 3–6 yrs.' exp. reqd.

(1) Contract Administrator (St. Louis): Degree plus A/E/P exp. reqd.

(1) Marketing Coordinator (St. Louis): Degree plus Ventura Publisher exp. reqd.

(1) Sr. Land Planner (Seattle): 8–15 yrs. exp. in major projects reqd.

(1) Utilities Engineer (Seattle): 2–6 yrs. municipal project exp. reqd.

(1) File Clerk (Dallas): No exp. reqd.

(9) Total positions open.

If you are interested in being considered for any of the above positions, or if you know of anyone you think might be interested, please contact the corporate human resources dept. in Dallas.
Thank you.

Marshall Zebowitz
Director of Human Resources
MCZ/ems

FIGURE 2.3   Sample job posting

filling the position. Fees range anywhere from $200 to $2000 and are paid out after a waiting period—usually three to six months after the new employee starts work. Some firms pay out a portion of the referral fee when the new employee starts and the remainder at the end of the waiting period.

Although many design industry experts preach the benefits of recruitment referral fees, they do have some drawbacks. They may engender negative feelings if an employee refers someone whom he or she thinks is qualified but the applicant is not hired. The employee may decide that the firm failed to hire the person just to avoid paying the referral fee. Thus referral fees may have the exact opposite of the intended effect; they may demoralize staff when the intent is to provide a staff benefit.

Another danger is that managers may abuse the system. One major engineering firm's HR director found the firm's regional office manager was abusing the company's referral program. He had a deal with employees to split the referral fee on just about every candidate the office hired. It turned out that no matter where the candidate came from—through an ad, an unsolicited resume, or whatever—

the company got stuck for a fee. The bottom line is that recruitment referral fee programs may be one avenue to generating candidates, but think long and hard before putting one in place. If you do, make sure it is monitored for abuse.

2.5 RESUME/APPLICATION DATABANKS

One of the best, least expensive, and fastest ways for a design firm to generate qualified candidates for a position is to develop and maintain a resume/application databank. This databank should include the resume, application for employment, or recruitment notes for every single person who has applied to the firm.

It can be either a computerized or manual system. There are a number of excellent computerized resume/application tracking systems available for PCs, and a few for mini and mainframe systems. Packaged PC-based software for resume and application tracking can be purchased for as little as $395, whereas the mini- and mainframe-based software packages can cost as much as $70,000. But before you go charging off to invest in hardware and software systems, consider whether file folders and a good manual classification scheme will suffice. It usually makes sense to put a manual system in place first, anyway, before computerizing.

Start your databank by collecting all of the resumes, applications, and interviewing notes from everyone in your firm who might have any. Tell whoever opens the mail to direct all unsolicited resumes and letters concerning employment to the person in charge of your firm's hiring activities—preferably, the HR manager. Then classify every existing and incoming resume according to a predetermined scheme.

Whatever scheme you develop, it's important that you try to set up categories that are pretty much mutually exclusive. You don't want to have to look in five places for candidates to fill one position. It's also recommended that you adopt a comprehensive list of categories, even if your firm doesn't employ people in all of them. You'll probably find that you will still receive resumes from engineers if you're an architectural firm (and vice versa) and you'll want to have some place to file those resumes. The other reason for categorizing all resumes is that your firm may some day decide to get into a new discipline or service area. Your resume bank may provide you with some candidates for the new discipline area immediately. You may decide to refine the scheme each year to better reflect your firm's resume flow and specific needs.

An example of a group of categories for one discipline is as follows:

Electrical/Draft
Electrical/Design Technician
Electrical/Engineer
Electrical/P.E.

Each year, you should start a new set of files even if you don't change your classification scheme. This will allow you to review the most recently acquired applications first when a need develops. Move on to preceding years' files as necessary, looking in the second most recent year's files first, and so on.

After all resumes are collected and classified, create a cross reference system on note cards filed by last name. This way, if someone calls in to see what the status of his or her resume or application is, you'll be able to look them up quickly by last name in your file cards, which will tell you how you classified him or her and what year's files they fall into.

Usually, attempts to build a resume/application databank are hampered by skeptics who think that it's all a waste of time. Who wants applications that are two years old anyway? These people would rather just throw a fresh ad in the Sunday paper and see who is looking. These critics should consider the following real-life story: One firm had 29 positions open at the time they decided to set up a resume/application databank. After a couple weeks of intense effort, the databank was ready to be put to the test. Within two more weeks, three of the firm's past applicants were tracked down and hired, the first of whom had submitted his application to the firm almost three years before and had made a job change since his last application. Most design professionals will be flattered that a firm saved their credentials for such a long time and took the trouble to track them down.

A good resume/application databank, in place for a year or more and supplemented by some regular advertising in a few select publications, should be able to fill at least half of a design firm's openings. Half may sound like a lot, but the firm in the real-life story filled 76 positions in one year, spending less than $6500 on advertising and nothing on employment agencies or search firms. It wouldn't have been possible without their resume/application databank!

There's another benefit of a centralized resume/application databank if you do work with employment agencies or executive recruiters. The ability to prove that you already knew about an applicant before a search firm sent you his or her credentials could save you time and money in case of a dispute. Too often referring agents sue firms for placement fees even though the firm did indeed have prior contact with the candidate.

Your goal should be to get virtually everyone in your competitor's firms into your resume/application databank over time. Never throw away a resume. Every one of them could prove valuable some day.

2.6   EMPLOYMENT ADVERTISING

The most used and least consistent method of producing qualified employment candidates for a design firm is advertising. This doesn't mean you shouldn't advertise! It does mean, though, that you should think about how you are using your ad budget to get the best return on your advertising dollar.

If it is properly handled, advertising can be one cost-effective component of a recruitment plan. Assign one person in your office the responsibility for all recruitment advertising. This will keep you from running the same ads in the same publication at the same time because of poor internal communications—a total waste of money, yet it happens. This practice will also enable you to get any frequent advertiser discounts you are entitled to.

Consider consolidating your position openings. Try placing fewer, larger ads. Larger ads will enable you to benefit from economies of scale, since you won't have to repeat the company name and benefit or contact information in each smaller ad. Also, in most publications the more space you take the less the cost per column inch, providing you with further economies.

Try running regular advertising for the position types you have historically had the hardest time filling, especially when running larger ads where the extra position listing won't cost you much to add. Build up your resume/application databank and receive the added benefit of the higher unsolicited resume flow that your firm will get from having wider name recognition in the design community.

Design firms should also advertise consistently in the same publications. Being seen in the same place all the time helps build name recognition of the firm. This name recognition increases the likelihood that even those who aren't looking to change jobs now may contact you when they do get into the job market. You may also get quantity discounts for being a frequent advertiser. Ask.

Ads should be designed so that they will attract the reader's attention quickly. Leading off with your firm's address may not be the best way to catch a reader's attention. Something on your firm's opportunities for home ownership or low cost of living might. For example, "Come to beautiful Seattle, Washington, where $80,000 still buys a three-bedroom, two-bath home in a neighborhood where you won't have to worry about your kids playing outside after dark." It's also good to provide your ad readers with information on any unusual benefits the company offers—such as fully paid insurance or relocation benefits.

Make sure not to oversell your company or your opportunity. There have been lawsuits brought by employees who felt misled by an employment ad and switched jobs because of it. Don't give the position you are advertising a title that misrepresents its real duties and responsibilities (i.e., calling a secretary a "marketing management administrative specialist"). Too many firms think this is a good idea but end up wasting a lot of their time and the applicants' time. Be sure not to include any discriminatory language or language that might be construed as discriminatory (e.g., "attractive," "young," "he," etc.), in your ad. One ad spotted recently was for a company seeking "a young engineer, 25 to 28." Another kept referring to the ideal candidate as "he." These are common mistakes that can lead to trouble.

Use the media that will reach the audience you're interested in. There are a number of sources available to design firms interested in finding specialized talent. Figure 2.4 is a partial list of A/E/P trade publications and their advertising addresses.

Be sure to request details on candidates' current compensation packages, but don't include your salary range in the ad. Salary ranges can only do two things: You'll get unqualified applicants because the salary sounds high, or you'll preclude someone qualified from responding because it seems low. There's nothing wrong

Architect's Clearinghouse
521 America Street
Baton Rouge, LA 70802
(504)387-23359

Architectural Record
Classified Ad Office-A/R
1221 Avenue of the Americas, 42nd. Floor
New York, NY 10020
(212)512-2556

Consulting-Specifying Engineer
Classified Department
1350 E. Touhy Ave.
Des Plaines, IL 60018-5080
(708)390-2088

Engineering News-Record
Classified Ad Office-ENR
1221 Avenue of the Americas, 42nd. Floor
New York, NY 10020
(212)512-2556

Progressive Architecture
P/A Classifieds
1100 Superior Ave.
Cleveland, OH 44114
(216)696-7000, Ext. 2584

PSMA Ascent
Job Bank
Professional Services Management Association
1213 Prince Street
Alexandria, VA 22314
(703)684-3993

SMPS Marketer
Positions Open Advertising
The Society for Marketing Professional Services
99 Canal Center Plaza, Suite 300
Alexandria, VA 22314
(800)292-7677

FIGURE 2.4 Advertising media list

with *asking* ad respondents to include a breakdown of their current compensation package, including base salary, overtime and bonus. However, do not ask them for compensation *requirements*.

Include your company name, address, and phone number, as well as your company contact person on every ad you run. If you have a toll-free number, use it for your out-of-state advertising. The idea is eliminate all barriers to make it is as easy as possible for your prospects to respond. Also, be sure not to use that tired old line, "Send your resume and a cover letter detailing your interest and qualifications for the position." This may deter someone who is only considering making a move from contacting you. Many of the best candidates are not actively looking. They may not even have a current resume, and if they do, the need for a cover letter could keep them from taking action.

Make sure your receptionist, switchboard operator, or secretary knows what to do when someone calls in or comes to your office in response to your ad. If a registered electrical engineer from your chief competitor calls, make sure he or she isn't simply told, "Send in your resume and we'll call you if we're interested." It's worth shortcutting your normal process for hot prospects.

Track the responses to each advertising effort to determine which medium produces the best numbers and quality. One good way is to put a code in your reply address that identifies the date and name of the publication you've advertised in. For example, "Send all resumes to Mark Zweig & Associates, 43 Main Street,

1. Assign the responsibility for all recruitment advertising to one person in your firm.
2. Consolidate your position openings into larger ads.
3. Advertise continually for the types of positions you have historically found the hardest to fill.
4. Advertise repeatedly in the same publications.
5. Track your responses to each advertising campaign effort in order to determine which medium produces the best numbers and quality.
6. Design ads that will quickly attract the reader's attention. Be different. Too many recruitment ads disappear into the clutter when they should jump out and generate excitement.
7. Use the media that will reach the audience you're interested in.
8. Include your company name, address, phone number, and contact person on all ads.
9. Ask for current compensation package details in all ads, but don't put salaries or salary ranges in your ads. Also, avoid asking for ad respondents' salary requirements.
10. Sell prospective candidates on your firm by advertising any unusual benefits the company provides to employees, but never oversell your opportunity.
11. Make sure your receptionist, switchboard operator, or secretary knows what to do when a call comes in or someone shows up at your office in response to your ad.
12. Do not include any discriminatory language or language that might be considered discriminatory in your ads. Put "E.O.E./M/F" at the bottom of all recruitment ads.
13. Never give the position you are advertising for a title that misrepresents its real duties and responsibilities. Do not, for example, call a secretary an "administrative coordinator," or an office runner a "technician."
14. Don't set up barriers for prospective employees to respond to your ad. Examples of barriers would be a request for a cover letter or insistence that interested applicants call only at normal business hours.

FIGURE 2.5   Employment advertising guidelines

BG-34, Natick, MA 01760." The "BG-34" stands for Boston Globe, March 4th edition.

For companies not knowing how to design employment ads, or for those who want to do something a little nicer than an in-column classified, there are advertising agencies who can help. One of the best is a firm by the name of Nationwide Advertising Service, Inc. (NAS), an employment advertising-only firm, headquartered in Cleveland, Ohio, with offices in 38 locations throughout the United States, Canada, and the United Kingdom. Nationwide Advertising puts out a *Recruitment Ad Guide* each year, a tremendous resource that lists all U.S. regional newspapers, with their circulation and employment advertising rates, and shows literally hundreds of sample recruiting ads. This book is free to anyone requesting it.

In addition to the traditional ad design and placement services, some of the other services available from ad agencies are box and blind box response options, telephone answering and prescreening services, market research, and newsletters on recruitment and employment trends. Fees for ad agency services vary greatly. Some companies will essentially design and place an ad free of charge. They get their commission directly from the publication that prints the ad. Others charge hourly rates for design and clerical services and reimbursables, in addition to getting their commission from the publication. Just as in the A/E/P business, extra service from ad agencies costs money. As a whole, ad agencies are probably underutilized by design firms looking to make the best use of their advertising budgets, but whether you use an agency or place recruiting ads yourself, the guidelines listed in Figure 2.5 will help.

2.7 SEARCH FIRMS AND EMPLOYMENT AGENCIES

Just about every design firm has used the services of either an employment agency or executive search firm at some point. At last count, there were over 20,000 executive search firms, professional recruiting firms, and employment agencies operating in the United States, with the numbers growing each year. If you haven't used one of these companies, you've undoubtedly been called by them in an attempt either to sell you their services or recruit you for one of their openings.

Because of the misunderstanding that surrounds executive search firms and employment agencies, because of the tremendous amount of money design firms spend on these services without really understanding them, and because a discussion of these services can help a firm's in-house recruitment efforts, this section examines in some detail how these firms work, the people that work in them, and the relative effectiveness of the varying approaches they employ in filling positions.

Both executive search firms and employment agencies are commonly referred to by the unknowing as "headhunters," a term that really applies only to true executive search firms who do not try to place job hunters. Employment agencies, by contrast, will represent candidates in an effort to find them a job. They do this in one of three ways. They will mail or FAX a resume to your firm, most likely without the candidate's name on it, hoping you'll give them a call with a show of interest. Or they will put out a regular mailer, or "laundry list," of biographical data on a number of their candidates. Or they will call you on the phone to tell you about someone (commonly referred to in the business as an MPC—most placeable candidate) even when they aren't under contract to perform recruitment for you.

One of the saddest of such experiences was the time a 300-person consulting engineering firm HR director got called by an agency with a "high-voltage A.C. engineer." Not knowing what that was, the poor HR director asked the voice on the other end of the phone for more details. It turned out the woman from the employment agency was trying to place an HVAC engineer, or heating, ventilation, and air conditioning design engineer!

Not every firm can be neatly classified as either employment agency or executive search firm. There are firms that normally work as executive search firms but occasionally slip into an agency mode for one reason or another. Maybe they turned up a number of excess candidates on an assignment, some of whom may be desirable but simply weren't needed by the original client. Or perhaps their search assignment activity is at a low point, and because there is no other revenue-generating activity to spend time on, they make MPC calls. The most prestigious firms, however, would never send a blind resume or make an MPC call for fear of damaging their reputations.

Another way to distinguish between employment agencies and executive search firms is by how they get paid for their services. Employment agencies tend to do everything on a contingency fee basis. If you hire one of their candidates, you owe them a fee. Their fees are usually based on some variation of the 1 percent per thousand dollars of first year's earnings basis, with a maximum fee of 30 percent of first year's earnings. For example, if you hired a secretary for $25,000 per year, the agency would collect a fee of 25 percent of $25,000, or $6250.

Executive search firms usually require a retainer from their clients. The retainer may take the form of a portion of the total fee up front, with the balance due upon filling the position. Or, in the case of old-line, traditional executive search firms, the retainer could be one-third of the estimated total fee up-front, one-third 30 days after starting, and one-third 60 days after starting.

Executive search firms, too, most often base their total fee on a percentage (usually 20 to 35 percent) of first year earnings. However, it is becoming more and more common for search firms to set flat fees for recruitment projects. Flat fees make the most sense because who is to say that just because a position pays more, it will be more difficult to fill? A shoreline protection engineer for a firm in southern Maryland at $40,000 per year may be much tougher to find than a Boston branch manager for a nationally recognized architectural firm paying $80,000 per year. Some executive search firms will also work for clients on an hourly fee basis. In the last few years, the largest executive search firms have begun to market (not entirely successfully) "unbundled" research services designed to provide clients with a list of potential candidates for them to attempt to recruit on their own. Just about all executive search firms charge for reimbursable expenses, as is traditional among consultants, at cost times some multiplier. A few firms estimate expenses and bill them on the front end of the project.

The main factor distinguishing executive search firms from employment agencies is their approach to filling a position. Employment agencies usually go about it in one of two ways. They advertise and see who responds, or they work their databank of resumes (see Section 2.5). Rarely do they actually contact someone and attempt to woo them away from his or her present employer. As a result, employment agencies tend to deal with a greater number of unemployed or extremely unhappy candidates than would a traditional executive search firm. Executive search firms, on the other hand, fill most of their positions through direct recruitment of individuals they identify in their client's competitors. They, too, will maintain databanks to supplement their research and direct recruitment approach. Occasionally, executive search firms will practice what they call "indirect recruiting," where they call or write potential candidates to ask them if they know of anyone who may be interested in the position they are currently working on. They do this in the hope that some will throw their name in the pot for consideration. If enough of these contacts are made, someone usually does.

Executive search firms and employment agencies are also distinguished by the types of people they tend to employ. Although it is impossible to generalize for all cases, employment agencies are usually not as selective in their hiring practices as executive search firms. Agencies tend to hire people who have come to them looking for a job. They throw these people on the phone with little or no training, knowing that most will fail quickly but that a few will make it. Employment agencies are characterized by extremely high turnover because of their hiring practices and because so few individuals are cut out for the business. Not many people with other career options will tolerate a steady diet of heavy telephone work and plenty of rejection from apprehensive potential clients five days a week. Two of the highest income generators for a hybrid agency/search firm which served the design industry years ago came from sales backgrounds. One had previous experience selling encyclopedias door to door, and the other at first sold pots and pans door to door and then used cars at a Chevrolet dealership before getting into the business of recruiting design and construction professionals. Today, one of the two has his own firm operating out of an office in the basement of his home; the other sells training tapes and seminars to other recruitment firms.

Executive search firms like to hire people out of the industry they will be serving as search consultants. The best search firms in the design industry have principals and staff who have come¹ directly out of the design business and know what the various types of people in a design firm do. Of their front-line consultants, some are retired principals, some are technical staff members who wanted a career change, and some are former HR directors or in-house recruiters. The larger firms also employ professional research support staff. By and large, most executive search professionals are college educated, and many hold advanced degrees.

Compensation practices affect the quality of staff working in employment agencies and executive search firms. Employment agencies, as well as many executive search firms, pay their counselors or consultants some form of commission. In an employment agency, the typical arrangement is for the counselor to have a draw against commission. That means that the company will advance the counselor a certain portion of his or her commissions each month. The draw is based on some estimate of what it would take for the person to get by until they begin generating income, or it's based on the proven ability of the counselor or consultant to generate income over time. Some agencies pay a small salary plus commission. Most larger agencies pay out to the counselor somewhere between one-third and one-half of fees generated, while smaller operations are usually in the 40 to 50 percent commission (or commission plus salary) range.

Executive search firms' compensation practices vary widely. While some pay consultants a salary plus commission, others pay a salary plus a year-end bonus, and in a few cases there are firms which pay straight salary. Complicating the compensation issue for executive search firms is that, unlike employment agencies, they tend to have more than one person involved in the process of completing any given search assignment. They may have one person who sells the job and acts as a principal in charge of sorts, another who serves as the day-to-day project manager, another who does the research, and yet another who handles the recruiting. This kind of division of labor is pretty much limited to the larger firms, of course, and there are lots of one- and two-person operations out there performing legitimate executive searches.

The last major distinction between employment agencies and executive search firms is the kind of positions they work on. Each may be appropriate for a design firm to use, depending on the nature and level of the need. Employment agencies don't tend to specialize in one industry, although there are no doubt some that do. Their counselors are typically generalists or specialists within broad categories, such as technical work, engineering, or computers. They will work on any position, but usually concentrate in the $20,000 to $50,000 range, depending on the nature of their business. For administrative, support, and computer people, there are agencies that can be extremely effective. There are a few who work quite well filling positions in architecture, interior design, and consulting engineering as well, although they won't usually commit to filling the position because of the fee arrangements with their clients. It used to be commonly accepted that agencies worked only in local markets, or at least were much more effective in their own back yards. That is no longer the case; both the larger agencies and those specializing in technical people work all over the country. Figure 2.6 summarizes the distinctions between employment agencies and search firms.

Executive search firms servicing the design industry tend to specialize in that field alone, or at least they have one or more persons who do. Some are multidiscipline management consulting firms that offer executive search services as a part of their total service menu. Their specialization usually makes them more effective than their non-specialized counterparts, since the research they have performed on countless previous assignments may benefit their work on your project. They know the industry, and the firms, and they usually have a number of sources in any given specialty whom they will call for help.

Executive search firms work nationally, with some even interviewing all candidates face to face before presenting them to their client. Face-to-face interviewing by executive search consultants used to be more common than it is today. Most clients don't want to pay for the privilege of having someone else personally interview their candidates before they do. They know if the person looks good on paper and has the right education and experience credentials, the only real concern

Employment Agencies

Typically work on contingency fee basis.

Tend to be generalists or specialize in broad areas under headings like "technical."

Have less skilled staff.

Pay staff on commission.

Have high staff turnover rate.

Advertise and use in-house resume bank to fill positions.

Will market employment candidates to companies not knowing if an opening exists.

Have fee schedule usually based on a 1 percent per $1000 in salary or some derivative on this formula.

Tend to work in their local market.

Work on positions up to $50,000, with the bulk in the $20,000 range.

Executive Search Firms

Also known as "headhunters."

May work on either contingency or retainer depending on skill of search consultant and current workload.

Charge fees ranging from 20 to 33 percent of first year earnings, with the best firms charging well over 20 percent.

May work on a flat-fee basis.

Typically charge for reimbursable expenses.

Have more highly skilled consultants. The best work on salary plus bonus; the others typically work on some salary plus commission.

Tend to specialize in one area only, for example, mechanical/electrical contracting, A/E, and the like.

Never or rarely market candidates to companies on a speculative basis.

Fill most positions through direct recruiting methods.

Work on positions with salaries over $50,000, with the majority between $60,000 and $85,000.

FIGURE 2.6   Employment agencies vs. executive search firms

is chemistry, and that's something that they themselves will be best equipped to judge.

Executive search firms serving the design profession tend to work on positions in an annual salary range of $50,000 or more, with the bulk in the range of $60,000 to $85,000. To pay a search firm a 25 percent fee on a $65,000 position means a $16,250 expenditure. Add that to the cost of relocation, and a design firm with a normal industry profitability factor of 7 percent will have to collect over $300,000 before approaching the break-even point on hiring costs. Because of this expense, the risk in making a bad recruiter selection, and design professionals' preference for self-sufficiency, design firms need and want to minimize the use of employment agencies and search firms. But with the incredible difficulty of finding qualified professionals in just about every discipline, how is this possible? The best way is to establish a sound HR program in your firm following the recommendations of this text, but even without your own HR program, there are four major steps you can take:

1. Establish a company policy of not using executive search firms or employment agencies, and make everyone in the company with the authority to hire aware of it. The CEO can always authorize an exception in special cases.

2. Plan for needs before they occur so that when an opening develops, the firm isn't thrown into a crisis. It is precisely the crisis management approach that mandates the use of outside sources to fill a position.

3. Assign one person in your firm the responsibility for hiring. This is the concept of the hiring process manager, which will be discussed in depth in Chapter 4 (Section 4.2). For now the point is that by assigning one person in your firm the responsibility for all hiring, you'll make sure that all employment agency or search firm inquiries are directed to one individual who knows your policies, knows the status of hiring for any position, and knows what recruiting firms the company will use.

4. Have no budget for payment of employment agency and search firm fees. If the money isn't there, you'll have to seek out other methods for filling the job.

Despite the best of intentions to maintain a completely self-sufficient recruitment process, there may be times when you still need help filling a critical position. In that case:

1. Select the *best* firm for the particular need. Use an appropriate specialist who is most likely to succeed. A list of recruitment firms specializing in the A/E/P industry accompanies this section (see Figure 2.7).

2. Check references. Unless you have prior personal experience dealing with the firm and the recruiter on a recruitment project, you should always go through the process of checking references with past clients. Don't buy the line that "all of our client relationships are confidential." That's a sure indicator the recruiter has no successes to point to and will be learning at your expense.

3. Be willing to pay a retainer and reimburse expenses. Face it: The best professionals in any field don't need to invest their time on a purely speculative basis. They perform a service and expect to get paid for their time. By the same token, design firms charge separately for professional services and reimburseables, so why shouldn't recruiters?

4. Go through a formalized process of determining whether a staffing need exists, and use search firms and employment agencies only for real needs. Like design professionals, they don't want to invest time in a project that isn't for real.

Career Opportunities, Inc.
    734 Walt Whitman Road, Ste. 210
    Melville, NY 11747
    Contact: Joseph Shupack, (516)549-0425

Claremont-Branan, Inc.
    2150 Parklake Drive, N.E., Ste. 212
    Atlanta, GA 30345
    Contact: J. Phil Collins, (404)491-1292

The Coxe Group
    2 Mellon Bank Center
    Philadelphia, PA 19102
    Contact: Weld Coxe, (215)561-2020

Fox-Morris Associates
    Mercantile Towson Building
    409 Washington Avenue, Ste. 704
    Baltimore, MD 21204
    Contact: Chip Saltsman, (301)296-4500

The Fuller Group, Inc.
    5252 Westchester, Ste. 275
    Houston, TX 77005
    Contact: David or Ruth Fuller, (713)663-6073

Larsen & Lee, Inc.
    7315 Wisconsin Avenue
    Bethesda, MD 20814
    Contact: Don Larsen, (301)657-1330

McNichol Associates
    P.O. Box 534
    Philadelphia, PA 19105
    Contact: Jack McNichol, (215)922-4142

C. M. McReynolds
    19 Suffolk, Ste. "A"
    Sierra Madre, CA 91024
    Contact: Chuck McReynolds, (818)798-4287

Michael Latas & Associates, Inc.
    1311 Lindbergh Plaza Center
    St. Louis, MO 63122
    Contact: Michael Latas, (314)993-6500

The Viscusi Group, Inc.
    220 East 57th Street, Ste. 2D
    New York, NY 10022
    Contact: Stephen P. Viscusi, (212)371-0220

FIGURE 2.7　Recruitment firms serving the design industry

5. Give the recruiting firm well-defined, written position criteria. Clearly communicate what the firm wants. Don't make substantial changes in the criteria after starting the search unless absolutely necessary. If changes in direction are required, tell your recruiter as soon as possible.

6. Ask for feedback from the recruiting firm on how realistic your criteria appear to be. A good recruiter, someone who specializes in filling the types of positions that you are using him or her for, is in the hiring marketplace every day. Chances are he or she will know even better than you what people are likely to be earning, what kinds of diversity in skills is available, and so on.

7. Make use of the recruiters' ability to provide feedback throughout the hiring process. Don't cut them out of the picture after the interview is set up or before an offer is made. A good recruiter will be in touch with all candidates from the time each is first contacted until after the new employee reports to work. He or she will be able to advise you along the way of the candidates' concerns, needs, motivations, and hidden agendas.

8. Return all phone calls from your recruiter promptly. Nothing kills a recruiter's enthusiasm for filling your position like an uncommunicative client. Treat your recruiter as you or any other professional would like to be treated.

9. Keep your promises. Call candidates on the dates and at the times you've committed to. Send out information you have promised to send. Keep up your end of the project, and don't kill your recruiter's credibility with the candidates he or she has recruited.

10. Respect the perishable nature of recruited candidates and what your recruiter has gone through to find them. Proper follow-through is essential to keep candidates from pulling themselves out of the hiring process.

11. Give honest feedback to the recruitment firm if they appear to be missing the target. Even the best recruiters may get off track occasionally. But don't hesitate to pull a search away from an obviously incompetent firm.

12. Give the search firm any information they request or that you think would be helpful to them on both your firm and your geographic area.

One thing some design firms have done successfully is work out discounted fee arrangements with a recruiter for a longer-term relationship than just filling one position. Some design firms work on this basis with an independent recruiter. Others actually bring the recruiter into their firm and provide him or her with an office under a contractual relationship.

One mid-size, full-service firm has a executive search company that they pay a small monthly retainer and reimbursable expenses. The company then pays a preset, flat fee for each person they hire through the recruiter. Because of the volume of business they do together, this fee arrangement saves them over half of what they would normally pay.

There are some excellent recruiters who will agree to an arrangement like this; they are service providers who battle cash flow just like their design firm clients.

Also, they know the benefit of having a long-term working relationship with a client—they can better address their client's needs when they are more intimate with them. This type of arrangement is not advised, however, when the design firm/recruiter relationship has not been fully tested. These arrangements work out best when a more typical project relationship has existed for some time and there have been a number of successful assignments already completed.

There will probably always be times you will have to use an outside source to find people. Being careful in your selection of a consultant, approaching your relationship in a cooperative spirit, and taking the dozen steps outlined above will help you make the best use of their services.

2.8 FENDING OFF OUTSIDE RECRUITERS

The flip side of the search firm problem is protecting your staff from being recruited by consultants working on your competitors' behalf. Beyond making sure that your firm is the best possible place for any design professional to work, there are a few things that you can do to minimize the likelihood your best staffers will be bombarded with recruiters' calls.

For one, any search firm or agency that you pay a fee to should provide you with a guarantee in writing that your firm is off limits for two years. Insist on it. Also train whoever answers the company switchboard to be on the lookout for people fishing for names. Switchboard operators would be wise to be a little less helpful when someone calls who "can't remember the name of a really sharp young health care design architect who works there" or to be less willing to tell a caller "planning a seminar" who all the HVAC design engineers are. For whatever reason, firms in New York City seem to really have a handle on this problem. Most of their switchboard operators simply will not give out any names over the telephone. If you want to slow down recruitment from your firm, have these callers connected to someone in the HR department or ask them to submit their request in writing.

You should also reconsider the accessibility of a company directory of everyone in the firm, including their titles and home telephone numbers. Some companies do this as a convenience for their employees or to help make the company more accessible and responsive. The bottom line, however, is that although there is no way to ensure your best people won't be called by a recruiter, you shouldn't make it easy for them to end up on a recruiter's list of potential candidates. When either a recruitment company or recruiter in a competitor's office gets a hold of one of these directories, it can be devastating. The cost of one of these in-house phone directories can be far greater than the expense to produce it!

2.9 DIRECT RECRUITING

At a 1985 stockholder's meeting for a major multioffice design firm, the HR director made a presentation on why and how the firm could start up a direct recruitment program. By direct recruitment, we mean directly contacting currently employed individuals to find out if they are interested in learning more about your open position. The discussion went around the table for maybe 20 minutes, with terms like *proselytizing* and *stealing* used freely. Just when it appeared the idea would be shelved, the company chairman, who hadn't said a word since the discussion started, suddenly threw his notebook and stack of papers on the conference table and said, "Goddamn it. We've sat here for the past twenty years and watched our best people get wooed away by our competitors. I'm tired of getting [expletive deleted]! We've got to get the best athletes." And with that, he quickly ended discussion on the topic of whether the company should recruit directly from its competitors or not!

The point is, there has always been a raging debate on whether direct recruiting is ethical or not, although more and more companies apparently see nothing wrong with it. Both opponents and advocates of direct recruiting sometimes refer to it as stealing people. But slavery was outlawed in this country in 1863. If people can't be bought and sold and therefore aren't owned, how can they be stolen? The answer has to be that you can't steal people. Individuals are responsible for their own actions; they are captains of their own ships. You can't force anyone to do anything he or she doesn't want to do, and nothing is wrong with extending an invitation to get acquainted unless you are misrepresenting your company or the opportunity in an effort to get someone to jump ship. Frankly, if you want to find good people without resorting to search firms and agencies, sooner or later you'll have to do some direct recruiting. For those that are ready to try, here are some recommendations how to go about it.

Design firms wanting to get into this business first need to set up a company information database, a place where every bit of information on competing firms' staffs is filed. Just as was the case with the resume/application database described earlier, the firm's information database can be stored manually or on the computer. If you don't have ready access to a terminal or a nice database program designed for maintaining the kind of information you'll need, a simple manual system will suffice.

Your firm's information database should contain the name of each of your competitors; the location of their home office and all branch offices; a list of the services they offer; who their principals are (if available); how many staff members they have; and any specific information you have on the company's employees. Directories such as the AIA *Profile*, or the *ACEC Directory of Member Firms* are good places to start for information on your competitors. Each time you learn about someone, your firm's information database is where you should keep a record.

One good way to keep your firm information database is on 5" × 8" lined note cards filed alphabetically within specialty service or geographic categories. As it becomes necessary, simply staple additional cards together for more room to write. Figure 2.8 shows a sample card.

To develop specific information on your competitors' staffs, monitor the business or real estate section of your newspaper, talk to your employees who have come from other firms, track firm announcements and company newsletters, and attend

John Coleman Hayes +Assoc.
Nashville, TN

(615) 385-3484

JOHN COLEMAN HAYES
AND ASSOCIATES, INC.   35
104 Woodmont Blvd.
5th Floor
Nashville, TN 37205
(615) 385-3484
FAX: (615) 385-1918
Principals: John Gilmore, Jr., P. E.
Activities: Civil, environmental, sanitary engineering, architecture, interior design, and city planning; investigations, reports, EPA 201 studies, airport master planning; design and inspection of water and wastewater systems, natural gas systems and storm drainage; airports, highways, streets, bridges, residential and recreational facilities; site planning and development. Criminal Justice facilities, commercial and retail buildings.
Ownership: Privately-owned Corporation

Bill Wilson - Civil P.E. - approx.
10 yrs. exp. - site work

Tom Grau - "Grow" - VP-head
of environmental dept.

FIGURE 2.8 Sample direct recruiting source card

professional association meetings. If you go through this process systematically and apply some creativity to your research, you'll be amazed how much information you'll amass in six months or less.

Occasionally, secondary information sources aren't adequate. You may have a critical need in a particular area for the first time, no internal candidates, nothing in your resume databank, and no other budget for advertising or recruitment fees. You've decided to go the direct recruitment route, but though you have all of your competitors identified and know where to look, you don't have any specific names of people to call. You now have to do what's commonly referred to by recruiters as *sourcing*. There are a number of things you can do to develop your recruitment prospect list.

One is simply to call your competitor's office and ask for the name of whoever is in charge of the area you're interested in. Most people are surprised how easy it is, and this is a tactic used every day by professional recruiters. Or, as many recruiters have done, you can develop elaborate scripts for eliciting different kinds of information (see Figure 2.9 below).

Situation 1 (one person in the position):

COMPANY: Biswanger, Holden & Morris.
RECRUITER: Could you help me? I need to know who your chief shopping center architect is.
COMPANY: Eric Van Husen.

RECRUITER: What is his exact title?

COMPANY: He's our chief building engineer.

RECRUITER: I'm sorry. You must have misunderstood me. I'm looking for whoever is in charge of shopping center architecture.

COMPANY: It could be Jerry Deane. He is a principal with the firm. I'll connect you.

RECRUITER: Excuse me. I must be looking for the person who works directly under him.

COMPANY: That would be Fred Ernst. He's the architect on the Cleveland Galleria project.

RECRUITER: That's him. What's his exact title and your mailing address.

COMPANY: He's an Associate, and our address is 52 Main, Burke, IL 62901.

Situation 2 (one person in the position, tough switchboard operator):

COMPANY: Good morning, ABC & Associates.

RECRUITER: I wonder if you could help me. Can you tell me who is in charge of electrical engineering at your firm?

COMPANY: Who is calling?

RECRUITER: This is Mike Lawson. Who is in charge of electrical engineering there, please?

COMPANY: Why do you need to know?

RECRUITER: I'd like to add him or her to my list. Who is in charge of electrical engineering there?

COMPANY: You need to talk to Susan Terry—I'll connect you.

RECRUITER: Is she the Electrical Engineering Manager?

COMPANY: Yes she is—I'll connect you.

RECRUITER: Excuse me. I just wanted to get her name, title and mailing address.

COMPANY: "It's Susan Terry, spelled T-E-R-R-Y, and her title is Electrical Department Manager. The address is ABC & Associates, Inc., One North Main St. Anytown, MO, 99999.

RECRUITER: Thank you for your help.

Situation 3 (multiple people in the role):

COMPANY: Good afternoon, Lazurus Associates.

RECRUITER: You have a young architect working for you—about 26 or 28 yrs. old—a sharp dresser. What is his name?

COMPANY: That must be Bill Thompson or Eli Walton you're looking for.

RECRUITER: Bill Thompson. Is he about 26?

COMPANY: Bill is about 34 or 35.

RECRUITER: It must be Eli Walton I'm looking for. Is he about 28?

COMPANY: He's about 26 or so. He's our sharpest young architect.

RECRUITER: That must be him. What is his exact title?

COMPANY: His title is Senior Architect.

RECRUITER: Thanks. I'll add him to my list.

FIGURE 2.9 Sample sourcing call phone script

Another step mentioned earlier is to ask your existing employees for names. They may be able to refer you to someone they met at a project meeting, public hearing, through the YMCA basketball league, or from a past employer. Don't wait for your people to volunteer their help—call on them yourself.

Something that always seems to produce results but isn't always possible to do is to attend the same association meetings as your competitors. If you're discreet, you can make it look almost as if it was coincidental that you happened to meet your competitor's best young designer at the local ASID meeting. Prospects developed in this fashion are often quite receptive when called later to set up a "get acquainted, information swapping" session.

Another excellent source of names are the ITE, ASCE, ASLA, IEEE, and other professional association rosters. Some of these rosters list names, titles, and employers of potential recruits. It may be tedious, but you can get some good sourcing done with association rosters.

One aggressive recruiter of design professionals is known to hang out at the same watering holes as his competitor's employees (usually somewhere near their office). He gets to know their people and it all looks coincidental. This same fellow organized a sports league (in this case, basketball) for civil engineering firms in his city. As a result, he got acquainted with some of the younger engineers in each of his competitor's offices.

If you don't want to make sourcing calls yourself, you may be able to use an executive search firm to infiltrate a particular company or group of companies. Some recruiters will allow you to pay them on an hourly basis to source for you, although others feel that is the most important part of recruiting and won't provide this service separately.

A great but often overlooked way to find names is to research your marketing department's old proposal files. Look for copies of joint-venture or politically mo- tivated prime/sub submittals that your firm made with competitors, and see if any contain resumes of people you may be interested in.

One final secret source of names used by the best executive search professionals who serve design firms is registration rosters and directories. Some states, Texas for example, list the discipline and employer of everyone in their PE roster (see Figure 2.10 *a* and *b*). It may be tedious, but there's nothing to stop you from looking down each page of a registration roster until you see your competitor's company name, and transferring the name and discipline of the person working there to your company information database. Better still, for a fee some states will even print out their roster by company, discipline, or location. This is particularly handy for firms recruiting engineers in states that organize their registration by discipline. See Figure 2.11 for a list of sources for employment candidates.

Once you have these names, you have to contact your prospects in an attempt to find out more about them and to get them interested in your opportunity. This part of the recruitment process creates anxiety for some people. Again, a thought- fully worded script may make this easier (see Figure 2.12). The important thing to remember is that recruiting is not unlike any other kind of sales process. Your goal is not to get someone to commit to making a job change on the first call. All you

FIGURE 2.10a Sample engineering roster pages

are trying to do is get him or her to move ahead to the next step in the process, that is, to agree to get together with you or send you some biographical data. Even if you get nothing more than the standard company resume used by his or her present employer for selling the person's time, you'll have planted the seed and established some dialogue and a reason for a follow-up call.

ROSTER OF REGISTERED PROFESSIONAL ENGINEERS

24-MAY-1989

S/N	NAME/PHONE	ADDRESS		FIRM		BR
28080	COHEN, JACK H. 71-488-3415	15922 HEATHERDALE DR	HOUSTON	ASSURANCE TECHNOLOGY INTERNATI	TX 77059	A
34859	MARKS, VICTOR JAMES 71-488-7440	15711 HEATHERDALE	HOUSTON	G E GOVERNMENT SERVICES	TX 77059	A
48378	ALEXANDER, DAVID HARRY 71-488-7440	14919 PENN HILLS LN	HOUSTON	SINGER COMPANY	TX 77062	A
35548	BELSHAW, GEORGE WILLIAM 71-488-9080	15807 LA CABANA DR	HOUSTON	ILC SPACE SYSTEMS INC	TX 77062	A
29571	HEUER, RONALD D. 71-280-2512	16107 DIANA LN.	HOUSTON	BOEING COMPANY (THE)	TX 77062	A
35830	HUMPHREY, GEORGE THOMAS, III 71-280-4662	14919 BROOKPOINT DRIVE	HOUSTON	SINGER COMPANY	TX 77062	A
50509	MCSWEENEY, RICHARD KING 71-488-2728	15530 TORRY PINES	HOUSTON	RKM ENTERPRISES	TX 77062	A
61149	REUTER, GERALD JAMES 71-483-4520	15702 FATHOM LANE	HOUSTON	NASA	TX 77062	A
33148	ROGERS, WILLIAM FRANKLIN, II	1430 NEPTUNE LN.	HOUSTON	NASA-JOHNSON SPACE CENTER	TX 77062	A
56756	STUMP, WILLIAM RAMELLE, JR. 71-338-2682	1506 FESTIVAL	HOUSTON	EAGLE ENGINEERING INC	TX 77062	A
34789	URBANEK, WALTER ADOLF 71-440-7022	6623 GENTLE BEND	HOUSTON	FISH ENGINEERING & CONSTRUCTIO	TX 77069	A
30481	FROST, L. M. 71-524-8236	10914 VILLA LEA LANE	HOUSTON	SOUTHERN IMPORTERS	TX 77071	A
35543	MUSGROVE, JOHN GORDAN	7906 CHANCEL DR	HOUSTON	BECHTEL POWER CORP	TX 77071	A
44261	FRANSON, ROBERT EUGENE 71-333-6694	7602 TIMBERWAY	HOUSTON	LOCKHEED ENGINEERING & MGMT SV	TX 77072	A
15610	MOSS, WALTER L., JR. 71-461-3653	8910 BONHOMME RD.	HOUSTON	PRESNAL ENGINEERING CO	TX 77074	A
43369	GARDENIER, HUGH EMORY 71-626-1601	651 DIAMOND LEAF	HOUSTON	TEXAS ENGINEERING EXTENSION SE	TX 77079	A
31376	KORENEK, JOSEPH L. 71-676-4764	14426 CINDYWOOD	HOUSTON	BROWN & ROOT INC	TX 77079	A
32872	PRESNAL, A. L.	1730 ELMVIEW	HOUSTON	PRESNAL ENGINEERING CO	TX 77080	A
51627	THOMAS, JAMES RODNEY 71-467-1682	5003 LYMBAR	HOUSTON	ENGINEERING SPECIALITY SERVICE	TX 77096	A
34619	GARDNER, DENNIS COLE	% METROPOLITAN TRANSIT AUTH PO BOX 61429	HOUSTON	METROPOLITAN TRANSIT AUTHORITY	TX 77208	A
55965	BISHOP, ROBERT HAROLD 71-485-8246	PO BOX 58681	HOUSTON	CHARLES STARK DRAPER LABORATOR	TX 77253	A
31671	CLIFFE, RICHARD T., JR. 71-943-5314	PO BOX 58221	HOUSTON	SIP ENGINEERING INC	TX 77258	A
59723	KEETON, ROBERT ANDREW 71-280-7442	BOEING AEROSPACE OPERATIONS P.O. BOX 58747 HS-03	HOUSTON	BOEING AEROSPACE CO	TX 77258	A
27954	MORAN, ROBERT L., JR. 71-333-2847	P O BOX 58936	HOUSTON	ROBERT L MORAN JR P E	TX 77258	A
28656	WENDT, R. C.	158 MOBILE CT	CONROE	ENVIRONMENTAL IMPROVEMENTS INC	TX 77302	A
29386	PURSER, PAUL E. 71-852-3435	PO DRAWER 1599	HUMBLE	PAUL E PURSER P E	TX 77347	A
32870	NORTON, DAVID J. 71-367-1348	41 DOVEWOOD PLACE	THE WOODLANDS	HOUSTON AREA RESEARCH CENTER	TX 77381	A
33087	ETHERTON, BILL D.	3819 PECAN VALLEY DR	MISSOURI CITY	STUBBS OVERBECK & ASSOCIATES I	TX 77459	A

FIGURE 2.10b Sample engineering roster pages

Direct mail campaigns

"Positions wanted" listings

In-house direct recruitment efforts

Referrals from existing employees

Calling back former employees

College placement offices

Advertising in specialty magazines

Advertising in national newspapers

Advertising in association newsletters

Advertising in employment-only publications

Advertising in regional newspapers

Advertising in local newspapers

Lists from professional organizations

Announcements/bulletin board posting at religious institutions

Co-op programs

Referrals from past employees

Employment agency referrals

Executive search firm candidates

Outplacement firm referrals

Referrals from suppliers

Referrals from competitors

Referrals from clients

Alumni association listings

Trade show job fairs

State and local employment office referrals

Referrals from friends and acquaintances

Supermarket bulletin board posting

College and university bulletin board postings

Radio advertising

Television and cable TV advertising

Contract employment company referrals

Internal candidates

FIGURE 2.11   Sources of employment candidates

Both in-house and external recruiters frequently don't understand why someone does not have a current resume. Many times people who are currently employed and are not so unhappy that they are actively seeking to make a change don't have up-to-date resumes they can send you overnight. In those cases, it's either best not to worry about it and use some kind of recruiting form (see Figure 2.13) to guide your telephone or face-to-face information gathering, or to ask for a copy of the person's company resume.

RECRUIT: Hello. Talbot here.

COMPANY: Is this Gary Talbot?

RECRUIT: You got him. Who's this?

COMPANY: Gary, this is Barry Santos calling, and that's spelled S-A-N-T-O-S. How are you today?

RECRUIT: I'm fine. What can I do for you today?

COMPANY: I'm with Johnson & Hardwald here in Boston. Are you familiar with us?

RECRUIT: Sure, you guys are the big A/E firm over in Watertown. I have some friends over there.

COMPANY: Really—who are they?

RECRUIT: I know George Lewis from the MassPort Central Parking Facility job we did with you guys as prime, and also Peter Thomas. I knew him from the time he worked at City Hall.

COMPANY: George and Peter are two of our best staffers. The reason for my call, Gary, is that I've heard a lot of good things about you. I wanted to put a call in to you to see if you would be willing to meet with us confidentially to trade a little information and discuss what opportunities we might have for someone like you in our company.

RECRUIT: I appreciate your call. What did you have in mind?

COMPANY: We always keep our ear to the tracks, Gary. I'd like to have a chance to talk with you to find out more about the kind of things you like to do where you want to go with your career. When could we get together?

RECRUIT: How about before work some time—say for breakfast.

COMPANY: Certainly. How about getting together over at Denny's on North Main Street next Tuesday at 7:00 AM?

RECRUIT: Sure, I could do that. How will I know you?

COMPANY: I have a beard and glasses. I'll wait by the entrance.

RECRUIT: Great. I'm always open to talk. I'll look forward to meeting with you.

COMPANY: Super. Call me if you run into a problem with your schedule. My number is (617)555-9999. Rest assured, this won't go any farther than the two of us.

RECRUIT: Thanks, Barry. I'll see you next Tuesday morning.

COMPANY: Good bye.

FIGURE 2.12   Sample direct recruitment phone script

Direct recruiting may be more of an art than a science. It's generally best to talk very slowly, especially during the first few minutes of your telephone conversation, so your potential recruit has time to shift gears mentally and hear what you are saying. Spell out your name and your company's name, if necessary, so the person can write it down.

Always ask if the person on the other end of the phone is free to talk privately. If not, ask if another time would be better or if the person would like to call you back at his or her convenience. It's conventional wisdom that if you want to be an aggressive and successful recruiter, you have to be prepared to work in the evenings occasionally. There is some truth to this, but more often than not people will be able to switch to another phone or arrange to call you at a better time during the day.

 **RECRUIT FORM**

■ CONTACT

Name _____ Source _____ Date _____

Bus. Ph.# (_____) _____ Home Ph.# (_____) _____ Bus. Ph. OK? Y N

Firm _____ Location _____

■ ROLE

Title _____ Yrs in position _____ Yrs in firm _____

Ownership _____ Report to _____

Description of Role _____

_____

_____

_____

_____

_____

_____

_____

_____

_____

_____

_____

_____

_____

_____

■ EDUCATION & REGISTRATION

Education _____ Adv. Education _____

Registrations _____ Affiliations _____

■ COMPENSATION

Base _____ OT _____ Bonus _____ Car _____ Clubs _____

Paid Dep Cov _____ Dental _____ 401(k) & PS _____

Current Resume? Y N   Will send (date) _____

(over)

FIGURE 2.13 Sample recruit form

■ **PREVIOUS EMPLOYMENT**

_____

_____

_____

_____

_____

_____

_____

_____

■ **PERSONAL**

Home address _____

Location requirements _____

■ **PSYCHOLOGICAL**

Concerns with present postion _____

Goals _____

Motivation to change _____

Assessment of communication skills _____

Consultant comments _____

_____

_____

■ **FOLLOW-UP DISCUSSIONS**

Date _____ Note _____

Date _____ Note _____

Date _____ Note _____

■ **INTERVIEWS**

1) _____

2) _____

3) _____

4) _____

FIGURE 2.13   _(Continued)_

If you can get the potential candidate to call you back, you've already taken the first step toward establishing the kind of control you want to maintain over the hiring process. Experience will show you that people who call you back are more likely to accept an eventual job offer from your firm than someone you are constantly trying to track down.

A few final notes on direct recruiting. If your research is good, your technique smooth, and your firm's reputation solid, you should be able to get somewhere between 50 and 80 percent of those you contact to agree to talk with you. At the very least, you should be able to get together for a little "information swapping." If your direct recruiting succeeds in getting someone to make a move, he or she will probably last longer on the job than someone who approached you. The reason: People who make a job change after being approached with an opportunity do so only because they see the move as an improvement over their current situation. Not that people who make a change because they are terribly unhappy don't feel the same way. It's just that those who are happy have more to risk, and because of that, will make a better decision to change than someone who is either running away from a bad situation or is unemployed and needs to put bread on the table.

2.10 COLLEGE RECRUITMENT

Most design firms look on college recruitment as a necessary evil—and not without reason. Firms don't need greenhorns or know-it-all 22-year-olds; they need seasoned professionals who can step in and start making money for them. At the same time, every firm recognizes that if they only hired veterans, there would be no design industry of tomorrow, and that recruiting and training new college graduates is insurance for the future of their firm and the entire industry.

The most efficient and effective way to handle college recruitment is to concentrate on your co-op program (more on this in Chapter 7). Concurrently, you should establish relationships directly with the academic departments you recruit from in a few select schools so you can learn about their best and brightest upcoming grads.

It's really hard to justify spending several days on a college campus interviewing anyone who signs up to talk with you, but this is the most typical form of college recruiting practiced by design firms. Colleges and universities like this approach, because they know that's the only way some of their potential grads would ever get an interview. No firm in their right mind would talk to some of these people based on their resume alone. The problem is that some firms use college recruiting trips as a reward for their technical professionals. It may be fun, and some of your people might love the ritual of going back to their alma mater each spring, but it's probably not the best use of the firm's time.

To improve the efficiency of your college recruitment efforts, narrow the number of schools you recruit from to a reasonable number. This will allow you to establish relationships of mutual trust and benefit with professors, department chairs, or deans. With less schools to hire from, you're bound to hire more of their grads.

And with less people to stay in touch with, you're bound to call on them more often.

One time-saver is to always get resumes on new grads before agreeing to talk with them. Treat them no differently than any other prospective job candidate. If they don't meet your grade and experience criteria, don't talk to them. Why waste your time?

You'll save yourself lots of problems down the road if you don't hire structural engineering majors for your site engineering department, or for your hydrology group, when they are obviously interested in becoming structural engineers. By the same token, you shouldn't be hiring as construction administrators architectural graduates who really want to become designers.

Many readers will undoubtedly argue that *they* didn't specialize in the area that they now work in, and they did all right. No doubt there are successful people in many areas who didn't specialize in school in their chosen field of endeavor. However, the whole concept of consistently effective hiring is based on probabilities. People will last longer in the job if their functional assignments are consistent with their areas of interest. Most people in the consulting engineering business have seen the structural engineering major who, after working two-and-a-half years in a municipal engineering group, decides that it's time to move on so he or she can practice building design. Or how about construction majors working in design capacities who feel like they have to get their boots muddy? Any time you make an exception to this practice, you are raising the odds of a personnel problem down the road.

College recruiting, like all other recruiting, requires common sense and the self-discipline to wait until you find what you really want before hiring. But before moving on to the next chapter, one last observation about college recruiting and today's new college graduates: Design firms have never been nor will they probably ever be able to match the starting salary opportunities of other industries. As a result, in some engineering disciplines—those with heavy competition from big dollar industries like high tech and defense—the design profession gets left with the dregs from the graduating class, those whose grades weren't high enough to work for one of the major glamour employers. Couple this problem with the high expectations for responsibility and earnings new grads often have for their first job and you've got some serious obstacles to overcome if you want sharp new grads who are going to last with the firm.

Young people are all too often blinded by the high starting salaries of high-tech companies and defense contractors. In fact, graduates starting at a lower rate in an A/E/P firm may be earning *more* than their industry counterparts 5 or 10 years after graduation. This is especially true for those with the interpersonal, communication, and managerial abilities so sought after by design firms today.

As an industry, design firms have to improve their recruiting skills and refine their sales pitch to communicate the long-term opportunities of the design profession. And the design professions will have to lean on the educators to get their help in instilling in their students more reasonable expectations for a first job experience.

2.11   CONCLUSION

There is a shortage of real talent for most positions in design firms. Growing firms spend a great deal of time and money in recruitment, and design firms not aggressively recruiting will be surpassed by their competitors in the coming decade.

Having a recruitment philosophy, knowing when to look for a new person, understanding the differences in and how to work with search firms and employment agencies, dealing with college recruitment efficiently, and being able to recruit directly are all important to a design firm that wants the best possible staff and the lowest recruitment costs.

3

INTERVIEWING

Shake and shake the ketchup bottle. None'll come out and then a lot'l.

—John Wareham

3.1 INTRODUCTION

If there is one thing that will be reiterated over and over in the course of this text, it is the importance of a *consistent hiring process*. Interviewing is no exception to this rule (see Figure 3.1). Many design professionals seem to view interviewing as an impromptu, seat-of-the-pants proposition. However, a consistent approach to interviewing is one of the keys to consistent quality in *hiring,* and that's why a whole chapter of this text has been devoted to this subject.

As important as interviewing is to a design firm's overall employee selection process, too few companies have trained managers in the art of interviewing or put much effort into refining the interviewing process. Proper interviewing requires some specific skills that can be learned. It requires a familiarity with the questions that can and can't be asked, an understanding of how to prepare for an interview, and a knowledge of how to most attractively merchandise the benefits of the firm and the position.

Above all, interviewing requires good listening skills. If nothing else, it has to be acknowledged that interviews make people uncomfortable, no matter which side of the desk they're on, and that this discomfort is for the most part an obstacle and not an aid to an effective interview. Forget what you've heard about pressure interviewing. The key to interviewing is making people feel comfortable so they can open up and reveal their true inner selves—a skill that can and should be learned by anyone who participates in the interviewing process for a design firm.

1. Personnel Manager (or HR Director or whoever is responsible for the hiring process) makes the first contact with potential candidates on the telephone, inviting in those who meet predetermined criteria and prescreening those who don't. Those prescreened are sent a "no thanks" form letter.

2. HR Director develops the schedule for the interviewing session. Informs all involved in-house individuals of when they can expect to talk with the candidate and how much time they should allot. Coordinates all individuals' schedules. If air travel is required, HR Director sees to it that all travel arrangements are made when necessary and sends actual tickets and complete itinerary to candidate. Confirms that candidate has received tickets prior to meeting.

3. HR Director puts candidate in touch with the preselected relocation specialist to assist with housing as required prior to the interview session. Coordinates with relocation specialist as required to allot time to show candidate housing in the area.

4. HR Director meets all candidates coming in from out of town at the airport as required. Points out highlights of the city on the way and explains office location in relation to other things the candidate is interested in.

5. HR Director conducts initial meeting with candidate and evaluates candidate from all perspectives except technical ability. Specific questions asked include goals, likes and dislikes of present position, and motivations to make this job change, in addition to any others on approved company interview question list. Explores all gaps in the candidate's employment history. HR Director explains company history, company goals, fringe benefits, and so on, using the *Company Recruitment Information Booklet.* Provides candidate with a copy of the booklet along with selected company brochures and marketing materials. Takes the candidate on a brief tour of the company's offices. On the way, candidate is briefly introduced to Mr. Jones, Mr. Barker, and Mr. Thompson (the firm's three founding principals) if possible. HR Director takes anywhere from one to two hours for this part of the process. In the case of local candidates, HR Director cuts off the process at any point if the candidate does not appear to be a good prospect.

6. Candidates passing the prescreening process are presented to the division or department manager and his or her staff, who assess the candidate's technical abilities as well as compatibility with other department or group staff members. When finished, the division or department manager takes candidate back to HR Director. This part of the process takes anywhere from one to two hours.

7. If appropriate, the candidate should next be taken out to lunch at the company club by the HR Director and division or department manager and be given a brief driving tour of the city after lunch.

8. If the candidate is from out of town, he or she should get together with the relocation specialist to look at available housing. Candidate is not left to look around the city alone.

9. After returning to the office, the candidate is escorted to the front door—or taken back to the airport if flying—by the HR Director. Before leaving, the candidate is asked if he or she has any questions, encouraged to call with questions that come up afterward, and told when the company anticipates getting back to him or her with an indication of the next step in the hiring process.

FIGURE 3.1 Sample interviewing process

3.2   DETERMINING WHO TO INTERVIEW

If you were to interview every single applicant to your firm, you would have time for little else but interviewing. Whether formally planned or not, everyone has some method for screening applicants. And it is worth putting a little thought into this method, because otherwise you could end up turning away some of your best prospects and wasting your time with some of the worst. Or you could be seduced into making a bad hiring decision on a subpar candidate who happens to give a great interview. So before getting into interviewing skills, the issue of how to decide *who* to interview merits discussion. Just how important is this step? Consider the following real-life case.

With the help of an employment agency, a major A/E firm hired a 40-year-old engineer for a lead position in its traffic engineering group. The engineer, who had left a similar job with a large consulting engineering firm over a thousand miles to the south, was very personable on first impression and interviewed well with the firm's top people, including the president. He was also a good negotiator. After an initial offer of $55,000 per year, he negotiated his starting salary upward to $57,000 *and* got the company to sweeten the pot with a $1500 signing bonus. The company also paid full relocation expenses for him and his family, which totaled over $8000 when the final bills came in for house-hunting trips and meals and hotels en route to the new job. A 20 percent employment agency fee of $11,400 brought the total cost of hiring to a little over $20,000, excluding interviewing expenses.

After he had been on the job a short time, it became clear that the new engineer was alienating both staff and clients. Despite the positive impression he created in pre-employment interviews, his projects lost money and he was generally a poor performer. Both technical and managerial skills were sorely lacking. After 11 months he was let go. Added to the $20,000 cost of hiring the engineer were two weeks' severance pay, two weeks' accumulated vacation, and two weeks' notice—another $6600—plus the services of an outplacement consultant at $75 per hour (some people in the firm felt guilty about firing the guy).

In reviewing the case it was discovered that prior to joining this company, the fellow had had eight previous employers in a 15-year period. Also, although he had a master's degree in civil engineering, he somehow had never gotten his professional registration—not to mention the fact that his candidacy was based on the receipt of an unsolicited resume from an employment agency and his hiring would require a relocation, all occurring *before* the standard recruiting procedure (as outlined in Chapter 2) was followed.

The bottom line—the engineer was a $28,000-plus mistake for the company. Considering the firm's average profitability of 7 percent of gross receipts, it would take them $400,000 in business *just to make up for the hiring and termination costs*. The moral of the story is that if the firm had done their homework on the front end of the hiring process, this guy never would have gotten to an interview where he had the chance to make a good impression and, in spite of what common sense would dictate, get hired.

A thorough review of this candidate's resume would have identified a number of red flags, indicators of potential problems if he were to be employed. His pattern of making so many job changes should have raised an eyebrow. Not only had this fellow had eight previous employers in 15 years; he hadn't stayed anywhere (with the exception of a government position) more than two-and-a-half years, and stayed some places as little as eight months. This is not to say that frequent job changing is not sometimes unavoidable. There are companies in the A/E/P industry that hire without regard to long-term need and then use the LIFO (last in, first out) approach when determining who to cut. And, there are also situations where people have made a number of job changes, but when you further examine their responsibility and earnings progression, it's easy to see why. Unless each job change represents a step up, rigorously scrutinize job hoppers.

Another warning signal that there was potential for trouble was the fact that in spite of an advanced degree, this senior engineer had no professional registration. The lack of registration, despite a career based largely on working in private-sector consulting firms, should have been a tip-off to possible lack of ambition or basic technical abilities.

The last problem with this candidate was the cover letter that accompanied his resume, sent after the employment agency established interest on his behalf. Riddled with spelling and typing errors, in addition to having poor grammatical construction, it alone would have been reason enough not to interview him.

It should be clear by now that knowing what to look for in a potential candidate's employment background is an important part of the interview process. If you do a good job prescreening applicants, you'll waste less time and money interviewing people and do a better job at more consistently hiring the right people.

The simplest way to prescreen is to follow one rule: Don't interview anyone who doesn't meet your predetermined hiring criteria. Some design firm owners and managers would argue vehemently against this. They would maintain that an open mind is the key to hiring good people, and there's some truth to their perspective. These people will generally interview anyone who drops in and wants to talk about job opportunities with the company. These are the same people who are usually receptive to the concept of "information interviewing" advocated in so many of the current texts on job search and career changing.

In lieu of the first rule, a good corollary would be: Don't interview anyone whose resume sends off danger signals (see Figure 3.2). Otherwise, you simply increase the probability of making a bad hiring decision. And if you haven't seen a resume or application in the first place, as in the case with a drop-in candidate, you can't even make that determination. (The exceptions to this rule will be covered shortly.)

Beyond the intermediate- and long-term implications of making a bad hiring decision, wasting professional staff time and travel expenses interviewing the wrong people has an immediate financial impact. One good rule of thumb is to have an interview-to-offer ratio of around three to one. Any more than that, and you're probably wasting time and money talking to the wrong candidates. Any less, and you probably aren't generating enough alternatives to choose from.

1. Gaps in employment history or lack of specific start and stop dates for employment experiences.

2. Poor spelling or multiple typos in the resume and cover letter.

3. Lack of dates for degrees received.

4. Statements like "attended University of Colorado" that imply a degree but don't make an outright claim for one.

5. Lack of any increase in responsibility over a period of years or while with several different employers.

6. Not listing college GPA.

7. Excessive detail on everything the candidate has ever done ("attained Cub Scouting merit badge in kite-making," or ten-page resumes).

8. Statements of employment objective that are too broad (for example, "to obtain gainful employment in a technical capacity with either a government, institutional or private-industry organization of large or small size").

9. Resumes that describe the candidate in third person and use all kinds of glowing adjectives ("Mr. Jones is an extremely capable, bright, articulate engineer second to none in his highly in-depth knowledge of state-of-the-art building HVAC systems design and construction").

10. Salaries that are much less than you would think someone with that background should be earning. There's probably a reason for it.

FIGURE 3.2 Prescreening candidates: Watch for danger signs

An employment interview isn't all that different from a selection interview for a design consultant after an initial qualification submission from a number of firms. In the case of a selection interview, the assumption is that the firms who get to that stage are all qualified to do the job, and the interview represents an opportunity for all but one to disqualify themselves.

Similarly, candidates who get to an interview should be basically qualified. All they can do in the interview is either disqualify themselves from further consideration for the specific opening or remain a contender for final selection. This is why interviewers need to take a *negative bias,* that is, look for reasons why someone *shouldn't* be hired.

All of this discussion goes back to a central idea of this text: Let the probabilities work in your favor. The probability-based outlook is derived from experience in hiring hundreds of design professionals. If there are too many danger signals, wait until you have a better candidate. When you total up your successes in hiring good people over the years, a lot of it will have been due to your skill in keeping the bad apples out of the process. That is the mark of a real pro at hiring.

During the preceding discussion, some readers may have been thinking, what about someone who can't or won't supply you with a resume prior to an interview? How do you prescreen in these cases? Employment agencies and executive search firms, for example, will often push hard to get you to talk with someone without seeing his or her resume. They may be worried that on paper the candidate won't live up to the glowing characterization they've given you, or they may be dealing with a directly recruited candidate whose ego is sensitive and they don't want to deflate it or scare the candidate off by asking for a resume. However, it is still best to have in hand some sort of written record of education and experience before interviewing a candidate, especially when travel is involved. The possible exception to this rule would be a directly recruited candidate from the company's local area, where it might be a bit much to ask for a resume prior to getting together, although there are some really gutsy recruiters who do. Usually, the advantages of having a resume in that case do not outweigh the disadvantages of turning the candidate off early on in the hiring process.

If you are dealing with an outside recruiter, and he or she tells you that the person was a direct recruit who does not have a resume, ask him or her to put together one for you prior to agreeing to interview the candidate. Every good recruiter will be willing to assemble a biographical sketch on a candidate they are presenting to you. The best firms do it as part of their normal process. One other point: Although the recruiter may give you a biographical sketch as part of his or her process, always ask for a resume just the same, if they have one. You may learn more from the resume than the bio, as the recruiter will certainly try to put the candidate's best foot forward in their version of his or her track record.

To sum up, any written version of a candidate's credentials will help you decide if you want to have a telephone interview in the first place, and it will also help guide your questions when you do. If you can't get anything else, at least see if the candidate can't get a copy of his or her marketing resume, whatever his or her current employer uses to help sell time.

3.3 TELEPHONE INTERVIEWS

It is not always possible or even advisable to conduct a face-to-face interview with a candidate. These cases are when you'll be thankful for your telephone.

Telephone interviews are generally used under one of three circumstances. First, when it is anticipated that there will be a tremendous response to an advertisement, some prescreening is done on the phone rather than having everyone either send in his or her resume or come in. There aren't too many instances where a design firm anticipates this huge a response to an ad, with the possible exception of a support position in a region with high unemployment.

The second circumstance where telephone interviews are appropriate is when you've run an ad for a tough-to-fill position, and to avoid setting up barriers that would prevent a currently employed person from responding, you list a phone number and instruct potential candidates to call for more information. At that point, you simply want to ascertain each respondent's basic qualifications (or lack of qualifications). On the basis of this phone interview, a decision is made regarding whether to call the person in for a face-to-face interview.

The third time to use a telephone interview is with a candidate from outside your area, where a face-to-face interview would represent a significant investment in travel time and money. This is probably the most common application of telephone interviewing in a design practice. Telephone interviewing can be an extremely effective technique for finding out more about a candidate without going to the expense of a personal interview. In this sort of telephone interview, all of the rules of interviewing apply, except you don't have the benefit of being able to use any of your senses other than hearing to size up the candidate.

Not all telephone interviews are the same. Some are conducted very casually and serve only as a major screening. Others can be quite structured and in-depth, lasting an hour or more. Advantages of telephone interviews include their low cost, ease of scheduling, and simplicity of structure. Disadvantages are the inability to see the candidate and assess the candidate's interpersonal skills, as well as the telephone interview's somewhat impersonal nature. Telephone interviews are highly useful to design firms when travel is required. They become less useful in local market situations.

3.4 WHERE TO INTERVIEW

Assuming you've decided to conduct a face-to-face interview, you now must decide where to meet.

1. In your own territory.
2. In the candidate's territory.
3. On neutral ground.

FIGURE 3.3 Where to conduct the interview

You may choose to conduct the interview in your office. This has many advantages for your firm. First, it's easier to schedule. Second, it will cause only minimal work disruption for those of your staff who will be involved in the interview. Third, and an important plus to this approach, is that it allows the candidate to see the facilities and what some of the firm's staff look like other than those who are conducting the actual interview.

Before you invite a candidate to your office, take a good look around. The appearance of the workplace is becoming more and more important to all professionals, but it is particularly important to design professionals, many of whom are actively involved in the planning and design of office facilities for a living. If your office facilities are a plus, be sure candidates know it by inviting them in. If surroundings are a negative, be sure to acknowledge that immediately and disarm the candidate by telling him or her that offices aren't important in your firm and that you'd rather spend more money hiring better people, training them, and getting better computer equipment. Another effective technique to overcome poor office space is to forewarn the candidate before he or she even comes to the interview that your offices aren't great. That way the candidate won't be disappointed upon seeing them.

The last option for interviewing in your office is not available to all companies. Hold the interview in another of your offices, perhaps a nearby branch, where the space is more attractive. One firm based in Fort Worth successfully used this approach several years back. Because their main office was less than stunning, they arranged interviews with Dallas-area candidates in their Dallas branch's super class-A, high-rise office space, even though the candidate might have been looking for a position in Fort Worth. This allowed the firm to put its best foot forward and still control the interview environment.

Some interviewers prefer to go where the candidate lives for the interview. They believe that if you can see where someone lives and meet the spouse and the rest of the family, you'll learn more about him or her. No doubt there's some truth to this, but when you consider the practical applications, it's rarely possible. You can't really ask a candidate to have you over for dinner. You're on shaky ground to tell a candidate you want to see where he or she lives and meet the rest of his family. And, it's expensive and time consuming to travel somewhere for an interview when, if you do have any further interest in the candidate, you'll have to bring him or her to your office for at least one interview, anyway.

One sensible case for interviewing at the candidate's location is when it is outside your region and you have a number of different people you want to interview in that particular location. In this case, it may be more efficient and economical to go there than to have each of the candidates come to you. Also, if you have some other reason to be in the area and the interview is not your sole reason for the trip, it is probably worth considering doubling up your appointments.

If you've decided against conducting the interview in your office and don't want to venture into the candidate's territory, your only remaining option is to choose some neutral territory, perhaps a restaurant for lunch or dinner. Some of the recruitment gurus will tell you that watching how someone acts in a restaurant will tell you all sorts of things. The advantage of interviewing over lunch in a restaurant is that the informality of the situation may encourage the candidate to open up. It also gives you the opportunity to check on the candidate's social graces, important if client contact is a requirement of the job.

One young architect unknowingly cost himself a position with a top development firm because he cut up all of the meat on his plate before eating it. Another project manager lost a department head position by ordering $25 worth of crab legs for lunch. The interviewer figured if the candidate was that careless with the firm's money before being hired, he would probably be a bigger abuser as an employee.

Be careful when selecting a restaurant to meet with a currently employed candidate. Don't suggest meeting somewhere too near the candidate's current office. Others from his or her firm may like to dine there, and the candidate may act strangely out of fear of being discovered talking with the competition. This is especially important when dealing with design professionals, where the mere thought of talking with a competitor is enough to send many to the confessional!

This is as good a place as any to bring up the subject of an interview log (see Figure 3.4). This is something every design firm should have. There are two reasons for keeping one:

Sample Interview Log

OFFICE: _____

NAME OF CANDIDATE	DATE SET-UP	DATE MEET	PURPOSE OF MEETING	WHO TO MEET WITH	LOCATION	EVALUATION	RACE	SEX	HANDI-CAPPED	VEV	HIRE

FIGURE 3.4 Sample interview log

1. You need information on race, sex, handicap, and Vietnam-era Veteran status to put together your EEO plans.
2. The interview provides the information you'll need to compute your interview-to-offer ratio, as well as your offer-to-acceptance ratio, two important HR-management performance statistics discussed in Chapter 1.

Not to dwell on it, but it can't be stressed too much that someone has to make sure this data is collected. Maintaining a current interview log is easiest for firms having only one office and one person in charge of their hiring activities.

3.5 PREPARING FOR THE INTERVIEW

When you're selective about who you ask in for an interview, you can put more thought and effort into each interview, thereby increasing the probability of a good selection and long-term match. The first steps to a good interview actually start before the interview even begins.

Start with a timely invitation, because this is not a place where foot dragging will be rewarded. No matter where the candidate is coming from, it is best not to wait too long to arrange the interview. Experienced recruiters know that time is their worst enemy and that when a good candidate is identified, the time to arrange an interview is now. Smart companies know that by acting quickly to arrange the interview, they achieve two goals. First, they flatter the candidate and show their interest by reacting so quickly. Second, they make sure that another firm can't snap up the candidate before they have had a chance to look at him or her.

Even if you can't conduct the actual interview within a week to ten days, it's best to arrange it quickly. Candidates with other employment offers who have interviews already scheduled with your firm will usually stall their decision until your interview is over. It is usually best not to wait more than a week to invite someone in who has sent a resume in response to an ad. Allow even less time (two to four days) for those who have been directly recruited by either the firm itself or an outside recruiter.

Once the interview date has been set, get ready. In the case of an interview in your firm's offices (where the majority of employment interviews take place), make sure that all the staff who are going to be meeting with the candidate know when the candidate will be there and what their own roles are in the process. They should be ready at their scheduled time to talk. Nothing sours a candidate more quickly than to have to sit outside someone's office or in a lobby for a half hour or more while the person he or she is supposed to meet with deals with a crisis or just plain doesn't keep his or her end of the appointment. It's rude, and there's no excuse for a company to treat candidates as if their time is not as valuable as the company's.

Conversely, candidates who are late for an interview should rarely be given second chances. Obviously, for those coming in from out of town, travel delays can excuse tardiness, but for candidates who are in the local area and who can't make it to the interview on time, there are few excuses. One experienced A/E/P industry hiring professional has a rule that he doesn't interview someone who is more than one-half hour late to the interview. He simply doesn't grant a second chance, figuring that if the candidate can't make it to the interview on time before he or she even has the job and when he or she is trying to make a good impression on the firm, what is likely to happen *after* he or she is hired?

3.6 HOTEL AND TRAVEL ARRANGEMENTS

When employment interviews require that candidates travel, always have your secretary or travel agent make all of the arrangements and handle the ticket purchase. Make it easy for candidates to come see you, and make sure that everything goes smoothly by handling the travel yourself. You'll also be sure not to pay too much for the tickets. The only disadvantage with this approach is that you'll miss out learning which candidates handle their personal finances so poorly that they can't afford to buy the tickets themselves—a bit of knowledge that may help you make your final decision.

The same thing applies for lodging and car rental. Take care of the arrangements yourself, making sure you get a fair price and that the candidates stay where you want them to, preferably in a nice area near your office. Never put candidates up in a dangerous neighborhood, and don't be so cheap that you make them stay at the Motel 6 fifteen miles from your office when a Holiday Inn is around the corner. You don't need to be extravagant in your choice of a hotel. A safe, moderately priced and conveniently located hotel or motel with whom you have negotiated a long-term discount room arrangement is the best bet.

The following story is a good argument for a firm handling all travel arrangements. A Texas-based firm was flying an architect in from Philadelphia to interview for a key position and decided to leave it up to the candidate to make his travel and hotel arrangements. The candidate, a 37-year-old hot-shot project manager from a nationally known firm, had just gotten married, so he decided (on his own) to bring along his wife for the first interview at the company's expense. He picked the most expensive hotel in town to stay for *two* nights and, upon arriving, had room service deliver lobster and champagne for two. The rental car he selected was a Lincoln Continental. Needless to say, he didn't get the offer that he probably would have had he not been so extravagant with the company's money. The firm also decided to make all interview travel arrangements themselves from that point forward.

Rental cars for candidates shouldn't be encouraged or provided until a second interview or later. The last thing you want is to have a candidate driving around in your area not knowing where he or she is going and possibly seeing things you don't want him or her to see. Companies frequently have trouble when they rent a car for an employment candidate to use while visiting their city, and the candidate rides around in his spare time to check out the housing. All too often, candidates end up in the most expensive section of town, which looks great. Then they find out what it costs to live there, and they think yours is the most expensive city in the country. Or, they end up driving around in neighborhoods that are below their expectations or too generic, in which case you have again allowed the process to get out of your control and risked disappointing the candidate.

When candidates are flying in from out of town, it's a good idea to have someone from the company pick them up at the airport. The candidate's anxiety will be eased knowing that transportation from the airport to the office is taken care of. Also, making the extra effort helps establish early in the interviewing process that the firm cares. Another reason for picking up candidates at the airport is so you can control what the candidate sees of your city. One A/E firm in a southern city always has candidates driven "the long way" between the airport and the office in order to bypass the blighted part of town.

The trip from the airport to the office is usually a good opportunity to become acquainted with the candidate in an informal setting. It may also be a chance for a brief whirlwind tour of your area, one that puts the interviewing company in total control of what the candidate sees. The better your area looks to the candidate, the greater the chances your offer will be accepted, should you eventually make one.

When you reach the office, be sure to bring candidates in through the front door. You want their first impressions of your company to be good. Nothing is worse than bringing in a top design architect from out of town for an interview, parking in the employee lot at the back of the building (which overlooks a scrap metal warehouse), then entering through the back door, which is shared with the survey field crews and all their muddy boots and equipment. In that situation, what is the architect likely to think about the company? Be conscious of the impressions you are creating.

Your goal early in the interviewing process should be to make the candidate feel comfortable, to break the ice and establish some rapport. It's always good to talk about innocent topics like weather or sports. Whatever you do, stay away from emotional topics like politics or world events at this stage!

3.7   INTERVIEWING TECHNIQUE

There is no mystery to good interviewing. It is a matter of putting the candidate at ease, asking the right questions, and listening carefully and attentively.

Twenty-five or 30 years ago, a concept of *stress interviewing* gained popularity in American industry. The stress interviewers advocated placing prospective job candidates under artificially induced stress to see how the candidates would perform. Although this school of interviewing still has a few followers, it is a more widely accepted practice today to make candidates feel as comfortable as possible so they will open up and reveal their true selves during an interview.

Nevertheless, some design professionals seem to derive a perverse sense of satisfaction from making employment candidates squirm in their seats. Obviously, when put on the defense, people reveal themselves only reluctantly. The interview degenerates into a game of cat and mouse and you've defeated your purpose of finding out what the candidate is really all about. So, if nothing else, try to avoid "interrogating" candidates and, for that matter, don't interview by committee, either. It has the same effect.

One candidate for the newly created director of HR position in a major consulting engineering and land planning firm was grilled by eight of the firm's principals simultaneously on his first interview. What's more, this was after *they* sought *him* out and directly recruited him for the position! An experienced interviewer himself, the candidate told the interviewing committee that if they wanted to improve their success in recruiting, the first thing they would have to do would be to change their interviewing process. That line got not only a few laughs, but also a job offer representing a 20 percent salary increase! The moral: Don't have any more than two people interview any one candidate at the same time.

You don't need to turn an interview into an interrogation to get the information you need. Far more important is learning to be a good listener. Good listeners are attentive, act interested in what the other person has to say, and talk a lot less than they listen. They don't tolerate inconsiderate interruptions from others outside the conversation. They make sure they are hearing what the other person is saying by asking for confirmation when required. They don't have annoying habits like tapping, humming, shaking the table, or staring off in the distance when another person is talking. They don't make it a practice to constantly bring the conversation back to the topic of themselves.

Listen to what the candidate says without interrupting, and take copious notes. Keep candidates talking about themselves. One effective technique for any interviewer to use is to get in the habit of saying "uh-huh" and "I see" periodically to show the candidate that you are listening. Another good habit is to ask questions like, "Why do you feel that way?" or, "Could you be more specific?" over and over. Statements like, "Tell me more," and "Give me an example of what you're talking about," are also useful in eliciting the true feelings and attitudes of the candidate.

Don't show approval or disapproval of anything a candidate says. You don't want to turn him or her off, nor do you want to inadvertently guide his or her responses. Some people have a bad habit of finishing sentences for candidates, getting them to say what they want to hear. Your best posture, once the interview is underway, is to say no more than necessary to keep the candidate talking. Also, once underway, minimize the number and length of interruptions, including phone calls. Interruptions are another example of the all-too-common rude treatment design firms give to employment candidates.

Without going into great length on the subject of body language, there are a few points worthy of discussion. You always want to show those you are interviewing that they are important. An attentive and interested expression and posture will help communicate this. Don't slouch in your chair, but instead, try to sit on the edge of your seat, back erect and head held high.

Do not fold your arms across your chest in a defensive or disapproving manner. Try arranging seating for the interview so that the candidate is at a 90 degree angle to you, as opposed to directly opposite. And, if the candidate will be seated across from you, make sure there isn't too much territory between you, as would be the case with a six-foot-wide conference table. Remove all barriers to effective communication. Interviewers who sit at desks with piles of papers, desk accessories, or desk lamps between themselves and their employment prospects are artificially adding to the distance between themselves and interviewees.

This last issue is a touchy one. Too little distance between the interviewer and job candidate is as bad as too much distance. Nothing will make someone clam up faster than the feeling that you are invading their personal space. Beyond that, in some rare instances, it could get you into trouble. Personal space needs are a combination of cultural norms and individual preference and may vary widely.

A midwestern firm's Vice President had terrible breath and made a habit of getting very close when he spoke with anyone. Although those he interviewed never verbalized it, one can only surmise that his lack of oral hygiene coupled with his tendency to invade others' personal space hurt his ability to interview effectively.

One young hot-shot section head working in a multidiscipline firm in the southeast had a bad habit of constantly feeling his crotch through his pants. Needless to say, he had a very hard time successfully hiring female professionals, who thought he was communicating something they didn't want to hear.

On the subject of note-taking, somewhere someone got the idea that there's something wrong with taking notes, as though it were less than considerate. The fact is that when you write down what another person is saying you are flattering them, encouraging them to continue. After all, what the person is saying must really be important if you are writing it all down, or at least that's what the candidate is likely to think subconsciously. Beyond that, any experienced interviewer knows that notes come in handy later when you try to remember exactly what a candidate said.

3.8 QUESTIONS AND ANSWERS

Most people who conduct many interviews have a set of questions they routinely ask (see Figure 3.5). A list of suggested questions accompanies this chapter. As you ease into an interview, you should start by filling in any information gaps you didn't take care of prior to the interview. Get the specifics on each position the candidate held, starting with the most recent or current position first. When did the candidate start working there and when did he or she leave? What prompted the departure? Was it initiated by the candidate or by his or her employer? What did the candidate like about the position? What did the candidate dislike? What did the candidate learn from the experience?

As you progress, ask more open-ended questions. Look for specific accomplishments in the candidate's employment history. The best indication of what someone will do in the future is what that person has done in the past. Everyone has heard the old cliche, "Success breeds success." It's true in most cases—not in all cases, but in most. Many design firms have strict criteria on the grades for new graduates for which they make no exceptions.

1. Tell me all about yourself. [A great opener]

2. Tell me your greatest strengths. Greatest weaknesses? [If a person doesn't know what his weaknesses are, how can he or she do anything about them?]

3. Why did you go into the [candidate's] field in the first place?

4. What are your goals? Short-, medium-, and long-term? What do you want to be doing 3, 5, and 10 years from now? What is your ultimate goal?

5. What do you enjoy most about your work? What do you like least about your work?

6. What kinds of reading do you do? What are the last few books you've read?

7. Can you work evenings and weekends if the job requires it? How do you feel about working overtime in general? Is it something you like? How long is a typical work week for you now?

8. What is driving you to make a change? [If the candidate is currently employed but was not directly recruited.]

9. What would conceivably motivate you to make a change? [If the candidate is currently employed and was directly recruited.]

10. What do you like and dislike about the company you now work for [or the last firm you worked for]?

11. How important is it to you to become an owner in this or any other organization? Why or why not?

12. If you worked for our firm and we asked you to live in Kuwait for three years to manage a major project, what would your reaction be?

13. What are you currently earning in terms of base salary? Are you paid hourly or on salary? How often do you get paid? When is your next pay review scheduled? What happened on your last pay review? Do you get paid overtime? Is it straight-time or time and one-half? Is overtime paid for nonbillable work as well? Have you ever received a bonus? If so, how much was it? Do you expect to get a bonus this year? If so, how much do you think it will be?

14. Do you have any unusual benefits? Does your company pay for all of your insurance? How much do you have to pay for your coverage? For your dependent coverage? Do you have a 401(k) plan? Does the company match, and if so, how much? How vested are you in the plan?

15. Do you have a company car? What kind is it? Is it yours for personal use? Do you have to pay for any of the expenses associated with it? How much do you think the car is worth to you?

16. Tell me about your most important accomplishments. Why are you proud of them?

17. Tell me about your worst failures. Why did they happen? What have you done to make sure they don't happen again?

18. Do you plan on continuing your formal education? If so, in what field? Have you though about a business degree? What else are you doing now to improve your skills in your field?

19. How long is a typical work day for you? What does it consist of? How much of your time is job chargeable? What percentage was chargeable over the last year? How do you feel about that?

FIGURE 3.5 Interviewing questions to ask

20. What turns you on work-wise? What turns you off work-wise? What do you like to do in your spare time?

21. What's more important in the success of a design professional in your eyes—design, communication, or management skills? Why do you feel the way you do?

22. What is more important to you—getting along with people or getting things done? Would you say you are a "people person?"

23. What do you know about our company? What good things have you heard about us? What bad things have you heard?

24. What do you feel are the most critical issues facing the design profession today?

25. What kinds of projects do you like working on? Do you like to do the same kinds of projects every day, or work on different things?

26. How do you feel about CADD on [candidate's specialty] projects?

27. Are you willing to travel? If so, what percentage of your time could you see spending on the road?

28. What kind of supervisor do you like to work for? What kind do you dislike? Could you tell me who your supervisors were at your previous employers? What do you think they would say about you? Would you mind if we called them? Do you have their phone numbers?

29. How do you feel about working with people you don't like? How do you deal with that? What would your co-workers tell us about you?

30. If we made you an offer, when would you be available to start?

31. What, if anything, would keep you from coming to work for us? What concerns do you have at this point?

32. What do you think makes you uniquely qualified for this position? Is there anything else you would like to tell us about yourself?

FIGURE 3.5   *(Continued)*

Ascertain likes and dislikes of past and present jobs and companies. These will help you assess the likelihood for a long-term employment relationship between the candidate and your firm. Ask yourself, "Does our company sound like that? Is he or she likely to feel any differently about our position?"

By and large, design professionals tend to be honest and straightforward people. Unfortunately however, there are exceptions to this rule, and because of these few bad apples you must always be on the lookout for dishonest candidates. Some of them are unusually adept at the interviewing process. You should be suspicious of candidates who answer questions with a question or who answer a different question from the one you asked. A candidate who is asked why he or she picked HVAC design as his or her career might turn it around and ask you why you went into it. Or the interior designer who is asked why he or she was let go from his or her previous employer will proceed to tell you why he or she went into interior design in the first place.

Look out for things that your intuition tell you just don't add up. A candidate for a 200-person A/E firm's financial manager position looked good on paper, had an MBA and appropriate undergraduate degree, and had only two previous positions in the preceding 10-year period. But his pork-chop sideburns and deteriorating Cadillac in the visitor's parking lot tipped off the savvy HR director, who, upon attempting to verify the fellow's education found out he was a complete fraud who had only attended one semester of college! Don't ignore your intuition. It comes from experience.

Every interviewer gives some thought to the questions he or she will ask, but *answering* questions is an equally important—yet largely ignored—part of the interviewing process. The best candidates will have the most questions, and they can be tough. Candidates who have no questions are usually duds, and if you encounter one of these, it should be viewed as a red flag.

Using the accompanying list of questions to be prepared to answer (see Figure 3.6 below) as a guide, think about how you would address candidates' questions. Add to the list any others that you might anticipate, based on yours or others' experience. Develop the best answers for them, too. Again, see to it that each person who gets involved in interviewing knows what the company wants to say when asked any of these questions by a job candidate.

1. What would I be doing if I worked in this position at your firm?

2. What do you see as the major threats to MZ&A Group in the next few years? The opportunities?

3. What do you see as the weaknesses of MZ&A Group? The strengths? What are you doing to overcome your weaknesses and build on your strengths?

4. What is your company staff turnover rate? Why is it so high/low?

5. How are your performance appraisals handled? Who would review me? How about pay reviews? When? What kind of increase could I expect if I perform well?

6. Do you pay bonuses? Would I be eligible? What do you base a bonus on? How much could someone like me expect to get in a typical year? When are bonuses paid?

7. Who would I be working for if I worked here? What is his or her background? What are the other people in the group or department like? Do they want to see someone hired? Why or why not? What can you tell me about their backgrounds? How do you think they feel about their boss? Could I talk with any of them?

8. What is the next step up beyond this position? How long would you expect it to take for me to get there? How long has it taken others?

9. What does it take for someone to be considered successful at MZ&A Group? What would your expectations of my performance be?

10. Has anyone been particularly successful entering the firm at this position? What kind of background did that person have? What other personality characteristics did he or she exhibit?

11. What kinds of projects would I be working on? What would my role be? Who are your clients? Who is your best client?

12. What kind of computer/CADD equipment do you have? Would I be expected to work on the system? Do you train? Would I be able to use the system? When and how much?

FIGURE 3.6 Questions to be prepared to answer

13. Do you have a business plan? Could I see it? What is the mission of your firm? What are the goals of the firm?

14. What are *your* own goals? What can you tell me about your background?

15. Why do you work at MZ&A Group instead of somewhere else? Why should I work for MZ&A Group instead of another firm?

16. What kind of training programs do you have? Do you pay for college tuition? Is training done on company time?

17. Could you give me some information on the firm's financial performance?

18. Who are your biggest competitors?

19. What is your fringe benefits program? Can you give me some written information on it?

20. How does your insurance company deal with pre-existing conditions?

21. Is there a waiting period on insurance?

22. Do you have a profit-sharing or retirement plan? Do you have a 401(k) plan? Can I roll over my retirement money into your plan? What is your vesting period? What does the term "vesting" mean?

23. What is the salary (or salary range) for this position? Do you have a bonus program? What would you expect someone like me to make in a typical year for a bonus? Do you pay for overtime? How much overtime would I have to work in a typical week?

24. What can you tell me about the other candidates for this position?

25. Who owns the company? How many principals are there? How does one go about becoming an owner? What does it mean to be an owner? How long does it typically take?

26. Can I take home one of your company policy manuals?

27. What is your severance policy?

28. What is your relocation policy?

29. Do you do business with South Africa?

30. What is your smoking policy? Policy on AIDS?

31. What are your hours of work? How many holidays do you provide?

32. When will you be making a final hiring decision? What is your schedule for getting someone on board? What is the next step in the hiring process?

33. When do you think I will hear back from you?

FIGURE 3.6 *(Continued)*

There is one more topic that merits discussion before moving on, and it's a literal time bomb waiting to go off in the face of many design firms. The problem is illegal interview questions. Federal and state laws prohibit asking about a candidate's age, race, religion, and marital status. See Figure 3.7 for a list of questions to avoid. Other types of questions may be prohibited only in certain states. If someone is passed over for hire and has been asked *any* illegal questions, you may have a tough time proving that they weren't discriminated against. And you could end up with a hefty settlement obligation to pay. So err on the cautious side, because it's just not worth it!

1. What church do you attend? What is the name of your priest, rabbi, or minister?
2. What is your father's surname? What [in the case of women] is your maiden name?
3. Who resides with you?
4. Who will care for children while you are working?
5. Where does your husband/wife/parent live or work? [You may ask whether relatives have been or are employed by your firm.]
6. Do you own or rent your home?
7. Did you ever have your wages garnished or attached?
8. When did you graduate from high school?
9. Are you married? [You may ask Mr., Mrs., Miss, or Ms.]*
10. How many children do you have? What are their ages?*
11. How old are you? When were you born?*
12. Have you ever been arrested? [You may ask about convictions in some states; in others, you can't.]*
13. What is your race?*
14. Where were you born?*

Note: Asterisked questions may be asked *after* hiring if required for benefit administration or for preparation of EEO reports or affirmative action plans. Check with your employment counsel for a current list of prohibited questions.

FIGURE 3.7 Prohibited interview questions

Everyone who participates in the interviewing process should have a list of illegal questions at his or her desk to remind him or her of what he or she can't ask. Firms are advised, however, to seek out the advice of their labor counsel on this subject for a current list reflecting any changes in federal employment legislation and the state statutes for each of their office locations.

3.9 DISCUSSING MONEY

If you haven't done so before this first meeting, the first interview is the time to get all of the details on the candidate's current compensation package, including specifics on base salary, bonus, overtime, insurance benefits, car allowances, and other perks. You'll need this information later when deciding whether to make an offer and what it should be.

Don't be bashful when asking about compensation. If candidates are reluctant to reveal what they make, simply tell them that you understand their cautiousness but must have that information before you can move ahead to the next step. Then repeat the question. Fortunately, when you ask for compensation data matter of factly as though you fully expect to get it, you will rarely encounter any objections. Instead of refusing, a candidate will more often throw out some nebulous statement like, "I make something in the fifties," or, "I make in the low to mid-forties." At that point, ask the candidate to be more specific.

Also, be sure to find out when the candidate's next pay review is. Little is worse than making an offer to a final candidate only to find out that he or she was up for pay review at his or her present employer two days after you first contacted him or her, and he or she just got a $5000 raise, pricing him or herself completely out of contention for your job.

If a candidate tells you he or she gets paid for overtime, get all of the details. Ask if the overtime pay is for all hours over 40, or just billable hours. Find out if the candidate is paid straight time or time and one half for overtime. Find out how much the candidate earned in overtime (in total) this year and last year. The same thing applies to candidates who tell you they get bonuses. Find out how often bonuses are paid, when they are paid, and what they are based on. Find out what the candidate expects this year, and what he or she received in each of the past two years.

Although it's rarely necessary, if the candidate tells you he or she is earning considerably more than you think someone with that particular background would earn, you may in some cases want to ask the candidate for a pay stub as confirmation. Again, you can't always do this, but for a low-level position or perhaps a technician's position, it may quickly identify someone who has been dishonest with you. A better approach, though, for getting at the truth is to ask how the figure he or she quotes breaks down in terms of bonus, overtime, benefits, etc. At this point, about half of these highballers will come clean and tell you how much of their pay isn't salary, and how much is in the form of benefits and other things that don't show up on a pay stub or W-2. Fortunately, because of the basically honest nature of design professionals, you probably won't have too many problems in this area.

Don't, however, ask how much money the candidate will need to make a job change. No one who is halfway savvy about negotiation would give you a figure. If he or she gives a figure that is less than what you are willing to pay, the candidate knows he or she is leaving money on the table. If it is more than what you are willing to pay, the candidate may be prescreened and taken out of the process right then and there, which means that *no* offer will come from you at all. Either way, it's to the candidate's disadvantage to provide you with a specific dollar figure. Beyond that, this problem is compounded when the question is posed early in the hiring process when the candidate probably knows very little about you, your company, and your credibility. If you simply must find this out, wait until the end of the interviewing process when the candidate is more likely to provide you with a realistic figure.

Younger candidates, such as new college graduates, and lower-level technical people might ask what the salary or salary range is for the position sought. Seasoned professionals may as well, although it is generally regarded as poor form to ask this question. Your response should be that you have no set salary or salary range for the position and that you will make the best offer you can afford to make to someone, depending on your assessment of his or her credentials, what you think it will take to get him or her to accept, and what your other people of similar backgrounds in similar roles earn. This rather lengthy explanation usually satisfies candidates, allowing you to move on to other matters.

3.10   SELLING THE COMPANY AND THE AREA

The interview is more than a time for getting information; it's also a time for giving information. The information you give in interviews and the impression you make will have a direct bearing on how candidates feel about your firm and, as a result, how many of your offers are accepted. This, after all, is the point of the whole hiring process: To make a fair offer to the right candidate and have it enthusiastically accepted. But giving information is not limited to how you answer candidates' questions. There is a lot more you can do to be sure that you have all possible success getting your offers for employment accepted.

The most effective recruiters are also the best salesmen. Whoever heads your firm's hiring activities should also be one of your company's most upbeat, enthusiastic ambassadors. This lead recruiter should be able to sell the proverbial snowballs to Eskimos.

One common misconception is that a recruiter needs to be a design professional to be effective. After all, don't design professionals want to hear what a position is all about from someone who understands their language? If the person who is in charge of your firm's hiring activities happens to be a design professional, great, but it shouldn't be a requirement. The most important thing is to have the personality and interpersonal and communication skills to be an effective recruiter.

Even the best recruiters will need written materials to aid them in their selling. Every firm should put together some basic recruitment materials. There's no need for an expensive recruitment brochure, although they're nice for the firms that can afford them. It's completely acceptable to have something on the order of a statement of qualifications, designed to be used as a presentation aid when the sales pitch on the company is made at the end of the interview. This need not be any more than a GBC-bound document, containing several important pieces of information for anyone considering a job change. It may include:

1. A description of the firm, including age, disciplines, number and location of branch offices, ownership, and so forth.
2. A statement of the firm's mission, if available.
3. An overall company organization chart, including something that shows where the candidate would work in the firm, if eventually hired.
4. Summary tables outlining significant events in the firm's history, as well as its growth in terms of staff, fee billings, or dollar value of constructed projects. (As long as this data makes the firm look like a good place to work; if it doesn't, don't use it.)
5. A summary of all of the firm benefits, including vacation, sick leave, medical insurance, and so on, with a disclaimer that benefits can change at any time.
6. Anything else you think would be helpful to sell your company, the position, or the area. Testimonials from actual employees on what a great place your company is to work are often included.

You should be able to go over this material in no more than 10 or 15 minutes, and all candidates for employment should be sent away with one of these booklets in hand. Later, if an offer is made, you can refer to the company information booklet that the candidate was provided with on his or her visit.

The importance of these materials can't be overemphasized. Everyone who interviews with your company should be given the same information on benefits, in particular. If your information is not prepared in advance, miscommunications will occur and all sorts of special exceptions are likely when offers are made.

Some design firms produce special videos on the firms to help sell job candidates. These videos should be professionally designed and shouldn't be any more than 5 or 10 minutes long. Firms unable to afford videos often put together a standard slide presentation for interviewees, showing their projects and management philosophy.

It wouldn't be right to bring up the subject of selling candidates—out-of-town candidates, in particular—on your firm and region without discussing the relocation consultant. Make arrangements with a competent residential real estate relocation expert in your area to handle your out-of-town candidates' real estate needs. A good real estate person is as effective as anyone in selling candidates on the good points of your area. These consultants have the ability to ferret out concerns about more than just housing, too, and can be a real resource when it comes to understanding the candidate's spouse's concerns and feelings.

Select a real estate professional the same way you would any other professional with whom you do business. Get referrals from people you know, and interview the best prospects to find one person who will deal with all your out-of-town candidates. Your real estate relocation expert should be able to supply you with cost data on your area compared to where the candidate is coming from, not just in the way of real estate but also in the areas of health care, food, taxes, and so on. Your relocation pro should be fully willing and able to provide a tour of your city for all incoming employment prospects. Many relocation experts have films or other A/V presentations that they show to those visiting from the outside.

A relocation pro should be adept at figuring out what kind of housing the candidate wants and needs and directing the candidate to the best area within your city to meet those needs. In other words, if the candidate is in the market for a $100,000 house, your pro won't be showing him or her homes costing $150,000. By the same token, if your candidate is a top executive coming out of an expensive residential area and has $400,000 to spend, your pro won't be showing him or her $175,000 tract homes in a subdivision that the agent has an exclusive contract to sell.

As soon as you have arranged an interview with an out-of-town candidate, put your relocation expert in touch with the candidate. That way, the homework on the housing issue can be done early in the interviewing process, and you may just save yourself a second airline ticket to check the area out before a decision is made on your offer. Beyond that, if you're going to have a problem with cost of housing, it's better to find out early in the process so you can prepare for it. There is more on the subject of relocation in Chapter 4.

3.11 CLOSING THE INTERVIEW SESSION

If the candidate looks like a good prospect, close the interview session with a brief presentation on the firm, and supply the candidate with your recruitment materials. If the candidate does not appear to be a good prospect, you may want to cut the interview process short by handing the candidate a copy of your recruitment materials, telling him or her that all of the information on the company's history, organization structure, and benefits is in there and that he or she may read it at his or her convenience.

Be sure not to make an offer or commit yourself to anything during a first interview. There's no way you can get the input of those involved in the interviewing process, adequately check references, and verify education and registration credentials. Beyond that, there are psychological reasons why moving too quickly can work against you (more on that in Chapter 4). Be sure candidates don't leave an interview feeling a job is theirs, unless you have actually extended an offer. You may hurt your negotiating posture and chances for an eventual offer acceptance.

Conclude all interviews by saying that you will get back in touch with the candidate by a specific date. At the conclusion of the meeting, the candidate should be asked what his or her feelings are that point. Follow this up with something to the effect of, "We appreciate the opportunity to spend time with you. As you can imagine, we are talking with a number of candidates for this particular position. Let us put our heads together and get back in touch with you within the next few days." Never tell the candidate, "Go home and think about it." Candidates have nothing to think about until you have formally extended a specific job offer. Local candidates should be escorted to the front door and seen off the premises. Out-of-town candidates should either be taken back to the airport by a company employee or have cab or limo transportation arranged by the firm.

After the interview, don't deceive or string people along. Tell all candidates that you are talking with other people and that they should call if their situation changes or if they have any questions before the time you get back to them. Don't say you'll do something by a certain date and then fail to do it without at least relaying to the candidate the fact that there will be a delay and why. Experienced recruiters know that this can be the kiss of death for a good candidate. The best people simply don't accept that kind of treatment; they honor their commitments and expect you to do the same. Anyone who will accept being strung along is telling you something about how desperate (and desirable) he or she is (or isn't).

Last but not least, don't let candidates pull themselves out of contention before you do. Some companies seem to pride themselves on setting up all sorts of obstacles for people who are interested in employment with their firms. They feel that if someone can tolerate a long wait to get an offer, go through filling out a lengthy and cumbersome employment application, or submit themselves to impersonal and degrading drug tests, they are somehow tougher or more interested than someone who won't. That kind of thinking is really silly in a highly competitive labor market where demand for talent far exceeds supply.

Your goal throughout the entire interviewing process should be to keep yourself in the decision-making position. To do that, you can't have candidates coming to the conclusion that they don't want to work for your firm even if they get an offer. But that's what will happen if you don't sell every candidate on the benefits of your firm and your open position and treat them with care and respect at every step in your process. (See Figure 3.8 for an interview checklist.)

Be prepared for the interview.

Make candidates feel comfortable.

Take complete and accurate notes.

Don't make candidates wait to see you.

Be conscious of impressions.

Listen without interrupting.

Keep candidates talking about themselves.

Don't show approval or disapproval of anything.

Get the details on the candidate's current compensation.

Don't ask how much money the candidate needs to make a job change.

Look for accomplishments in the candidate's past.

Try not to interrogate the candidate too intensely or put him or her on the defensive.

Be sure not to finish the candidate's sentences for him or her.

Be honest and communicate clearly.

Don't tolerate interruptions during the interview.

Don't have more than two people interview any one candidate at the same time.

Look out for candidates who answer questions with a question or who answer a different question for the one you asked.

Sell all candidates on your company and area.

Be sure not to make or commit yourself to an offer during an interview.

Be sure candidates don't leave an interview feeling the job is theirs, unless you have actually extended an offer.

Conclude all interviews with a statement to the effect that you will get back in touch with the candidate by a specific date

Don't ignore your intuition.

Don't let candidates pull themselves out of contention before you do.

FIGURE 3.8   Interviewing checklist

3.12   SECOND AND THIRD INTERVIEWS

Some design firms have hiring processes that mandate two, three, or even more interviews. A two-stage interviewing process is best for local candidates. The first session may be a meeting to determine mutual interests, get all the details on the candidate's background, and set the stage for the next meeting with the technical person responsible for the area the person would be working in.

Limit out-of-town candidates to one interview, if possible. Try to schedule the candidate to arrive early in the day, even if he or she has to be flown in the night before. Get the interview over by early afternoon, and plan some time to show the candidate around later in the day. Get the candidate out by the end of the day. If an offer is eventually made to an out-of-town candidate, a second ticket or pair of tickets may be necessary to close the deal. But don't make this part of your regular process. It's a waste of time and money.

3.13   CORRESPONDENCE THROUGHOUT THE INTERVIEW PROCESS

As discussed in the preceding chapter, all resumes and applications should be sent to one person in your firm for classification and filing in your recruitment database. The same person can take care of routine correspondence during the interviewing process. Don't underestimate the importance of these simple written acknowledgements. Anyone who sends a resume or fills out an application for employment with your firm deserves a prompt, courteous response. Standard letters stored in your word processor will suffice, telling candidates either that you have no openings for them currently but will keep their credentials on file, or that you are currently in the review process and will get back to them at some point in the future. Standard letters should also be created for handling rejection after an interview, or for conveying that a position has been filled. Personally sign every letter.

These letters are one more step toward ensuring that everyone who comes into contact with your firm has a favorable experience. They will help ensure a positive response if you ever contact the candidate in the future on another position. Once your system for cranking them out is in place, the cost is minimal compared with the benefits. Design firms that maintain good correspondence throughout the interview process can testify to their candidates' appreciation of the personal treatment these letters communicate.

Some design firms attempt to shortcut the process by using mailing labels and postcards or letters addressed to "Dear Sir/Madam" with no inside address. This kind of impersonal treatment may have the opposite of its intended effect; it may create the impression that the firm is nothing more than a cold, bureaucratic place that doesn't really value people (see Figures 3.9 through 3.13 below for sample correspondence through the interview process).

Date
Mr. Bill Smith
Address
City, State Zip

Dear Mr. Smith:

We received the resume you sent us recently. Your interest in Mark Zweig & Associates is greatly appreciated.

FIGURE 3.9   Form Letter: Resume received but no interest at this time

Unfortunately, as interesting as your credentials and background may be, we have no openings at the present time for which you are being considered. We will, however, enter your resume to our confidential resume/application databank for review in connection with any openings that may develop here in the future. If a potential match develops, we'll get back in touch with you.

In the meantime, good luck with your job search.

Sincerely,

MARK ZWEIG & ASSOCIATES

Anne O'Brien
Director of Human Resources

AMO/slc

FIGURE 3.9   *(Continued)*

Date
Mr. Bill Smith
Address
City, State Zip

Dear Mr. Smith:

We appreciate the time you spent filling out an application for employment with us, and also the interest you have shown in Mark Zweig & Associates.

Unfortunately, as interesting as your credentials and background may be, we have no openings at the present time for which you are being considered. We will, however, enter your resume to our confidential resume/application databank for review in connection with any openings that may develop here in the future. If a potential match develops, we'll get back in touch with you.

In the meantime, good luck with your job search.

Sincerely,

MARK ZWEIG & ASSOCIATES, INC.

Anne O'Brien
Director of Human Resources

AMO/slc

FIGURE 3.10   Form letter: Application filled out but no interest at this time

Date
Mr. Bill Smith
Address
City, State Zip

Dear Mr. Smith:

The purpose of this letter is to acknowledge receipt of your resume/employment application in response to our recent recruitment advertising.

We received a tremendous response to our ad and have not yet been able to review each resume/application. Hopefully, we will be in a position to get back in touch with you within a few weeks.

If you have any questions concerning the status of your application, please call me. Thank you for your interest in Mark Zweig & Associates.

Sincerely,

MARK ZWEIG & ASSOCIATES, INC.

Anne O'Brien
Director of Human Resources

AMO/slc

FIGURE 3.11 Form letter: Response to ad, application pending

Date
Mr. Bill Smith
Address
City, State Zip

Dear Mr. Smith:

We appreciate the time you spent meeting with us, and we enjoyed the opportunity to get acquainted with you.

As interesting as your background may be, we have no current openings for someone with your specific skills and interests. We will, however, enter your credentials into our confidential resume/application databank for future review. We'll re-contact you should any opportunities develop.

In the meantime, best of luck to you.

Sincerely,

MARK ZWEIG & ASSOCIATES, INC.

Anne O'Brien
Director of Human Resources

AMO/slc

FIGURE 3.12 Form letter: After personal interview, no interest at this time

Date
Mr. Bill Smith
Address
City, State Zip

Dear Mr. Smith:

The purpose of this letter is to inform you that the position of _____ with our firm has been filled.

We sincerely appreciate the interest you have shown in Mark Zweig & Associates and will keep your information in our confidential databank for future reference. Rest assured, we'll be back in touch with you should a potential match between your background and our needs develop.

In the meantime, good luck with your job search.

Sincerely,

MARK ZWEIG & ASSOCIATES, INC.

Anne O'Brien
Director of Human Resources

AMO/slc

FIGURE 3.13   Form letter: Position filled

3.14   CONCLUSION

A consistent approach to interviewing is one of the keys to consistent hiring, yet too few design firms have trained managers in interviewing and defined their interviewing process. Interviewing skills can be learned. Effective interviewing requires interviewing the right people in the first place, knowing the questions that can and can't be asked, knowing how to prepare for an interview, and understanding how to most effectively sell the benefits of the firm and the position. It also requires good listening skills and diligent follow-up.

4

HIRING

The doctor can bury his mistakes, but an architect can only advise his clients to plant vines.

—Frank Lloyd Wright

4.1 INTRODUCTION

It's not failing to capitalize on every opportunity that comes along that kills design firms; it's mistakes. A bad hiring decision is one of the most costly mistakes a design firm can make. With an average staff turnover rate in the 20 percent range for the design industry, a typical 100-person design firm will have to replace 20 people each year; that is, it will have 20 opportunities to make major blunders. Developing a process that helps you decide who to hire is the first issue addressed in this chapter.

Getting your employment offers accepted is the next major obstacle. A great deal of time and money can go into finding and interviewing employment prospects. Once the best candidate rises to the top, those hours and those dollars will be completely wasted if he or she turns down your job offer. That doesn't mean you have to offer more than you can afford. This chapter will cover how to maximize your closing rate without giving away the store.

4.2 THE CENTRALIZED HIRING PROCESS

The only way to get consistent results in hiring is to have a consistent hiring process. You need consistency in recruiting, consistency in interviewing, and consistency in selecting candidates and extending offers. And there's only one sure way to achieve the required consistency—*centralized control*. One person needs to be in control of your firm's hiring activities. That's why more and more firms have a full-time, professional HR manager. But whether or not your firm has an HR director, someone must take responsibility for this crucial process. Let's call this individual the Hiring Process Manager (HPM).

If you have an HR manager, he or she should be the HPM. If not, select one of your firm's principals or managers who pays attention to detail, who is sensitive to the potential liabilities in the employment process, and who has some selling skills. Make sure that whoever you select is sincerely interested in the job and committed to the benefits of having someone in the role.

Be careful not to assign the HPM role to just anyone. If your personnel person is largely an administrator or record-keeper, he or she may not be the best person for the job. Don't just carelessly assign the hiring process responsibilities to someone to appease your conscience. The HPM, together with each of your firm's branch managers, should select an individual to act as an HPM in each branch or to assist the HPM in all matters involving each branch.

The HPM should manage the entire recruitment, interviewing, and hiring processes described in the first four chapters of this book; the HPM is responsible for:

1. Determining whether a need to hire someone from the outside actually exists.
2. Developing reliable sources for temporary or subcontract help.
3. Managing the internal recruitment process.
4. Maintaining the resume/application databank.
5. Buying all employment advertising.
6. Dealing with all employment agencies and executive search firms.
7. Acting as a direct recruiter.
8. Coordinating the college recruitment program.
9. Managing the process of determining who to interview.
10. Prescreening of any sort.
11. Maintaining the interview log.
12. Making the presentation on the company and its geographical area to all employment candidates.
13. Seeing that all correspondence pertaining to the hiring process goes out.
14. Selecting and coordinating with the firm's relocation consultant.
15. Extending and confirming all employment offers.
16. Selecting and monitoring the performance of the designated regional HPMs or the local HPM assistants in each of the branch offices.
17. In general, acting as the company liaison throughout the hiring process.

There are many benefits to selecting one person to act as HPM (see Figure 4.1). First, with all interviewing activities flowing through one individual, it's easier to make sure that all interview statistics are kept for both EEO and performance-measuring purposes. When anyone in the firm can set up and conduct interviews, there just isn't any control, making it an almost impossible task to keep the proper records.

1. Allows greater control over how interview statistics are kept.
2. Minimizes employment agency and executive search firm fees.
3. Minimizes employment-advertising expenses.
4. Keeps the bad apples out of the hiring process through quality prescreening.
5. Saves time of managers who otherwise would do the hiring.
6. Delivers consistent sales message to prospective employees, keeping the firm from making unintentional commitments.
7. Makes employment offers that get accepted, while conserving firm resources and avoiding potential future liabilities.
8. Provides a vehicle for accelerating the firm's expertise and sophistication in the hiring process.
9. Overall, makes the firm's hiring process more consistent and easier to manage.

FIGURE 4.1   Benefits of the Hiring Process Manager (HPM)

Having all hiring activity go through one person also makes it considerably easier to avoid paying too many fees to employment agencies and executive search firms. When all other steps in the recruiting process are routinely taken first, outside recruiters will be used only when absolutely necessary. The HPM is also better able to tell an outside recruiter whether the company already has someone's resume in its system because he or she is the one who maintains the firm's in-house resume/application databank.

The benefits of centralizing employment-advertising purchases include a greater assurance the company won't be buying unneeded advertising, and a method for ensuring that your company gets all quantity discounts you are entitled to. By the same token, it also facilitates consolidation of all position openings in the firm's employment ads.

One of the most important duties of the HPM is to keep the bad apples out of the hiring process, especially candidates who have a knack of masking their obvious shortcomings with a polished presentation. By thorough prescreening, the HPM can minimize the chances that an individual hiring manager will come under the spell of one of these candidates and make a hiring mistake.

With one person making the firm's sales pitch to job candidates, you're less likely to generate confusion and false expectations. Because of a lack of confidence and sales skills, some technical managers tend to make outlandish promises that can't be kept and oversell both the company and position. This can create incredible liabilities for your firm! Though the company information or recruitment booklet is a critical element in the process of delivering a consistent sales message to prospective employees, what your company agents *say* is every bit as important.

The HPM is also a great asset when it comes to structuring employment offers and extending them enthusiastically. The HPM will be sensitive to the phrasing of written offers so as to avoid inadvertently making long-term employment obligations that the firm has no intention of keeping.

Last but not least, consider the following. In a firm that has five different managers hiring a combined total of 20 people each year, each manager will on the average make four hires per year. If one person is involved in all hiring, that person will be accumulating experience and judgment *five times* faster than a manager who participates in the process 20 percent of the time. It is through this concentration of experience that the skills of the HPM grow quickly. The bottom line to this discussion is that whatever the formal hiring process is for your firm, having one person (and the *right* person) in control of it makes it easier for you to manage and increases the probability that each step along the way will be followed.

4.3 CHECKING CREDENTIALS AND REFERENCES

If you sometimes neglect to check credentials and references of employment candidates because it seems uncomfortable or unprofessional, consider the following anecdote. One full-service A/E/P company hired a supposedly degreed and licensed civil engineer for their office in Anchorage, Alaska, a branch started as a project office to handle a large asbestos abatement construction services project. The engineer's degree and license weren't initially necessary for the asbestos work the firm was doing, but a year or so later when the contract was nearing its end, home-office management thought it would make sense for him to market municipal engineering services in the area. Something came up that required the firm have proof of his registration, and the engineer was unable to produce it. When the firm attempted to verify his registration and education, both turned out to be misrepresented. One of the firm's vice presidents then flew to Anchorage and confronted the engineer, who stormed out of the office, vowing to go over to the school and "get everything squared away now." He never returned, leaving all of his personal effects in his office.

The moral of the story is that this guy never would have been hired in the first place if the firm had taken the trouble to verify his education and registration. Before any candidate can be fully evaluated, all academic credentials and professional registrations *must* be confirmed. Most colleges and universities keep student records filed by social security number. It's not a bad idea to ask for the social security number on your firm's regular application for employment. That way, all you will need to do is give the candidate's complete name and social security number to the school to confirm any degrees. The same thing applies for registrations. Always ask employment candidates for their registration numbers. State registration bureaus are more than happy to confirm the registration of anyone who claims to have it. All it takes is a five-minute phone call.

Just as important as verifying education and registration claims is a thorough check of the employment references of all candidates who make it to the point of final consideration (see Figure 4.2 for sample reference check form). At least two references, preferably from former employers, should be checked. Personal references from the candidate's minister, rabbi, or next-door neighbor mean next to nothing, and you shouldn't waste your time talking to these people. Who would give you the name of someone as a personal reference who would say anything bad about him?

If a job candidate is still employed, informal reference checks should be conducted confidentially and with the candidate's full knowledge and permission. Checking references without permission creates the potential for lawsuits from job candidates you don't end up hiring. Former employers are the best sources of information on a currently employed candidate. Past supervisors who made job changes themselves are another possibility. Unfortunately, not every candidate has a previous employer (or employers). And former employers from the distant past are of questionable value as references.

Some companies like to check references from professional peers or clients as well. These references may provide valuable insights into a candidate. The danger, again, is that all references should be checked *only* with the permission of the candidate, and candidates who are currently employed may hesitate to tip off clients that they are considering making a job change.

One more option for dealing with employed candidates is to make any offers extended to them contingent on your getting good references from their present employers after they turn in their official notice to leave. Proceed with caution here, however! The employer, feeling scorned, may not give good references on a staff member who is leaving to go to work for a firm perceived as a competitor.

Unemployed candidates are considerably easier to deal with from the standpoint of securing references. For the unemployed, insist on getting the names of all former supervisors in all former employers, at least those from the previous 10-year period. While you're at it, you may want to ask for current phone numbers where those people can be reached. In some cases, former supervisors may have made job changes themselves, and having their current phone numbers can be a real time saver.

Develop a standard reference form with a corresponding list of questions that you can use regularly. Ask how the potential employee was perceived by clients, peers, subordinates, and superiors. Ask whether the employee had an absenteeism or attendance problem. Ask how the employee's performance was evaluated and whether the employee is eligible and would be considered for rehire by the company. Confirm dates of employment, titles held, and last compensation, if you can. Also ask, "Is there anything else I need to know about [candidate's name]?" This kind of open-ended question may turn up all kinds of information you wouldn't have gotten any other way.

Reference Check Form

_____, I'm calling to check a reference on someone who used to work for you. Your honest comments will be sincerely appreciated. Rest assured, anything you say will be held in the strictest confidence.

We are considering hiring _____ for a position of _____.

Candidate: _____   Date: _____

Position Applied for: _____   Office: _____

Name & Title of Reference: _____

Company: _____   Location: _____   Phone: (___)_____

1. How long have you known _____? _____

2. How long did _____ work there? _____

3. How would you rate _____ technically?
   ☐ Below Par   ☐ Average   ☐ Excellent

4. How would you rate _____ managerially?
   ☐ Below Par   ☐ Average   ☐ Excellent

5. How would you rate his/her overall job performance?
   ☐ Below Par   ☐ Average   ☐ Excellent

6. Did he/she get along well with his/her:
   ☐ Supervisor?   ☐ Peers?   ☐ Subordinates?   ☐ Clients?

7. Did he/she miss work often? _____

8. Did he/she have any drug or alcohol problems to your knowledge? _____

9. Did he/she have any other problems that you are aware of? _____

10. What else I should know about? _____

_____

_____

_____

11. Providing you don't have a policy against rehiring former employees, would you rehire
   _____?   ☐ Yes   ☐ No

Thank you for your help. Rest assured your comments will be held in strict confidence.

FIGURE 4.2   Sample reference check form

Your technique in checking references will greatly affect the quality of information you are able to extract. Always start the reference check call with a thorough (and slow) explanation of who you are and why you are calling, making sure that you are completely clear about whose reference you are checking, and what position you are considering that person for. Tell the reference provider that any comments he or she makes will be held in strictest confidence and will remain solely between the two of you. This is an important step, because many design firms are so scared of the possibility of a lawsuit from a former employee that they simply won't give out *any* reference information. (Refer to Chapter 12 for an explanation of why these fears exist.) Some verbal reassurance may go a long way toward alleviating these fears.

If you have reached this point in the process, you are impressed with the candidate and are seriously considering extending an offer. However, you still need to find out anything that could indicate a potential employment problem with him or her. It's your job to have a "negative bias": Look for reasons why you *shouldn't* hire the candidate, as opposed to why you *should*.

In the few cases where a former employer won't tell you anything, go back to the candidate and ask him or her if there is anyone else in the company that you might be able to talk with. Maybe there is another supervisor in the firm who will talk to you, or one who has left and is now working elsewhere. By the way, even though you hope to get the information you need when checking a reference, when *you* get called to provide a reference, be careful not to say much. More on the reasons for this double standard in Chapter 12.

One word of caution. Some dishonest candidates like to develop their own recommendation letters. They take some of their firm's blank letterheads on the way out the door, then type up a glowing recommendation for themselves. Don't accept written references without verifying them. In any case, there's no need to tell the referrer that you have anything supposedly written by him or her. In fact, it's probably best that you don't, because no one wants to look like he or she was less than honest when writing the reference in the first place.

Don't get so wrapped up in the process of checking references that it impedes your ability to get offers out expeditiously, and you end up losing good candidates because your process is so cumbersome. But don't shortcut this important step either. Reference checking is no fun, but it's a crucial part of the overall hiring process for a design firm. The consequences of making a mistake are just too big. Don't ever hire anyone without checking references.

4.4 COMPARING CANDIDATES

When a firm has done everything within its power to recruit the best possible candidates and has effectively prescreened, thoroughly interviewed, and completely checked out each one, there comes a time to choose which candidate gets the offer. It's best if you can generate three or four good candidates for each opening. That way, you have some basis for comparison, increasing your chances of making a good decision to hire the best one. It just stands to reason that if you have several choices, each one qualified, you'll make a better decision than if you have only one choice.

Obviously, there may be cases where you can't generate a number of possibilities and are forced into taking the best of a limited number of currently available candidates. This, however, should be the exception, not the rule. Too many design firms take the first person who comes along as a matter of normal practice. As a result, they make lots of bad hiring decisions.

Sample Candidate Comparison Matrix
(Weight x Rating = Score)

Selection Criteria	Weight	Rating	Score
Technical skills/qualifications in discipline ares			
Management skills qualifications.			
Potential to advance.			
Ability to attract in light of current compensation.			
Ease of relocation (if required at all).			
Communication/ Interpersonal skills.			
Educational credentials.			
Professional registrations.			
Quality of references			
Likelihood of long-term employment			

FIGURE 4.3 Sample candidate comparison matrix

One A/E firm needed a new marketing director to replace a principal who wanted out of the role. An employment agency sent the firm a resume on someone; the firm interviewed him and hired him at a $70,000 starting salary, despite some concerns of a few of their owners over the likelihood of his success in the role. Ten months later, after wreaking havoc on the marketing department staff, business development force, and the firm's principals, he was fired. All of the plans, processes, reports, and print materials he developed were scrapped, and the company had to start all over again. The point is, if more than one possibility had been generated by the firm prior to making a decision to hire this person, they might have made a better choice and saved a good deal of time, money, and lost opportunities.

One good way to compare candidates is to use what we'll call a *candidate comparison matrix*. This matrix allows you to assign a weight to each of your selection criteria for a particular position, rate a candidate on each criterion, multiply the individual ratings by the selection criteria weights, and sum the scores to come up with an overall ranking. You can then compare two or more candidates by their overall ranking.

Selection criteria you may want to use include technical skills in the appropriate discipline area, general management skills, potential to advance, communication/interpersonal skills, ease of relocation (if required), current compensation in light of your salary constraints, educational credentials, professional registrations, likelihood of long-term employment, and quality of references. You may also have other criteria that you want to use, depending on the particular position being filled (see sample matrix, Figure 4.3).

It may seem cumbersome to go through this comparison process every time, and it's not always necessary to do so. But it's an especially good idea to go through it when you are not overly experienced in hiring or when other people are involved in the decision and you want to use the candidate comparison matrix to help educate them.

4.5 DETERMINING THE OFFER

If you've conscientiously carried out the recommended hiring process all the way from recruiting and interviewing to reference checking and decision making, you've probably wound up with an excellent candidate—one you would feel great about bringing into your organization. Now you face the considerable challenge of developing an employment offer that this outstanding candidate will accept without blowing your bank account or wreaking havoc on your existing salary structure.

Formulating offers may, in fact, be easier if you're willing to hire just anyone—the more desperate, the better. The consequences of making a bad hiring decision, however, far outweigh any possible savings of time and trouble during the recruiting and hiring process. Find the best people and make the best offers you possibly can, and don't be apologetic even if you secretly believe it may not be enough. Some firms are afraid of making an offer to an outstanding candidate for fear of rejection, but unless you ask, you'll never know. If you've done a good job of reading your candidate and selling him or her on the position and the firm, you can shift the odds in your favor. That's why it's worth spending some time formulating your offers.

Assuming the position title, responsibilities, and location remain as originally discussed with the candidate during the interviewing process, there are several important compensation variables to consider in your employment offer. Together, they make up the total compensation package.

1. Base salary (or hourly rate) and date of first pay review
2. Overtime compensation (if any)
3. Signing bonus (if any)
4. Bonus or other incentive compensation (if any)
5. Fringe benefits
6. Company vehicle or vehicle allowance (if any)
7. Relocation package, if required (if any)

All of these variables have to be considered individually and collectively when trying to come up with an offer. It is precisely at this point in the hiring process that the information you got on the candidate's exact compensation package during the recruitment and interviewing phases becomes so critical. If you still don't have the exact current or most recent compensation information on your chosen candidate, you need to call the candidate to get it. Tell the candidate that he or she is under serious consideration for an offer at this point, but before you can make your decision and formulate an offer, you need *all* of the details on his or her compensation. (Refer to Chapter 3 for more hints on how to get compensation data from candidates.)

In most cases, base salary or base hourly rate is by far the most important of the compensation variables. People usually think of their compensation in terms of their base salaries. That's what they see each pay period on their checks, and that's what becomes their regular expectation or "entitlement." (There's more on this topic in Chapter 9.) Overtime pay, for those earning lots of it, will also become part of this perceived entitlement. It's important that this concept be accepted and understood by everyone who will actually help determine employment offers for design professionals.

As experience will tell you and as most recruiters serving the design industry will confirm, there are a couple of rules of thumb that are useful in determining employment offers. First, currently employed candidates who are making a job change will expect at least a 10 percent increase in base pay for a local move. The longer someone has been at the same company, the more critical this 10 percent becomes, because they feel they have more to risk by making a bad decision. With relocation, the expected raise will probably be 15 percent or higher. While there are exceptions to these rules, if you track your offer-to-acceptance ratio over a period of time, you'll be amazed at how accurate these percentages are.

Unemployed candidates are a different story. A candidate without a job is in a very different bargaining posture. Unlike employed candidates, it's not a question of whether they are going to start a new job, but when. Some are going to accept the first job they get offered. In any case, they are not in a position to expect a raise, and many will settle for even less than their last job paid. Of course, some unemployed candidates may have very unrealistic expectations, but on the average you should not be paying them increases of 10 or 15 percent. You need to judge each case individually. Was the candidate fired or did he or she quit? Does he or she have any other offers? How much are they for?

Coming from a high cost of living area to one that's considerably lower may not make a difference. A great deal depends on how badly (if at all) the candidate wants to get out of his or her present position and company, whether the candidate has a spouse or a spouse's career to consider, and whether the candidate owns real estate. These variables may drive the usual 15 percent increase up or down.

The problem comes when companies in regions with a relatively low cost-of-living start to think that everyone in Los Angeles, New York, or Boston will be clamoring to make a move involving little or no increase in pay just because their cost of living might drop. Unfortunately, it doesn't work that way most of the time. Whether it's rational or not, people don't want to move for little or no increase in base pay. Perhaps it's egotism; perhaps it's a fear of losing ground if things don't work out. Whatever the case, don't assume that a lower cost of living is that big of a factor for candidates currently employed in more expensive parts of the country. Unemployed candidates, however, are in a completely different frame of mind. They may not have as many options. In any case, as a group, they certainly have less to risk than candidates who are currently employed. Because they are more willing to pick up stakes and move, it may be easier to sell them the advantages of a lower cost of living. Generally, when a candidate is going from a low-cost-of-living area to one that is much higher, the same rules of thumb on base salary increases apply. However, you may have to sweeten the deal with a more generous relocation allowance or with a signing bonus to get the candidate to take your position. There will be more about relocation in Section 4.6, but for now, consider the issue of signing bonuses. Long popular for athletes and then spreading to the more visible positions in big industry, signing bonuses have gained in popularity for some of the larger and more successful design firms in the last decade or so. A signing bonus is a cash sum paid to a new employee upon starting to work or over some short time period thereafter, such as 3 to 12 months.

Signing bonuses allow design firms who don't want to ruin their existing salary structure or billing rate structure to hire someone they may not otherwise be able to attract. The main advantage of signing bonuses is that they really *do* provide an inducement to make a change. What's more, it's a lot more economical to offer a $2500 signing bonus than $2500 in additional salary; you pay the signing bonus just once, while the salary would be paid year after year. On the other hand, there are two major disadvantages of signing bonuses. First, other employees may find out about a signing bonus, which can be devastating to morale. Second, a candidate might take a job just to collect the signing bonus and then quit after a short tenure.

If you can overcome the possible disadvantages, signing bonuses can be a useful part of your hiring arsenal. To preserve morale, start by plugging up information leaks in the accounting, secretarial, and payroll departments. Hire trustworthy people for those departments or threaten sanctions, up to and including being fired, for divulging confidential compensation information to others in the firm. Second, if you pay a signing bonus, have the new employee sign a reimbursement agreement that would require repayment of a prorated portion of the signing bonus should the employee depart on his or her own accord within a specified length of time (see Figure 4.4).

Understanding that MZ&A Group, Inc., has made substantial investment in my hiring, I, _____, agree to the following: Should I terminate my employment with MZ&A Group, Inc., through my own choice at any time prior to my one-year employment anniversary, I will be obligated to reimburse MZ&A Group, Inc., for any signing bonus costs incurred by them on a prorated basis (based on a 12-month period calculated to the nearest whole month) for my relocation. I understand these costs include gross bonus and all applicable company-required payroll taxes. Repayment will come through either deduction of the amount from my salary or other compensation promised to me by the firm, or by personal reimbursement on the date of my departure.

I further understand that should I fail to satisfy this agreement—causing legal action on the part of MZ&A Group, Inc., to enforce my obligation—all legal costs incurred will be included as a portion of the amount due the company by me.

I am signing this with full knowledge of my obligations under this agreement.

_____   _____
Employee Signature   Date

Note: This sample agreement is only intended as a guide. Consult with your legal counsel on the legality and exact wording of such an agreement in your state.

FIGURE 4.4   Sample signing bonus reimbursement agreement

Overtime pay is another important compensation variable. Although it's becoming less prevalent for professionals, some firms still pay it. For other positions, paid overtime may be legally required (see Chapter 9). For now, just remember that some people consider overtime part of their regular base pay. If you ignore the issue of overtime, it will come back to haunt you in the form of offer rejections. That's why it's extremely important in the interview phase that you probe into how much overtime the candidate receives, how the overtime rate is computed, at what frequency overtime is paid, and how he or she feels about overtime. Would he or she rather trade off the earnings for more time with family or other non–work-related activities?

Don't assume that every candidate shares your values with respect to overtime—especially candidates who earn a significant amount of overtime compensation and who are considering a position in your firm that doesn't normally include overtime compensation. If the overtime pay is essential to maintain a candidate's current standard of living, you'll have a hard time attracting him or her unless your base salary offer reflects the typical overtime amount *plus* the expected increase. No signing bonus (unless huge) or promise of incentive compensation eligibility is likely to overcome this loss of overtime unless the candidate is willing to trade dollars for free time.

What most firms call incentive compensation is really some form of purely discretionary profit distribution. Bonuses in most A/E/P firms are based largely on the overall company profitability combined with some subjective evaluations of individuals' performance. Their value in attracting candidates is limited. Unless you are prepared to guarantee a specific bonus for someone, or a recurring bonus each year, it is doubtful that your bonus program will be a major draw for most recruits. One possible exception would be for candidates from companies that do not pay bonuses at all. However, these days it is a rare firm that doesn't pay bonuses, at least for those at a professional level.

Fringe benefits and perquisites are the last form of compensation that must be considered at the offer stage (relocation will be treated separately). For the purpose of this discussion, fringes will include medical, dental, disability and life insurance; vacation and sick leave; profit sharing and 401(k) plans; paid parking; and so on. Perquisites are extras reserved just for certain people in a company, such as country club or athletic club memberships, company automobiles, and use of the corporate time-share condo, to name a few.

Some design firms have a bad habit of making exceptions in the fringe benefits area for new hires, and in all but one situation, it's probably a mistake. To start with, there are state and federal laws that prohibit bracketing certain benefits (for example, medical insurance) based on someone's salary or position in the firm. It's not acceptable to give paid dependent medical coverage to executives if you don't offer it for everyone. Second, it's a morally questionable practice to make exceptions for new people in matters of basic fringe benefits when existing staffers don't have the opportunity to renegotiate their benefits. Beyond that, in design firms these things always seem to get out, and they can cause morale problems such as resentment of the new employee, which in turn makes it doubly difficult for him or her to settle in and become a productive member of the organization.

The one possible exception to the rule of avoiding exceptions may be vacation benefits. If an individual is coming from a position where he or she currently has more annual vacation leave than your firm's policy would provide to a new employee, you may want to make an exception so the new employee doesn't have to step back. This shouldn't be given away automatically, however; if possible, the matter should be discussed before making any offer to find out how important it is to the candidate. Obviously, for the person who never uses all of his or her annual leave, it's not going to be a major stumbling block—unless, that is, the candidate is allowed to trade unused vacation for cash in his or her current situation.

It should be apparent by now that coming up with an offer is not always a simple and straightforward process. There are three ways design firms deal with this predicament:

1. The firm can approach the candidate at the conclusion of the interview process and ask, "What is it going to take for you to come to work for us?"

2. The firm can quickly come up with a lowball offer under the assumption that the candidate will want to negotiate compensation anyway.

3. The firm can analyze all of the facts concerning the candidate's current compensation and location as well as the compensation of comparable existing staff members. Combining this data with an intuition of what it will probably take to get the person signed up, the firm can make the best offer under those conditions.

The first alternative is not advised for the simple reason that it puts the candidate in the uncomfortable position of having to second-guess what you are willing to pay versus what he or she really needs to make the job change. Too often the candidate is not an experienced negotiator and, not wanting to leave money on the table, he or she comes up with an outlandish figure that either scares off the company or puts them in a position of potentially disappointing the candidate with the actual offer.

The other possibility is that the candidate won't want to appear too demanding or scare off the company. In that case, he or she comes up with a figure which is really *less* than what he or she needs to make the move. The company then makes the offer he or she suggested, and they are surprised when he or she eventually turns down the job after a little more reflection.

Alternative 2, or *lowballing*, is also not recommended. Rarely is a good long-term employment relationship founded on the company trying to screw the candidate for whatever it can get. It is generally an overzealous stinginess that leads to the adoption of this strategy. However, it all too often backfires when a candidate simply turns the job down without producing a counterproposal for the firm to consider.

The third alternative is the best strategy. Assess all the variables in the situation and make the best affordable offer that has a chance of being accepted. Again, this is most effective when you have one person, the Hiring Process Manager (HPM), involved in making all hiring decisions and determining all employment offers. The experience acquired through repeated hiring will help develop the intuitive judgment necessary to come up with offers that get accepted and yet don't waste the firm's money or hurt its cost structure. In most firms, the offer itself should be determined by the HPM, the candidate's slated immediate supervisor, and the principal in charge of the area that the person will be working in. For lower-level positions, the HPM and the immediate supervisor should determine the dollar offer.

4.6   RELOCATION

Some design firms, especially smaller firms, simply don't do anything for new hires in the way of financing their relocation. These companies are not in the majority, however. Most firms, at least ones that are selective in their hiring practices, will at some point need to relocate a new hire. Relocation is almost always costly. The burden is usually shared by the new employee and his or her company.

There are many expense variables to consider in the relocation process, all of which figure into the total relocation cost (see Figure 4.5).

1. Physical moving costs of all household goods.
2. Interest differentials.
3. Closing costs.
4. House hunting trips.
5. Return home visits.
6. Purchase of the employee's existing house.
7. Spouse job assistance.
8. Temporary housing expenses.
9. Miscellaneous expenses.

FIGURE 4.5   Relocation package issues

1. *Physical moving costs.* This is the cost of physically relocating a new employee and his or her family, along with their personal possessions, to the area where your job is located. Considerations for the physical move include the maximum dollar amount the company will pay for the move, the maximum weight the company will pay to move, whether packing is paid for, whether unpacking and appliance set-up are paid for, whether ground transportation of autos is paid for, and whether insurance on belongings while in transit is paid for and to what extent (maximum replacement coverage, deductible, and the like). It must also be decided whether the company pays for lodging, meals, auto mileage, and other expenses while in transit, and if so, what the limits are on those items.

2. *Interest differentials.* Mortgage interest differentials are yet another component of the total relocation package. A mortgage differential is the difference in the percentage rate of the employee's old mortgage and his or her new mortgage. Considerations here include the percentage amount of the differential, the maximum mortgage amount it will be paid on, and the length of time it will be paid for (usually three to five years.) Mortgage differentials became less common as mortgage rates fell throughout the mid- to late 1980s.

3. *Closing costs.* Closing costs are incurred by the employee to close on the sale of both his or her existing house and the new house. Subvariables within

this expense category include items such as broker's fees, attorney's fees, inspections, property surveys, and appraisals. Determine what portion, if any, of these expenses the company will pay.

4. *House-hunting trips.* House-hunting trips are frequently part of a total relocation deal. House-hunting trips are trips for the employee to find housing in the new location. You should determine who will be reimbursed for coming on the trips (spouse, kids, mother-in-law, for example), how many trips will be paid for, what class of airfare is allowed, whether rental cars are paid for (and what the limits on daily rate are), and whether lodging, meals, and other incidental expenses are covered while on the trips.

5. *Return-home visits.* Return-home visits are also considered part of the overall relocation deal. These trips are for the employee to return home to visit family (especially a spouse) left behind while the house is up for sale or kids finish school. Subvariables within this expense category include setting a maximum airfare per trip and limits on the number of trips.

6. *Purchase of the employee's existing house.* Some companies will actually purchase the new employee's existing house to make it easier for him or her to accept the new job. These firms should consider limiting the amount of the purchase, determining a method to establish the purchase price, and determining when the company will actually effect the transaction. In other cases, firms make bridge loans to new employees. This way, the equity from the future sale of the individual's existing house is available for use as a down payment on the employee's new house.

7. *Spouse job assistance.* There is also the question of whether the firm provides or shares in the cost of finding the hire's spouse a new job. Assistance may include the cost of employment agency fees, resume preparation expenses, career counseling, and so on.

8. *Temporary housing expenses.* Some firms pay for temporary housing while the candidate waits to find or move into permanent housing. If you choose this course, you will want to determine a maximum daily or weekly rate the company will pay; a maximum duration over which the firm will contribute; and whether utilities, laundry (dry cleaning) expenses, maid service, furniture rental, and other incidental costs are also paid for.

9. *Miscellaneous expenses.* Auto registration fees (the cost to register autos in the new state) are paid by some firms to a relocating employee. In other cases, design firms grant a miscellaneous allowance to help offset costs to the employee for things like auto registration and new carpet, drapes, and wallpaper for the new house or apartment.

There are so many places for a design firm to go wrong when striking a deal on relocation that it may seem amazing any firm would get involved in it. In fact, you are always better off if you can avoid it. The probability that a locally recruited employee will be on the job after five years is significantly higher than for a recruit who had to relocate. Intuitively, that makes sense. The employee, the spouse, and other family members may never completely settle into the new area; they may long to return to what they consider home, or they may be nomads who enjoy the adventure in moving. In any case, employees who are already in the area are less stressed by the job change and can settle into their new role more easily than someone who is changing jobs and moving at the same time.

That's why, unless you are absolutely sure what you are looking for doesn't exist there, all searches should start in the area local to your need. The problem is that with the tight labor market for specialized professionals in some specific discipline and geographic market areas, it can't be avoided.

Now for some company relocation horror stories. Design firms that have been involved in purchasing employees' homes are rarely happy with the outcome. One consulting engineering firm bought its new Huntsville, Alabama, branch manager's existing house in Baton Rouge for $76,000 as a part of his relocation deal. After sitting on the house for months, the company finally was offered $10,000 less than they paid for it. They took it, only to have the property significantly damaged in a major flood the day before the new owners closed. Not only was there no flood insurance, but the company got sued by the prospective new owners, who had moved all of their belongings into the garage the night before the flood!

In another case, a firm had a blanket relocation policy that paid for "the physical cost of the move." The electrical engineer they moved over 1000 miles to join their company interpreted that to mean the company would pay for moving the two cords of fire wood he had stacked behind his house! In another situation—one that's not all that uncommon in cases where companies have poorly worded relocation policies—a company ended up paying to move both of a new employee's cars on the moving company van. Then, the candidate, his spouse, their four children, and two live-in in-laws flew at the firm's expense to the new city.

One Massachusetts firm agreed to pay "all moving costs" in addition to giving the newly hired executive a $2000 additional allowance, paid out in four installments of $500 over his first four months of employment. Recruited away from his company in Texas, the executive had to sell his house quickly at a $23,000 loss just so he could afford to rent something in the new location. He and his family of three plus four pets then endured a three-day drive, during which they stayed in inexpensive motels and ate at fast food restaurants. Upon reporting to work and submitting the expense report of roughly $200 for reimbursement, the company president refused to pay it, stating that the four $500 installments he would receive were for just that purpose. This same executive had been relocated a number of years before when he moved to Texas, and in that case the company had paid for everything *and* given him a $9000 cash bonus at the start. Needless to say, the stark contrast to the treatment he received at the hands of this new employer immediately demotivated the new employee and led him to question the character of his new employer.

Without exception, far and away the easiest and best way to deal with relocation for a new employee is to offer some sort of a cash relocation allowance for the employee to use as he or she sees fit. This relocation allowance eliminates all potential for misunderstanding at the employee's end, allows the new employee to spend the money as he or she wishes, allows the company to know the full extent of its obligation, and minimizes paperwork and other administrative hassles. The cash relocation allowance is to everyone's advantage. It should be determined for each specific offer situation, based on what the company can afford and what will make the relocation as easy as possible for the new staffer.

It's not to say that there is no place for a detailed relocation policy. They make sense for firms wanting to have a fair and equitable way of treating current employees who are relocated. But even then it may not be wise to treat the relocation of a branch manager who is one of the firm's principals the same way as a drafter who either takes the opportunity to move to another office to fill a job at $9.00 per hour or else loses his or her current job due to lack of work!

The problem is that it's nearly impossible to come up with a policy sufficiently clear and detailed to deal with all possibilities and avoid existing or new employees feeling shortchanged.

Whether a cash allowance is granted or expenses are reimbursed, the new employee should be asked to sign a relocation expense/allowance reimbursement agreement (see Figure 4.6) that allows the company to recover some of its initial investment in cases where an employee departs the company prematurely. Experience will prove that you'll rarely need to enforce one of these agreements, as long as you're selecting the right people in the first place. (Consult with your legal counsel on the legality and exact wording of such an agreement in your state.)

Understanding that MZ&A Group, Inc. has made substantial investment in my relocation, I, _____, agree to the following: Should I terminate my employment with MZ&A Group, Inc., through my own choice at any time prior to my one year employment anniversary, I will be obligated to reimburse MZ&A Group, Inc., for the costs incurred by them on a prorated basis (based on a 12-month period calculated to the nearest whole month) for my relocation. I understand these costs include physical moving expenses, temporary housing, cash relocation allowances, and/or any other costs incidental to my relocating from my previous residence that were reimbursed by the company. Repayment will come through either deduction of the amount from my salary or other compensation promised to me by the firm, or by personal reimbursement on the date of my departure.

I further understand that should I fail to satisfy this agreement—causing legal action on the part of MZ&A Group, Inc., to enforce my obligation—all legal costs incurred will be included as a portion of the amount due the company by me.

I am signing this with full knowledge of my obligations under this agreement.

Employee Signature   Date

FIGURE 4.6 Sample relocation allowance/expense reimbursement agreement

---

One final point on relocation. Any money provided by you as an employer to an employee for relocation purposes is, at the time of this writing, considered taxable income by the IRS. The employee can offset the income by providing evidence of actual costs incurred in certain areas, up to limits specified by the IRS. Too many companies don't realize this and forget to report moving expenses they incurred on a 1099 form for the new employee at the end of the year. This is one more reason a single cash allowance makes things easier all around: It puts all the accounting obligation in the hands of the employee, who is in the best position to know all of his or her expenses (see Figure 4.7 for a summary of relocation pointers).

1. Relocation for new employees is best addressed through providing an individually determined cash allowance to be used as the employee sees fit. Avoid cumbersome, detailed policies except (possibly) when moving existing employees.

2. All relocation expenditures should be wrapped up under a relocation expense reimbursement agreement.

3. All relocation items reimbursed by the company are considered taxable income and can be offset only by actual documented expenses incurred as per IRS guidelines and up to maximum limits specified by the IRS.

FIGURE 4.7   New employee relocation pointers

4.7   EXTENDING THE OFFER

Prior to actually extending the offer to your chosen candidate, it's a good idea to re-evaluate your need and your decision. Raise and answer the following questions:

1. Will hiring this person meet our initial as well as anticipated future needs? How much potential does this person have to advance in our firm beyond this position? Should market conditions change, how flexible is this person and could we get full utilization of this person in some area other than that for which he or she is being hired?

2. Are we absolutely sure that we need this person now and can't make changes in current staff assignments of other people in the company, work overtime, or take any other steps that would allow us not to hire someone?

3. Are the probabilities for a successful hire in our favor? Is this person's experience directly related to the role he or she will be filling at our company? Is he or she coming out of a similar environment, making the adjustment a relatively easy one? (See Chapter 5 on the subject of corporate culture.)

4. Is this really the best person for the job, or are we kidding ourselves and seriously compromising our original criteria in our rush to get the job filled? Are our expectations realistic or are we attempting to force fit this person into a job because he or she is likeable or available?

5. Have all relevant decision makers involved in or affected by this hiring been consulted on whether to make the offer?

6. Is the offer we are about to make the right one, based on the current supply and demand for this person's skills, what this person is currently earning, how badly we want this person, how this person will likely contribute to the

firm's profits, what the long- and short-term opportunity costs of not filling the position are, and what others with similar backgrounds make?

7. Have all effects of hiring this person on the other firm, department, or team staff members been considered? If someone is likely to be upset by our decision either to hire someone from the outside or this person in particular, has he or she been told why we are doing it?

Once all the answers to these questions have been looked at one more time and you are still comfortable with your decision to hire, you have reached the time to act. The offer has to be made!

Before getting on the phone or meeting with the chosen candidate to make your offer, be sure you have a clear understanding on what his or her title will be, who he or she will report to, and what his or her basic duties and responsibilities will be in that position. Believe it or not, some firms, adhering to the "best available athlete" principle, will hire good people when they see them without regard to how they will fit them in. Don't do it! Most candidates are scared off by this approach.

If you have multiple offices, especially in cases where interviews have occurred at different office locations, make sure you know which office the candidate is being hired for. One Twin-Cities firm made an offer to an engineer for a position in Minneapolis, when the company actually needed him to work in St. Paul.

Make sure all compensation issues are clearly understood. Will this person receive overtime; if so, at what rate? Is there going to be a signing bonus or relocation allowance provided; if so, for how much? Will the candidate receive a company car as part of the offer; if so, what are the details on it? Has the candidate been provided with all benefits information as part of the process? Will there be any exceptions in the offer? What will be the latest date for a decision on the part of the candidate, and, last but not least, how soon will you need him or her to report to work? (See Figure 4.8 for a summary of the points to address when making an offer of employment.)

In situations where the final candidate is local, bring him or her back into the office or meet somewhere in person to extend the actual offer, if possible.

1. Title, duties, and responsibilities of position, as well as the name and title of whom the employee will report to.

2. Salary or pay rate (hourly, weekly, or monthly). Frequency of paycheck distribution. Exempt or nonexempt status. Eligibility for overtime compensation. Method of calculating rate: straight time, time-and-a-half, other? When does overtime start? Date of first performance review. Date of first pay review.

3. Benefits. Company vehicle and relocation package details, if appropriate. Any exceptions to company policy.

4. Office location the employee will work out of and regular hours of work.

5. Deadline for candidate's acceptance or rejection of offer and anticipated start date.

6. Expression of sincere desire on the part of the company that individual will join the firm.

FIGURE 4.8 Points to address in employment offers

Otherwise, the offer should be made over the telephone. In any case, the verbal offer should be confirmed immediately in writing no later than the day after it is made, and preferably the same day.

Some design firms, particularly the older and larger companies, prefer to simply send their selected candidates a job offer in the mail with no warning. These same firms then wonder why their chosen candidate turns down their offer! This practice can only lead to a higher percentage of turndowns from candidates who receive the impression that the company is overly bureaucratic.

The offer itself should be extended by either the HPM or the manager that the candidate would report to if hired. It should not be extended by some person in the company who has never spoken with the candidate. It should not be extended by an outside recruiter if one was used in the process. It should only be extended by someone in the company who is authorized to make employment commitments and who knows the potential liabilities associated with doing so. Ideally, the offer should be extended within a week of the final interview. Postponing it any longer reduces the chances of getting an acceptance. The longer you delay, the more the candidate's interest wanes and the more likely the candidate will begin talking with another firm.

Employment offers should always be portrayed in the most favorable light possible. *Never* apologize for any offer you make to someone. Even if the offer is not as good as you think will be necessary to get an acceptance or what you think the company should be offering, don't let the candidate know you feel that way. Candidates will read that as a sign from you that the offer is an initial offering and that you are now ready to do some serious negotiating, when in fact that is the last thing you want to get dragged into. It's entirely possible that the candidate may not think it's such a bad offer, and only your apologetic tone will give him or her reason to wonder if he or she is worth more.

By the same token, don't inadvertently make promises and commitments or create expectations that won't be met. Do not under any circumstances oversell. One of the leading causes of voluntary turnover, which is usually preceded by a period of demotivation and declining productivity, is overselling candidates on the company and position. Examples of these promises are statements like, "You'll be our next principal," or, "We look forward to you having a lifetime career with our firm," or, "After a brief training period, you'll become the Architectural Division Manager for XYZ Associates." Don't make these kinds of promises unless you are absolutely sure they will be kept.

Also, be sure to express the base pay offer appropriately. If the individual will be a salaried employee, tell him or her so and also what his or her gross check will be *each pay period*. Consider a salaried project manager who on an annual salary basis would earn $52,000 per year paid weekly at $1000 per. The pay offer should be stated as "a salary of $1000 per week," not "$52,000 per year, paid weekly." Some courts in some states may interpret the latter statement as an employment agreement of one year or longer, obligating the firm to pay out the entire salary for the term of the agreement in the event of termination.

The offer should be stated clearly and without ambiguity. Any confusion or uncertainty on your part will contribute to doubts the employee may already have about his or her wisdom in considering a job change and will hurt your chances for an acceptance.

All details on other compensation and relocation provisions should be discussed so the candidate knows the full offer. Any special benefits should also be discussed when making the offer. After extending the offer, your first question should be whether the candidate has any questions about anything at all in the offer. All questions should be addressed, and if you don't have the answers you need or want to consult someone else on what you anticipate may be a problem area, tell the candidate you'll have to get back to him or her later, always specifying when he or she can expect to hear back from you.

Once the candidate understands the terms of the offer, it is time to nail down a decision-making date, providing he or she doesn't accept on the spot. (That rarely happens, even with the best of offers!) The question should be phrased, "When can we expect your favorable response to our offer?" Hopefully, the candidate will tell you that he or she will make his or her decision and get back to you within a couple of days. Of course, the candidate may tell you he or she needs as long as two or more weeks to make a decision. Once again, there is considerable debate on this subject. However, in general your best course is to give at least three days and no more than seven days for a decision. Your own experience will probably confirm that the longer you give candidates to make a decision, the greater the chances for an eventual turndown. After all, the candidate has more time to shop your offer if that's what he or she wants to do. The candidate would also have more time to think of all the reasons why he or she *shouldn't* take the job.

Candidates should be asked *before* it happens how they will react to counteroffers from their present employers. Candidates who tell you before the fact that they won't be receptive to counteroffers are making commitments that may actually keep them from seriously considering counteroffers if they are made. If necessary, warn candidates that their companies may make counteroffers only to keep them around until someone can be found to replace them. Contingency-type recruiters know how important this is, as their earnings depend directly on whether the candidate accepts the job. Don't forget this important step in the hiring process!

Make sure that you counsel candidates how actually to turn in their notices. Advise candidates not to sit down and allow themselves to be dragged into a long discussion about why they are leaving. Tell them to stay standing when they inform their current employers that they are leaving—and to state that their decision is final.

A lot of managers in design firms will feel funny about discussing with job candidates things like counteroffers and how to turn in a notice, but experience will prove that discussing these topics is an important tool in keeping down the percentage of offers accepted and then reneged on later.

The last question you need to address after making the offer is to find out if the candidate has any kind of preliminary start date in mind. In addition to testing the reaction to your offer, it may uncover a stumbling block if the candidate needs longer than you feel you can live without him or her. The important thing is that you should rarely give a candidate more than two to four weeks to report for work. Once again, to let the probabilities work in your favor, you should insist on a relatively prompt start date. Too many design firms that allow delayed start dates get burned when their chosen candidate calls at the eleventh hour and reneges on an initial acceptance. The firm has to start the hiring process all over again, by which time the back-up candidates are either gone or have pulled themselves out of contention.

As mentioned earlier, don't delay in getting the offer confirmation letter out (see sample letter below, Figure 4.9). Ideally, send via Federal Express or some other overnight carrier so the candidate sees you are serious and sincerely interested.

March 17, 1990

Mr. John Doe, P.E.
Address
City, State   Zip

Dear John:

Mark Zweig & Associates is pleased to confirm our verbal offer of employment to you.

As we discussed, your position will be that of Project Manager, working in the Natick, Massachusetts, headquarters office of our firm and reporting to Mr. Frederick D. White, Vice President. Your starting salary will be $1,346.00 paid bi-weekly, plus you will be entitled to all fringe benefits as outlined in the enclosed *Company Information Booklet.*

As an exempt-status employee, you will not receive any compensation for overtime hours worked. Your first performance and salary review will occur on your 90-day anniversary with our company.

John, we look forward to your acceptance of our offer no later than 4:00 P.M., Wednesday, March 21, 1990, and to your starting to work as soon as possible thereafter.

We are excited about the prospect of your joining our firm. Should you have any questions concerning this offer, please contact me at your earliest convenience.

Sincerely,

MARK ZWEIG & ASSOCIATES

Mark C. Zweig
President

MCZ/slc

cc: Mr. Frederick D. White

FIGURE 4.9 Sample letter: confirmation of offer

4.8   ACCEPTANCE, REJECTION, AND NEGOTIATION

If all goes well and the offer is accepted, the start date has to be firmly established. Two to four weeks notice is sufficient. Any longer than that is unsatisfactory and increases the probability that the candidate will change his or her mind. Nothing is worse than planning two or three months for someone's arrival, only to have him or her call a week before the start date and back out.

If timing permits, provide your new employees with all the forms necessary for their insurance, personnel processing, or whatever, to be completed prior to their first day of work. This will help the new hires hit the ground running on their first full day of work at your company.

Immediately after the verbal acceptance of your offer, send a letter out to confirm the acceptance and planned start date. You may also want to routinely ask candidates to put their acceptances in writing for you, as it reinforces their commitment to you (see Figure 4.10).

No matter how fair your offer may appear, you could end up dealing with someone who wants to negotiate. It's important that you be able to distinguish between serious problems with your offer and the candidate who is fishing for all he or she can get.

Generally speaking, with few exceptions, you should not have to be negotiating offers. If you have done your homework before making the offer, just about every consideration should have been addressed. It is possible that some oversight or new facts may enter into the situation, however. The candidate may have been promoted while you were courting him or her; the candidate may have received another employment offer that is being compared to yours; or you may just have a greedy candidate who wants to milk you for all you have to offer. In the last case, get firm! Don't allow yourself to get pushed around. You may need to tell the candidate that he or she has heard your final offer—take it or leave it.

The best practice is to make the offer, and if the candidate comes right out and asks if the offer is subject to negotiation, say it isn't. State that you made the best offer you could make and hoped the candidate would agree that it was fair.

Even when you have taken every possible precaution and done everything spelled out so far in this text, it is possible that you will be turned down by your top candidate. Before throwing in the towel, it's important that you don't let the candidate off the hook so easily. Ask him or her for a full debriefing, and probe into all of the reasons for your candidate's decision not to join your firm. It may be there is something that isn't completely understood about your offer. It is possible that it's something relatively minor that you might be willing to negotiate. If either of these appears to be the case, ask the candidate whether, if you get that issue resolved, he or she will accept. If the candidate balks or seems indifferent, find out what else is keeping him or her from joining your firm. At worst, you may learn something about your process or the people who were involved in the candidate's recruitment that you will want to change for the next candidate. At best, you may turn the candidate around by clearing up a simple misunderstanding or making a relatively minor concession.

March 21, 1990

Mr. John Doe, P.E.
Address
City, State   Zip

Dear John:

Mark Zweig & Associates is pleased that you have accepted the offer to join our firm.

As we discussed, your position will be that of Project Manager, working in our Boston headquarters office and reporting to Frederick D. White, Vice President with our firm. Your starting salary will be $1,346.00 paid bi-weekly, plus you will be entitled to all fringe benefits as outlined in the enclosed *Company Information Booklet*. As an exempt-status employee, you will not receive any compensation for overtime hours worked.

Your first day at work will be Monday, April 3, 1990. Please report to Ms. Anne O'Brien, our Personnel Administrator by 8:00 A.M. on that date. She will have some paperwork for you to complete on your insurance, as well as a few other forms for you to fill out.

John, in the event that you have any questions concerning the terms and conditions of your employment with Mark Zweig & Associates, please contact me. We are looking forward to having you on board!

Regards,

MARK ZWEIG & ASSOCIATES

Mark C. Zweig
President

cc: Mr. Frederick D. White
    Ms. Anne O'Brien

FIGURE 4.10   Sample letter: confirmation of offer acceptance

4.9 CONCLUSION

Even if you can't change your top candidate's mind, you've got other good candidates waiting in the wings, assuming you've followed the process described in the first four chapters of this book. That's another benefit of recruiting enough good candidates to give yourself a real choice: Even if your top candidate turns you down, the remaining candidates will meet or exceed your criteria, and there's no need to start the recruitment process all over again. It's also another reason you should keep the process moving and avoid wasting time. Your back-up candidates will start to lose interest or feel slighted if you spend too much time between interviewing and making an offer.

Make every candidate feel he or she is the top candidate. Get a decision as soon as possible after making an offer and, if the answer is no, move on to your second choice and treat him or her just as well as you did the top candidate. On the other hand, don't fail to learn from anything you mishandled with the first candidate. Make adjustments as necessary.

One final point. When you finally nail down the position, don't leave your other candidates hanging. You've gone through a lot to find them and cultivate their interest in your firm. Call each one and explain that, although you were very impressed with their credentials, they weren't quite right for this particular situation. Keep them feeling good about you and your firm. The next time you have a similar position open you'll be glad you did.

5

ORIENTATION, INTEGRATION, AND MOTIVATION

You can dream, create, design and build the most wonderful place in the world, but it requires people to make the dream a reality.

—Walt Disney

5.1 INTRODUCTION

The first three to six months on the job are probably the most critical time for a newly hired design professional. It is during this period that he or she will be assessing the wisdom of joining the firm. Likewise, the company will be scrutinizing the new employee to determine whether it did the right thing by hiring him or her, and to assess his or her long-term potential with the firm.

Orientation is an important part of the process for ensuring that a new employee will be as successful as possible in a new company. Most design firms pay little more attention to orientation than it takes for a new employee to complete the myriad of forms required.

Beyond orientation, the new employee must be successfully integrated as a productive team member into the rest of the organization, or the firm's corporate culture. This can't happen unless the existing staff *wants* the new employee to succeed rather than seeing him or her as a nuisance or a threat. It also can't happen without some extra attention from management and early feedback to the employee on his or her job performance.

Last but not least, after the company hires the best possible person for the job (the one most likely to work out), orients the new employee for a hot start, and successfully integrates him or her into the existing culture, the last challenge is to keep motivation high and avoid turning him or her sour on the firm. This requires a good understanding of what motivates and demotivates design professionals in the work setting.

109

5.2 ORIENTATION

Orientation is defined as the activities that introduce new employees to the organization and to their tasks, superiors, and work groups.

Consider the case of Jeff, a new field survey crew member. Twenty-one years old, just married, and fresh out of the Army, Jeff had never worked in a company setting before but was anxious to get settled into his new job. Arriving at 8:00 AM as his hiring letter from the company's personnel manager instructed, he went to the personnel department and waited for someone to show up. An hour later, the personnel manager, who since 7:45 AM had been in a long discussion with one of the firm's department managers, walked out of his office to find the surveyor sitting there. He had assumed Jeff would go straight down to the survey department that morning. Finally, by 10:00 AM, when all of the paperwork required for processing was completed, the new employee was sent down to the survey department. Upon seeing him, his new boss glared and said "We were wondering where you were. Late on the first day—you're off to a real good start. Now what am I supposed to do with you for the rest of the day?"

Or how about the case of Andy, a project manager on the first day of his new job with a 200-person A/E firm. After a brief discussion with the firm's executive vice president, who was responsible for hiring him, they went to look for "somewhere for him to sit." Andy ended up being stuck in a multistation cubicle in the most distant corner of the building, sharing desk space and a telephone with several of the firm's asbestos abatement field technicians. After lunch, he was rushed off to a project meeting where he knew no one, and he wasn't even able to hand out any business cards because they hadn't been ordered for him yet. An accounting clerk came by to see him the next day with some forms for him to fill out. He had no other orientation.

Anne, a newly hired interiors architect, after relocating her family and household over 500 miles, reported to the HR manager on her first day at work. She, along with several other new employees were welcomed to the company, given all kinds of forms to fill out, and introduced to the company policy manual. She was then given a five-minute tour of the building and was finally turned over to her new studio manager, who immediately gave her a project to work on.

In the first case, the new employee, despite his best intentions, starts with one strike against him. In the second case, the firm is obviously not ready for the new man. The last case, probably the most typical of a design firm, shows how little attention is paid to orientation even when firms do formalize the process.

The point is that formal orientation programs, effectively designed and administered, offer a number of benefits to design firms. These include:

1. *Reduced employee start-up costs.* Although an orientation program that delays using the employee for job-chargeable work ostensibly increases start-up costs, formal research on the subject has shown that properly oriented employees are considerably more efficient than those who are not. This makes it possible for new employees to meet company performance standards sooner.

2. *Reduced employee anxiety.* A job change is an extremely stressful situation for the new employee. Add relocation on top of a new job and you double the stress. Typical feelings for new employees include fear of failure, self-doubt, and second thoughts about whether the job change was the right decision. Effective orientation works to minimize this anxiety.

3. *Increased employee competence and effectiveness.* Proper orientation increases productivity because new employees know where things are, who to see for the variety of needs they might have, and how to use various office equipment such as computers, copiers, and telephones. All of these elements add up to more competent employees.

4. *Reduced turnover and corresponding recruitment costs.* Employees who are confident, competent, and free of anxiety tend to last on the job longer than those who aren't. With an average cost of over $6000 to replace just one professional, effective orientation contributes to the firm's profit.

5.3 HOW TO CONDUCT ORIENTATION

The formal orientation program is likely to be a new employee's first experience on the job in a new firm. This part of the overall orientation process should include:

1. A tour of the office facility and introductions to others with whom the new employee will interact. Introductions to the firm's principals are also a good idea.

2. A presentation on the company itself, including the firm's history, growth, organizational structure, and projects. Some firms are using films or A/V presentations to accomplish this.

3. A review of all employee benefits, along with completion of all associated forms required for insurance, profit sharing, payroll, taxes, and so on.

4. Provision of a company policy manual, along with any discussion or clarification required on the firm's policies, rules, and regulations.

5. Review and discussion of normal hours of work, lunch times, parking, building alarm or other security measures, and other company operation details.

6. Instruction on how to fill out the company time sheet and an explanation of how it is processed and how and when the employee will get paid.

7. Instruction on how to get a job or project number, how to read and interpret the firm's project management information system reports, and how to prepare invoices (if appropriate).

8. Instruction on how to handle printing and duplication, account for project reimburseables, order supplies, complete and get reimbursed for an expense report, use a company vehicle, and so on.

9. Instruction on how to use all office equipment, including copiers, FAX ma-

chines, telephones (including making a long distance call), paging systems, computers, KROY or similar machines, and anything else that's appropriate.

10. Instruction in any safety measures or precautions appropriate for someone in a given role.

11. Gathering of all information required to prepare a marketing resume on the new employee.

The initial parts of a firm's formal orientation process should be handled by someone in the firm's HR or personnel department or, in the case of smaller firms, by whoever handles the HR function on a part-time basis. This individual will solicit the required support and contribution from those in the firm's other functional areas that the employee will get involved with—secretarial services, reproduction, finance and accounting, and so on. A detailed orientation checklist can be extremely valuable at this stage in the process to help make sure that no important details fall between the cracks. An example orientation checklist is available in Figure 5.1.

Name/Title of Employee: _____

Office: _____ Department: _____ Start Date: _____

1. Human Resources Department:
   _____ Complete all required forms.
   _____ Provide company policy and procedures manual and get receipt.
   _____ Explain all insurance benefits/options.
   _____ Explain retirement/401(k).
   _____ Explain performance appraisal and salary review processes.
   _____ Explain parking.
   _____ Provide company organization chart.
   _____ Give tour of building.
   _____ Explain hours of work, breaks, holiday and sick leave.
   _____ Provide keys to building.
   _____ Explain alarm system.
   _____ Order business cards and name plate.
2. Payroll Department:
   _____ Explain pay procedures.
   _____ Explain time sheets, activity codes, and job numbers.
   _____ Explain exempt/nonexempt status and overtime pay.
   _____ Explain company credit union and direct deposit.
   _____ Explain how to purchase bonds through payroll deduction.

FIGURE 5.1 Sample new-employee orientation checklist

3. Finance, Accounting & Administrative Service Department:

_____ Explain how to get petty cash.

_____ Explain how to capture reimbursable expenses.

_____ Explain expense report processing, requirements, and frequency.

_____ Explain how to purchase stamps.

_____ Explain how to requisition supplies.

_____ Explain mail distribution process.

_____ Order company credit cards, if required.

4. Library Department:

_____ Explain reference library and check-out process.

_____ Explain job file system and check-out process.

_____ Explain drawing file system and check-out process.

_____ Explain how to order publications needed.

_____ Explain routing procedures for periodicals.

5. Word Processing Department:

_____ Explain how to request word processing.

_____ Explain correspondence standards.

_____ Explain other typing standards.

_____ Provide with recording/dictating equipment and instructions.

6. Reprographics Department:

_____ Explain how to request reproduction.

_____ Explain capabilities of department.

_____ Explain how to make rush orders.

7. Receptionist:

_____ Explain how to use telephone system and accounting codes.

_____ Explain inter/intra-office routing procedures and schedule.

_____ Explain how to request company vehicle for business use.

8. Marketing Department:

_____ Complete marketing resume work sheet.

_____ Provide with company marketing support materials.

_____ Arrange photo session/order announcements, if required.

_____ Explain company's full-service capabilities.

_____ Explain go/no-go and proposal generation process.

9. Contract Administration Department:

_____ Explain how to open a new project number.

_____ Explain company standard contracts/agreements.

_____ Explain contracting approval process.

_____ Explain project management reports.

_____ Explain billing process/schedule.

FIGURE 5.1 _(Continued)_

10. Department Manager:

_____ Assign individual to serve as integration aid.

_____ Introduce to all other staff members.

_____ Explain department-specific rules and procedures.

_____ Take individual to his or her new work area.

FIGURE 5.1 *(Continued)*

Perhaps more important to the employee's long-term success, the second stage of orientation is handled by the supervisor. This is where the employee-supervisor relationship is initiated and where the employee finds out what the job is all about. Typically, it is also where the employee is introduced to the other people in his or her immediate work group. This stage of the process, when handled properly, gets the employee off to a sound footing with peers and subordinates.

5.4 HINTS FOR MORE EFFECTIVE ORIENTATION

1. Start orientation with the more routinized and formalized matters and move toward more job- or position-specific matters in the later stages of the orientation.

2. Don't assume that one brief introduction to someone will be sufficient for the new employee to remember the person's name and function. Provide other opportunities for the new employee to have further interaction with key people beyond the initial encounter.

3. Do whatever it takes to bolster the new employee's confidence and reduce his or her anxiety early in the job experience.

4. Get the CEO or another senior person involved if possible. He or she can assure the employee the his or her door remains open if a problem comes up.

5. Prepare the employee to dismiss whatever false rumors or other negative information he or she is likely to hear about the company from the other employees.

6. Tell the new employee to be a proactive communicator, that is, to realize that because others are busy it may not be asked often enough whether he or she needs help. Tell the new employee that "the only stupid question is one that goes unasked," and that people will be glad to help.

7. Don't immediately force the new employee into a situation that tests his or her capabilities. Baptism by fire should be avoided if at all possible. Instead, let him or her gradually ease into new job responsibilities over a period of several weeks or more.

8. Follow up on the success of your orientation effort. Have someone meet privately with each new employee after 30 days on the job to be sure the employee isn't having any problems that need to be addressed.

Part-time and temporary employees are likely to have much shorter and simpler orientations than regular full-time employees. Nevertheless, many of the same benefits of formal orientation exist for them as well. The bottom line is that orientation, handled properly, will be one of the less expensive components of your firm's overall hiring process. Yet it offers some real benefits for firms wanting improved performance and longevity for their newly hired employees.

5.5 INTEGRATION AND CORPORATE CULTURE

Orientation is just the first phase of a design firm's overall efforts to successfully integrate a new employee into the firm. To be able to do this, a firm must have a good grasp of what is referred to as its *corporate culture* (see Figure 5.2). The firm has to hire the right people in the first place (those most likely to succeed in the culture), and then see to it that these individuals are properly socialized so that they can be assimilated into the culture.

Corporate culture is one of those management subjects so often misunderstood by design firm principals and managers. Corporate culture reflects the set of important understandings (often unstated) that members of an organization have in common (see Figure 5.3). It includes:

1. The often unstated but widely understood "way things are done around here."
2. The shared beliefs, values, and assumptions of those in the firm; for example, "If you work a lot of hours at this company, you'll get a big bonus," or, "The young guys who are good talkers and wear fancy suits are the only ones who ever get promoted at this firm."
3. What people talk about at work, how they dress, what kind of cars they drive, how conflicts between people are resolved, what employees' expectations for themselves are, which co-workers they associate with, and generally how people behave in the office are all ways to characterize a design firm's culture.

The process of integration requires successfully initiating each new member of the organization into its corporate culture. Some of the ways this is accomplished in a design firm include:

1. *Employee heroes*. Identifying the people who personify the firm's culture and whom others seek to exemplify. Communicating who these are to each employee.

Technology & Practice

The Threads of Corporate Style

Although corporate culture is one of the hot topics in management literature today, too few design firm owners and managers understand corporate culture or see the implications of their own organizations' cultures for their businesses. The definition we like best comes from Lawrence Peters of the Texas Christian College of Business, who likens corporate culture to the "fabric" of an organization. In other words, culture is made up of the threads that link your staff people. Woven together, these threads form a pattern and a texture consisting of the key values and assumptions of group members–in short, a sense of "the way things are done around here." Our consulting practice takes us into many design firms throughout the United States. We see all sorts of corporate cultures. There are stodgy firms and sloppy firms, nice ones and neurotic ones, square ones and slick ones. Although every situation is unique, we have found some common "threads" that we use here in a lighthearted, albeit serious-minded, characterization of five archetypical, or "off-the-rack," design firm cultures.

The Polyester Firm: The Polyester Firm, like the fabric for which it is named, resists change. It is stuck in the mid-70s era of management thought—or worse. The Polyester Firm is a production-oriented workplace, where doing what is technically best is valued over what clients want. Workers frequently pull all-nighters. Flashiness is not rewarded. Everyone drives a practical economy car and sports short-sleeved, wash-and-wear shirts (no jacket in the office). Conflicts are not resolved because confrontations are avoided at all costs. Profit is incidental to doing technically superior work. Typical specialty: environmental engineers or engineers doing work for architects.

The Blue Jean Firm: The Blue Jean firm appears laid-back on the surface, and no one gets his or her 100-percent-cotton (preferably pastel) attire into an uproar. People work with and for people they like, not just those they perceive to be on the fast track, and they admire eclectic nontraditionalists and loyal underdogs. Jeep Cherokees with ski racks are the vehicle of choice. People work out their problems by talking, and they favor consensus problem-solving. Working smarter is valued over working harder. Many Blue Jean firms are multidiscipline with a good balance of different specialties.

The Worsted Wool Firm: In the Worsted Wool Firm, good technical skills are taken for granted. Academic and experience credentials are outstanding. Good communication and presentation skills are coveted. High-ranking people wear Brooks Brothers suits and drive Black Forest cars. Principals wielding power clearly are at the top of the hierarchy, with all the requisite perks and privileges. Employees are ambitious, but not wildly so, and they concentrate on advancing through the hierarchy: associate by 35, principal by 45, managing partner by 55. Performance expectations are high and client relationships reign supreme. Typical

And what they signify.

By Frederick D. White

and Mark Zweig

specialty: multidiscipline firms serving corporate or industrial clients.

The Silk Firm: In the Silk Firm, style is valued over substance. Everyone tries to look busier than the next guy for fear of losing a big bonus, and brown-nosing is the approved means of career advancement. All nonbillable time gets charged to "marketing." Cocky young superstars expect to be CEO by 35. Those who bring in the work get all the rewards; those who grind it out are second-class citizens. Principals drive Mercedes and Jags and wear double-breasted Italian suits. The Silk Firm is characterized by a high turnover rate and specialization in "hot" project types.

The Tweed Firm: the Tweed Firm is stodgy, conservative, and slow-moving. Longevity, loyalty, and punctuality are valued above all else, and conformity is the way to get ahead. Young designers align themselves with an old-timer who knows how to get things done. Old-timers drive a Lincoln or a Cadillac. Dress for all is conservative preppy. Seniority resolves all conflicts. Performance is defined as working long hours and never using sick leave. The Tweed Firm produces the prettiest set of drawings—if not the most inspired designs—because it keeps all the old-line drafters instead of buying CADD. The Tweed Firm is most likely to be in pure architecture or prime basis engineering.

Some corporate cultures are remarkably sturdy; others should be marked "Delicate Cycle Only." But, almost invariably, the most successful and resilient design firms are marked by some kind of strongly defined corporate culture. We do not favor any of these cultures—whatever creates a closely-knit organization is good. On the other hand, a schizophrenic corporate culture can generate internal strife. Silk suits may infiltrate a Worsted Wool Firm and drive away old-line clients. Or, there may be firms within a firm, where each group or department has its own rival culture.

Unfortunately, the firm's corporate culture is not written down in the employee handbook or anywhere else. And often it is not clear, until the firm's corporate culture comes into conflict with its explicit organizational goals (such as making a profit). Then managers begin to take notice. At that point it may be too late, because riding roughshod over existing cultural norms is not likely to improve matters. As an example, we know of one Silk CEO who hired a Worsted Wool executive vice president to get the wrinkles out of his Blue Jean staff. Amazingly, the CEO was surprised when his laid-back staff mutinied under the new regime of law and order.

Take time to assess the weave of your own corporate culture. The sooner design firm management understands the critical importance of self analysis, the better off it will be.

Mr. Zweig and Mr. White are principals of Mark Zweig & Associates, a Natick, Mass., consulting firm specializing in the architecture/engineering/planning industry.

100 ARCHITECTURE/DECEMBER 1989

FIGURE 5.2   Corporate culture article

	Work Behavior	Trendsetters/ Role Models	Dress/Drive	Conflict Resolution	Personal Goals	Performance Expectations	Strategy for Change
Polyester Firm	■ Do whatever is technically best without regard to client's desires. ■ Pull all-nighters.	■ Eccentric genius types. ■ Computer jocks.	■ Wash and wear. ■ Short sleeve shirts with tie (coat not worn in office). ■ Drive practical economy car.	■ Don't talk about it. ■ Ignore problems. Maybe they'll go away.	■ Win design awards. ■ Become fellow in professional society.	■ Technical excellence. ■ Innovative design more important than profitability.	■ Sell group on logic of change.
Blue Jean Firm	■ Act "laid back" no matter what the circumstances. ■ Don't get in a hurry.	■ Likable, non-competitive types. ■ Eclectic Non-traditionalists. ■ Loyal underdogs.	■ 100% cotton, casual attire. Pastels. ■ Drive Jeep Cherokee, old Saab, or VW van.	■ Work it out by talking things through.	■ Do work you enjoy with people you like.	■ Work smarter, not harder. ■ Be loyal to the group.	■ Build consensus through meetings. ■ Broad participation in problem-solving.
Worsted Wool Firm	■ Delegate everything. ■ Don't rock the boat. ■ Do your paperwork.	■ Supermen/ women. ■ Seller/doer/ managers.	■ Brooks Brothers suits. Black shoes. Jacket kept on in office. ■ Drive Taurus, LeSabre, or new Volvo wagon.	■ Rely on hierarchy to resolve disputes. Highest level position wins.	■ Associate by 35. ■ Partner by 45. ■ President by 55. ■ Retire at 62.	■ Be perfect. ■ Don't antagonize clients.	■ Strategy handed from top down.
Silk Firm	■ Look busy. Appearance is valued over performance. ■ Charge all non-billable time to marketing.	■ Whoever is in power or gives out the rewards. ■ Clothes horses and flash kings.	■ Armani suits. Double breasted. ■ Pocket hankerchiefs. Rolexes. ■ Mercedes/Jags for principals.	■ Hardball Win/Lose negotiation. ■ Open confrontation with the gutsiest player winning.	■ CEO by 35. ■ Retire to resort community by 50.	■ Sell. ■ Sell. ■ Sell.	■ Schizoid combination of top-down and consensus, depending on situation.
Tweed Firm	■ Be punctual and reliable. ■ Avoid innovation. ■ Never miss a fee break.	■ The "old timers." ■ Whoever belongs to the right club or church. ■ Alumni of the chosen school.	■ Preppy. Blue blazers for both sexes. Cuffed slacks. Roll up sleeves in office. ■ Cadillac/Lincoln for principals.	■ Most senior person gets his/her way.	■ Never retire. Keep working well into 70s.	■ Never miss a day. ■ Keep neat work area. ■ Good drawing/drafting skills.	■ Move slowly. Avoid mistakes.

FIGURE 5.3 Corporate culture matrix

2. *Rites, rituals, and ceremonies.* The company longevity awards banquet, company anniversary celebrations, ringing a cowbell before each coffee break — these things reaffirm the key values of the firm.

3. *Special privileges or symbols.* More desirable offices, more convenient parking places, and titles such as *Associate* are privileges that can reinforce the characteristics or behaviors valued in employees.

4. *Organizational stories and myths.* Tales of incredible achievements, like one of the firm's founders redesigning a complete building overnight. Or the story might be something like how a sheet of drawings was ripped off a drafting table by the project manager in the middle of being worked on so the job wouldn't be turned in late, exemplifying the firm's commitment to on-time performance above all else.

Think about the impact of your firm's corporate culture on how new employees become productive members of the firm. Is your culture communicating to new employees something other than what you want it to? Is your idea of what constitutes acceptable job performance different from that of the majority in your company? Are you worried that your new employee won't achieve all he or she is capable of or, worse yet, that the new employee will be ruined by the organization's existing culture?

If you answered yes to any of the above questions, you have a serious problem that needs to be addressed. If you are the firm's Chief Executive and major stockholder, you are in the best possible position of anyone to change your firm's culture.

5.6 THE "BUDDY" CONCEPT

One orientation practice that has gained rapid acceptance in the design industry is to assign a "buddy" to each new employee, preferably a veteran employee who is the employee's peer. The buddy's role is to assist the new employee in his or her early days on the job and to work toward successful integration of the new employee into the firm.

Make absolutely sure the buddy is someone who sincerely wants to see the new employee succeed — not someone who was opposed to hiring the new employee and probably feels threatened. Also be sure that the buddy exemplifies the attitude and work ethic you want in the company. If not, the buddy concept can backfire.

In one case that comes to mind, a firm assigned its newly hired, degreed electrical engineer with four years' experience to a 20-year veteran, nondegreed electrical designer. The way this particular company handled it, the new employee and the buddy shared the same work space, in this case a large cubicle. When it became apparent that the young engineer's enthusiasm and attitude were quickly deteriorating, the firm's operations manager stepped in to find out what the problem was. A little investigation identified that the veteran employee was angered over what he perceived to be a lousy bonus from the previous year. He also was beginning to feel that as a nondegreed designer, there would only be so far he could advance in the company and that perhaps he had already peaked. His negative feelings toward the firm were rubbing off on the new man, who had developed a close personal relationship with this person to the point where the two of them became the best of friends at the office and away from work as well.

The new engineer was temporarily salvaged (he lasted a little over three years with the company) by moving him to a new cubicle and by having the firm's executive vice president, mechanical/electrical department head, and director of HR pay some extra attention to him. In spite of this attention and in spite of the fact he was the best-paid engineer with his level of experience in the firm, his attitude never fully recovered, and he ended up making a lateral move to join another company.

One last thought on the buddy concept. It doesn't cost much to give the buddy a budget for taking the new employee to lunch occasionally. Just tell him or her to let the new employee know that the company is picking up the tab!

5.7 MOTIVATION

The first months on the job are probably the most critical in terms of formulating the employee's long-term attitude toward his or her role and toward the organization as a whole. This attitude will be significantly affected by the firm's understanding (or lack of understanding) of the subject of motivation.

Just about everyone who is an owner or manager in a design firm is interested in learning more about how to motivate staff. There is probably more written on the topic of motivation than any other management topic. It is a widely held notion that one of management's primary duties is to motivate people. Of course, although a thorough understanding of the subject of motivation is beneficial to any manager, there are significant differences of opinion on the subject.

Some motivational experts maintain that each job and the entire organization should be structured in a way such that employees are trained to behave in certain predictable ways when a stimulus, like ringing a bell, is presented. Gaining more acceptance in the design industry is the contrasting notion that managers can't really motivate people in the work setting and that, instead of motivation, management's challenge is to avoid *demotivating* staff. Managers with this view see individuals as highly complex beings striving to interact with the world in a number of ways to satisfy a wide range of needs. They assume that they are hiring people who are already motivated from within.

Regardless of which side of the motivation versus demotivation issue you fall on, a thorough knowledge and understanding of motivation theory will help you manage human resources. Following is a look at some of the most well-known motivational theories.

In 1943, psychologist Abraham H. Maslow published what would come to be one of the most widely held theories of motivation. In his research, he identified certain needs in people and arranged them in a hierarchical order. Maslow believed that people were driven by multiple needs. He classified these from lowest

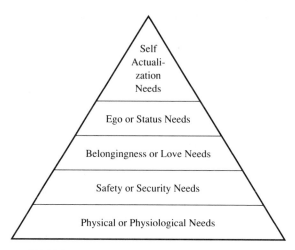

FIGURE 5.4   Maslow's hierarchy of needs diagram

to highest levels into physical or physiological needs, safety or security needs, belongingness or love needs, ego or status needs, and self-actualization needs (see Figure 5.4).

1. *Physical needs* relate to the basic necessities of life, such as food, clothing, and shelter. Related to physical needs are things like the office temperature and noise level, amount of work space allotted to individuals, availability of rest room facilities, and hours of work.

2. *Safety needs* motivate people to ensure against loss of some physical need fulfillment. Life, health, disability, and unemployment insurance programs, as well as retirement programs, all appeal to safety or security needs.

3. *Belongingness or love needs* include the need to work with, socialize with, or talk to others. They also include a need for friendship and camaraderie. Office space layouts, structured breaks, and company recreational activities all appeal to belongingness or love needs.

4. *Ego needs* have to do with self-esteem as well as someone's perception of how he or she is viewed by other people. Perquisites such as titles, special parking privileges, and well-placed private offices appeal to ego needs. Sometimes participation in special training also addresses ego needs.

5. *Self-actualization needs* are the highest-level needs. Self-actualized employees are free to express themselves and are creative and independent. Positions of power and participative management processes appeal to self-actualization needs.

The importance of Maslow's work lies in his hypothesis that individuals cannot move from one level to the next in the hierarchy without first satisfying lower-level needs. The implications for management lie in assessing where a specific individual is in the hierarchy in order to best appeal to his or her specific needs.

Frederick Herzberg, Distinguished Professor of Management at The University of Utah, asked 200 accountants and engineers what they found satisfying about their work in an effort to determine what motivated them. He called these measures of job satisfaction *motivators*. Herzberg also asked this group what it was that hurt their motivation, what made them unwilling to produce. He called these measures of job dissatisfaction *hygiene factors* (see Figure 5.5).

Hygiene factors (job dissatisfiers)	*Motivational factors (job satisfiers)*
Company policy and administration	Achievment
Supervision	Recognition for achievment
Interpersonal relations	Work itself
Working conditions	Responsibility
Salary*	Advancement
Status	Salary*
Security	Growth

*Although primarily a hygiene factor, salary commonly shows up as both a motivator and hygiene factor.

Source: Frederick Herzberg, *The Managerial Choice: To Be Efficient or to Be Human* (Salt Lake City: Olympus Publishing Company, 1982).

FIGURE 5.5   Herzberg's hygiene and motivational factors

The interviews produced some interesting results. Motivators turned out to be such things as the opportunity to achieve through work, recognition, promotion possibilities, and the chance to grow through additional responsibilities and learning opportunities. Dissatisfiers, or hygiene factors, turned out to center on complaints related to poor supervision, no chance to mingle with others on the job, uncomfortable physical work conditions, poor pay and benefits, and the feeling that there was no job security.

Although not all motivational experts agree with him, Herzberg's study leads one to the conclusion that motivating design professionals is a matter of providing the motivating factors rather than resolving hygiene problems. But, just because people aren't dissatisfied doesn't necessarily mean they're motivated; conversely, even if people are motivated, they may still be dissatisfied. The lesson for design firms is that you may have a staff of highly motivated and productive professionals now, but if you ignore the hygiene factors for too long, you run the risk of losing that staff.

5.8 MOTIVATORS AND DEMOTIVATORS

A new employee is bound to be a little more sensitive and insecure than someone who has worked in a company for a while. (Not to say that most professionals probably aren't less secure and less rational than they should be for their own good, anyway.) They require a little extra attention on your part to keep them turned on. Here are some specific hints for keeping your new staff members (or, for that matter, your existing staff) motivated:

1. Give staff members assignments that allow them to achieve some sense of closure. Design professionals get satisfaction from starting *and* completing a task. While this is relatively easy to accomplish for senior professionals, junior staff members have the same need and should be given simpler assignments that they can start and complete.

2. Don't assume that, because a staff member has not done a particular type of project or task before, he or she shouldn't be given a chance to do so. Design firms hate it when their clients do this to them, yet so many firms treat their own people this way.

3. Let staff members know where they stand in the eyes of others. Good feedback is especially critical in the first six months of employment. That's when staffers are the most anxious as well as the most receptive.

4. Get business cards, including title, made for a new employee as soon as possible. The same applies for those who have been promoted. Unnecessary delays in providing business cards can be demotivating.

5. Keep your staffers informed of events in the company, their department, and their project team. Be sure to deliver both the good and bad news on what is happening. Your honesty will be appreciated and you'll build credibility.

6. Move quickly to reinforce high job performance. Don't wait a full year to tangibly recognize someone who is clearly outperforming your expectations. Grant spot bonuses. Also use the power of praise to reinforce high performance.

7. Don't tolerate, or even worse—reward non-performers. Nothing is worse for the morale of your good people.

8. If a new staffer's motivation is not as high as you would like or as you expected it to be, don't rationalize. Have some faith that your hiring process will deliver good people in the first place, and accept it as your challenge to try to figure out how to unlock the potential in each of your staffers.

9. Excluding a new staffer from a meeting or training session can be a serious demotivator. Make the extra effort to include the new staffer in any meeting or session that he or she could conceivably benefit from. Feeling a part of what's going on is important to design professionals.

10. Also make sure that the new employee is not excluded from any parties or social get-togethers. One new employee was devastated by the fact that she and her family were not invited to the company summer picnic—she had joined the firm after the invitations went out, but before the picnic day. In another case, a firm's new Executive Vice President was hired (after a lengthy consultant-client working relationship and courtship), and though he had yet to officially start his new job, was excluded from a major affair honoring the company president's birthday.

11. Never chew out or yell at any employee in public. Although most people in the design business with even a shred of human relations skills take this for granted, that rare breed of management throwback from the pre-industrial revolution era will rear his ugly head occasionally. When he does, he'll completely devastate and demoralize the person he embarrassed in public.

5.9 LEADERSHIP

Inextricably linked to the whole concept of motivation and demotivation is the subject of leadership. History has shown that effective leaders can bring out both the best and the worst that human nature has to offer. They can inspire and motivate people to seemingly impossible achievements, as well as lead them down a path of complete self-destruction. No doubt, the quality of a design firm's leadership at all levels greatly affects its ability to motivate and retain quality staff.

All leadership situations involve the use of power—the ability of one person to influence the thinking or behavior of another. Leadership experts will tell you that there are five sources of power available to a leader:

1. *Legitimate power* is the power bestowed on someone by virtue of his or her position in the organization, or by law.
2. *Referent power* refers to the charismatic, or intangible quality that gives some leaders power over other people.
3. *Expert power* is the power that a leader has by virtue of his or her knowledge of a particular subject area. This power could be as a result of a technical specialization.
4. *Coercive power* is the power to punish someone for not doing what the leader wants.
5. *Reward power* is the power a leader has to grant rewards or other things that people want.

Leadership is a topic that people concerned with HR management in an A/E/P practice can't possibly learn too much about. There is so much conflicting information on the topic of what makes a successful leader that it's hard to put it to use, but one thing everyone can agree on is that there are vast differences in individuals' styles and abilities to function as leaders in design firms. Leadership style is no doubt influenced by the people being led, by the individual's own knowledge and skill at leadership, and by how much support and reinforcement the leader gets from those at a higher level in the organization.

To evaluate leaders, we often look to how well they fulfill their responsibilities, but what exactly are the responsibilities of leadership?

1. *Planning:* Leaders are responsible for developing the overall plan for their area of responsibility, whatever that may be. They are also the ones who set the direction for the efforts of whatever group they are leading.

2. *Setting priorities:* In every design firm, individuals face many conflicting demands for their time. The leader's responsibility is to establish the priorities for what problems need to be solved, what needs to be produced, or what has to be delayed in the face of conflicting demands.

3. *Communicating:* Leaders are responsible for communicating their plan and priorities in the context of the overall goals of the firm. Leaders in any area cannot set direction and establish priorities without ensuring that followers know what these are.

4. *Judging:* Leaders are often responsible for evaluating individuals' performance as well as distributing rewards. Although many people in managerial capacities in today's design practices are comfortable in the role of a reward giver, they often don't enjoy evaluating others' performances. Too often, they enjoy even less communicating that evaluation to those whose performance they are responsible for. By avoiding evaluation and communication, these managers shirk an important responsibility of leadership.

5. *Providing:* Leaders secure whatever resources their people need to meet their objectives. One of the most important roles of a leader is to get people the tools, equipment, material and labor resources they need to accomplish their goals.

6. *Solving problems:* Leaders are responsible for clearing roadblocks out of the way for their people. Whether it requires dealing with a nonperforming team member, a cantankerous secretary who refuses to make corrections to a piece of correspondence or report, or a principal who thinks his or her work should always come first, the effective leader clears roadblocks.

7. *Resolving conflict:* Leaders are responsible for resolving conflicts constructively. This doesn't mean avoiding or smoothing, the two most common, yet ineffective, ways to deal with conflict; it means finding out who or what is right, and then acting accordingly.

8. *Defusing negativity:* Leaders are responsible for defusing negativity. They know it only takes one negative thinker to destroy an entire group's morale and performance. Leaders understand that negative, "can't do" thinking cannot be tolerated and that negative thinkers should either be reformed by finding out what their problems are and addressing them (if legitimate), or be expelled from the group.

9. *Dispensing performance data:* Leaders are responsible for dispensing performance data. All too often, neglect of this responsibility at all levels in design firms leads to incorrect assumptions by group members and increased anxiety. A frequently cited demotivator of professionals in design firms is "not being kept informed." Good leaders understand their responsibility for ensuring that this doesn't happen.

10. *Anticipating future problems:* Leaders are responsible for looking to the future and anticipating problems before they occur. To fulfill this role, leaders continuously monitor both internal and external environments so action can be taken before crises develop.

Do good leaders share certain characteristics? Harvard psychology professor, David McClelland studied individuals' needs for achievement, affiliation (the need for close relations with others), and power—three needs present in varying degrees in all professional people. His research concluded that the most successful leaders had a high need for power and a low need for affiliation.

Experience in selecting and observing the leadership performance of hundreds of design professionals over an extended time period shows that the best leaders commonly share many of the following characteristics:

1. Good leaders are willing to take risks—not careless risks, but calculated risks—which the leader may not even perceive as risky.
2. Good leaders confront problems and conflict head-on. They aren't so concerned with how others perceive them that it affects their ability to do and say what is necessary.
3. Good leaders have deep inner convictions that their direction is true, and they can communicate this effectively to others.
4. Good leaders defend group members to those outside of the group. They assume that one of their own is right until proved otherwise.
5. Good leaders don't blame their own group members for poor performance, and instead accept responsibility for results.
6. Good leaders have the ability to bring people together to focus on a common goal, and they aren't afraid to promote intergroup conflict (competition) if the final results justify the tactic.
7. Good leaders set a positive example by not having a double standard for themselves and the rest of the group. They are hard workers.
8. Good leaders exemplify the characteristics of integrity and honesty. They don't lie, cheat, or steal in any form.
9. Good leaders are inspirational. They bring out the best in people through this intangible quality. They bolster the self-esteem of others rather than merely manipulating them.
10. Good leaders are positive, "can do" people who do not see themselves as victims of circumstance. They think of all the reasons why something will work, instead of otherwise, and they believe one person's efforts can make a difference. They do not feel helpless and don't communicate to others a belief that the future depends entirely on the market conditions or the whims of a few current clients. Effective leaders control the environment instead of it controlling them.
11. Good leaders have a sense of urgency and know that in the A/E/P business anything that will be accomplished must be done as quickly as possible. Good leaders have the philosophy, "Why wait until tomorrow to do what you can do today?"
12. Good leaders are people who can admit when they have been wrong or have made a mistake. They know humility builds credibility.

The question most often asked about leadership is, "Are good leaders born or made?" Whatever the answer, conventional wisdom tells you that more people probably have leadership potential than will ever realize it. An A/E/P firm's culture has to support and nurture the good leadership so essential to the firm's long- and short-term ability to attract and retain motivated staff. Environments that don't support leadership initiatives but instead undermine staff members' attempts to assert themselves in leadership roles usually have high staff turnover. When leadership is not supported and promoted, the firm's potential leaders either don't emerge or leave to go somewhere else where they can.

5.10 CONCLUSION

The first months on the job are critical for newly hired design professionals, and during this time they will be evaluating their decision to join the firm. The company, too, will likely have high expectations for the employee's early on-the-job performance.

Orientation can help ensure that a new employee will be successful. Most firms pay little attention to their orientation process. After orientation, new employees must be integrated into the rest of the organization. This requires an understanding of the firm's corporate culture. It also requires honest feedback to the employee on his or her job performance.

The long-term challenge faced by design firm leaders is to keep employees' motivation high through a thorough understanding of design professionals' needs in the work setting and a conscientious effort to address those needs.

6

PERFORMANCE APPRAISAL

I wish people who have trouble communicating would just shut up.

—Tom Lehrer

6.1 INTRODUCTION

If design firms are to get in step with the rest of American industry—which represents their greatest competition for qualified staff—they need to pay more attention to performance and performance appraisal. There are two sure-fire benefits to a good performance appraisal system. First, it can be one of the least expensive motivational tools available to managers. Second, it is essential to minimizing employment-related liabilities.

The process of performance appraisal in design firms almost never gets the attention it deserves. Too many design firm principals don't know what it is, why it's done, or how to do it effectively. It's often combined with whatever wage and salary review process the firm has. In addition, design professionals' natural reluctance to dole out either criticism or praise, coupled with the pressure to stay job-chargeable, results in many appraisals occurring either late or not at all.

Firms who do spend the time and money to come up with a formal performance appraisal process rarely train managers to use the system effectively. These firms frequently end up with a complex system too cumbersome to administer. Firms who don't develop any formal appraisal process often end up with no defense in a wrongful termination or discrimination lawsuit.

6.2   CASE STUDIES

A typical example of how badly performance appraisal is handled in a design firm is the case of Paul, a design architect in a 150-person full-service firm. Paul joined the company three years ago, after having spent his first five years out of architectural school with a smaller local firm.

Two of Paul's motivations for joining his present employer were that the company was growing quickly and that ownership opportunities were alluded to during Paul's pre-employment discussions with the firm. He knew that to become an associate, the first step in the ownership process, his performance would have to be viewed as stellar by the other principals in the firm. The problem for Paul was this: Although he was basically happy in his work and had worked on some major projects over the last three years, all of his work had been with one principal of the firm who had absolutely nothing to do with its management and who was now in the process of getting ready for retirement.

Although the company had a formal performance appraisal (P.A.) process that was supposed to occur at six-month intervals based on employees' employment anniversaries, Paul's only P.A. since joining the firm three years ago had been very brief. Paul had been shown a form with five or six performance categories on it, in all of which his principal had rated him excellent or above average. He didn't sign anything, and what happened to the form after his 10-minute discussion was a complete mystery to Paul.

In the design studio upstairs from Paul's worked Judy, an extremely aggressive and highly articulate young architect. Working on the same floor with five of the company's other principals gave Judy lots of exposure and many opportunities to work for a number of different people. She joined the firm the same month Paul did three years ago, although she had a couple less years of total work experience. Because Judy worked for some of the firm's more progressive principals, her appraisals were always completed on or close to schedule—a schedule that should have been the same for Paul's reviews.

Now Judy and Paul were friends, not close friends, but having joined the firm at the same time, there was a certain camaraderie that existed between the two of them. Judy had mentioned to Paul a couple months before that she had really gotten a super appraisal, that three principals sat in on her session, and that the review was so complimentary she had asked for a copy of the extensive comments to take home to show her husband. Imagine Paul's reaction when an announcement landed in his in-box one afternoon, an announcement that Judy and one of the firm's interior designers had just been made associates! That weekend, Paul started combing the classified ads, convinced that he was never going to be recognized and appreciated in *that* company.

The case of Marge, in her first job out of secretarial school, illustrates the lack of sensitivity some appraisers show toward those they are appraising. A high school honor student who lost first her mother and then her father to cancer and who had helped raise three brothers with little resources, Marge landed a position working to produce specifications in a three-person word-processing group for a major full-service firm. Despite what she considered to be her very best effort to do a good job, the "old battle-axe" who headed up her department, a supervisor with a history of causing turnovers, wrote in her 90-day appraisal that she was "very immature" and "must not be very intelligent." Upon reading this, Marge burst into tears. She had never been so embarrassed and angered in her life. After writing those insulting review comments, the supervisor had the audacity to tell Marge that she wasn't really unhappy with her overall performance, but that she "set very high standards for her girls."

The case of Rick illustrates what can happen if honest feedback isn't given on appraisals. Now 60 years old, Rick had been the fourth person to join what eventually grew into a 300-person company over a 35-year period. At one time a chief draftsman who supervised a drafting pool, in the last three years or so Rick just worked on projects. Everyone in the company knew he had a lousy attitude — he'd had one for years. Rick *never* did any more than he had to. He acted as if he hated every new employee. He fought every change management made, even when they were obviously in his best interests. He wouldn't even say hello to people in the hall unless they had worked at the company longer than he had (practically no one!). He had long since exceeded what the company could afford to pay someone with his skills and responsibilities. The problem was, no one had the guts to deal with him, and after all he was a "good draftsman."

When the workload and prospects for future work eventually fell off, the day came that Rick had to be let go. Called into his department manager's office, he was given the bad news, which he did not take well. He threatened suit at the meeting, pointing out that he had "always done a yeoman's job," that others should be cut before him, and that he was being discriminated against just because he "wasn't a young hot-shot who wore suspenders and drove a foreign car."

Rick's suit against the company revealed the fact that he had never had a poor review and that he couldn't have been compared objectively with others in his job category when the company made its cutback decision. Even the best performers in his job category had performance appraisals that were no better than his — if they had any at all.

Rick eventually received a $300,000 jury award based on age discrimination, retired to his cabin in the hills of Arkansas, and lived happily ever after. His former employers had to take out a second mortgage on their office building to cough up the cash!

These three cases illustrate the need for an effective and well-administered performance appraisal process. The sad fact is, these examples aren't really unusual in an A/E/P firm; others just like them happen every day.

6.3 BENEFITS OF PERFORMANCE APPRAISAL

Performance appraisal is the process used by management to inform employees individually how well they are doing in the eyes of the company. Performance appraisal goes by many different names in the industry and in the literature: performance review, performance evaluation, employee review, personnel review, performance rating, employee evaluation, employee appraisal, merit review, or review, among others. No matter what it's called, the process is usually formalized to the extent that any verbal feedback given by appraisers is accompanied by some written feedback, which is eventually added to employees' permanent personnel files.

Formal performance appraisal is a process established to evaluate employee performance regularly and systematically at all levels. Normally, the process includes the following steps:

1. Management establishes policies on how often and when to evaluate staff, who appraises staff, and what the criteria are for appraisal. The appraisal instrument is designed, and it is decided who will and who will not see the appraisals.
2. The HR manager, or his or her equivalent, trains appraisers in the process and sets a schedule for when appraisals are due.
3. Appraisers gather data on employee performance.
4. Appraisers consolidate inputs to develop the individual performance appraisal.
5. Individuals to be appraised prepare a self-evaluation (optional).
6. Appraisers meet privately with employees to discuss evaluation (and self-evaluation, if completed).
7. The written appraisal form or other documentation of the session is routed through all appropriate parties and finally put into the employee's personnel file.

Properly designed, the formal performance appraisal process can be quite straightforward and represents no great burden on managers or staff. There are a host of reasons why design firms should be doing regular performance appraisals on every staff member—far too many reasons for any firm not to have a formal appraisal process.

Regular performance appraisals reduce the employment-related liability exposure and protect the firm. Consistent, accurate, and well-documented appraisals lower the probability that the firm will lose a wrongful termination or discrimination suit. The firm needs a consistent history of evaluations on every staff member to minimize this potential liability. Although some authors on the subject feel this is a negative motivation for performance appraisal, the financial liabilities incurred by firms in employment-related lawsuits makes it a powerful one!

Another justification for performance appraisals is that employees should, in theory, be happier and more productive when they know where they stand and what is expected of them. In many cases a well-conducted appraisal session will lead to improved employee job performance. Although it certainly doesn't happen every time, an honest appraisal session, during which a manager identifies performance problems and weaknesses, may, in fact, result in an employee correcting or bolstering his or her performance in those areas. Also, the appraisal session offers an opportunity to provide further motivation to employees by confirming and reinforcing what it is they have been doing right.

Another good reason for formal performance appraisal is to identify the firm's high achievers, to bring them to the attention of others in the organization, and to justify promotion decisions. This is where routing becomes important.

The performance appraisal process provides an opportunity to discuss and develop mutually acceptable short-term goals and objectives for the employee. With the performance appraisal as the basis, the groundwork for what needs to be accomplished by the employee has already been laid, and setting short-term goals is the next logical step.

Yet another benefit of the performance appraisal process is that it provides employees with one more opportunity to express their concerns about the company and their positions. It should be a chance for the employee to voice questions and concerns in a one-on-one situation with the immediate supervisor. Whether or not anything is ever done about the issues brought up, giving the employee an opportunity to unload may afford a cathartic benefit.

Studies have shown that regular and effective appraisals can help reduce a firm's staff turnover rate. The key is communication. Performance appraisal is one of the few formal, two-way communication channels available to employees in design firms, and good communications are directly linked to lower turnover. Although turnover is no doubt necessary and sometimes even desirable, management should be in control of who goes and when (see Figure 6.1 for a summary of the reasons for performance appraisal).

One word of caution: There is nothing worse than scheduling appraisals and then not doing them when the time comes. This kind of negligence can seriously damage management's credibility with all employees. If a firm has a company policy to do performance appraisals on a regularly scheduled basis, it must do so.

1. The performance appraisal process can serve as a catharsis for employees with problems or concerns.

2. In theory, employees should be happier and more productive knowing where they stand and what is expected of them.

3. Performance appraisal should identify the firm's high achievers and bring them to the attention of others in the organization.

4. A well-conducted performance appraisal session can lead to improved employee job performance.

5. Performance appraisals provide an opportunity to formalize the process for setting short-term goals.

6. Regular performance appraisals can help reduce the firm's potential employment-related liabilities.

7. Effective performance appraisals can help reduce the firm's staff turnover rate.

8. If a firm has a policy to conduct performance appraisals on a regularly scheduled basis, not conducting them can seriously damage management's credibility.

FIGURE 6.1   Reasons to do formal performance appraisal

6.4 WHY MANAGERS AVOID PERFORMANCE APPRAISAL

Unfortunately, despite the obvious benefits for everyone concerned, the majority of those responsible for carrying out appraisals will fight the process every step of the way. Few people enjoy the prospect of criticizing another human being. Although the performance appraisal process involves far more than criticism, all too often apprehension and an ignorance of how to communicate performance weaknesses without deflating the employee's ego and motivation keep managers from using this important human resource management tool. It doesn't help that most firms with performance appraisal systems never train their managers to conduct appraisals effectively.

Design professionals especially, intelligent and sensitive as they often are, feel awkward about assuming a role as superior to someone else. According to the McClelland study (Section 5.9 in Chapter 5), effective managers tend to be high in the need for power but low in the need for affiliation. Yet design professionals as a species tend, by contrast, to be high in the need for affiliation and low in the need for power. This high need for affiliation results in a reluctance to deliver bad news.

But is it really fair to hold back feedback from an employee with a performance problem? How can someone be expected to improve under those conditions? The alternative to providing constructive criticism is, at best, to see someone waste time in his or her career and not achieve all that is possible for the organization. At worst, the day will come when the employee is fired without warning. Either alternative runs counter to the individual's and the organization's best interests.

Fortunately, the performance appraisal process in a typical A/E/P firm requires delivering good news more often than bad. There are, however, professionals who feel almost as funny about giving out praise as they do criticism. These misguided souls feel that professionals don't need praise, that as professionals they should get all of their satisfaction from the work itself.

This notion is not confined to the design profession. One Ph.D. psychologist working as a director of a nationally recognized day treatment program for emotionally disturbed adolescents called in a consultant to determine the cause for the poor morale and high staff turnover in her organization. After thoroughly examining the operation, it turned out that one of the major causes for the HR problems was the director's feeling that praise was unnecessary for psychiatrists and psychologists and that, being professionals, it would be unprofessional for them to operate in such an environment!

Everybody needs praise; everybody periodically needs validation that he or she is okay; and no matter how often someone is told that he or she has done a good job or that he or she is a valued employee, putting it in writing can have a more lasting positive motivational effect. At a recent seminar on principles of management conducted for a mid-sized A/E firm, one of the company's three division managers expressed the concern that giving too many strokes might raise individuals' expectations for increased compensation or promotion to artificially high levels which the company couldn't meet. This fear is keeping too many managers in design firms from using the performance appraisal process to reinforce what staffers are doing right.

Another excuse for managers' resistance to the performance appraisal process is the myth that appraisals take too much time away from more important activities. One HR manager in a big design firm consistently had problems getting a civil engineering team leader to do his appraisals. Yet the same manager who claimed he didn't have the time for appraisals was also the first to head out the door at 5:00 every afternoon, and he never missed a coffee break. It's easy to say that missing scheduled performance appraisals should simply not be tolerated by upper management. However, in this particular organization, the upper managers were also behind in the appraisals they were responsible for completing!

Finally, many technical professionals share the belief that if something is not completely objective and quantifiable, then it is worthless. The fact is that very little of what a design professional really accomplishes can be evaluated that objectively. But what's wrong with supervisors telling staffers their perceptions of the staff member's performance, when, under ideal conditions, supervisors are responsible for their staffers and control their destiny in the organization? The subjective opinion of an empowered manager is every bit as important to the individual and the organization as someone else's idea of what should be measured objectively.

Whatever the causes for managers' resistance (see Figure 6.2), it is up to whoever is in charge of a firm's HR management program to overcome these obstacles. The organization's managers need to understand why their resistance is not valid and why performance appraisal should be taken seriously.

1. Fear of delivering bad news.
2. Feeling that praise is unnecessary for professionals.
3. Performance appraisal takes too much time.
4. Performance appraisal is not objective and therefore meaningless.

FIGURE 6.2 Why managers resist doing performance appraisals

6.5 PERFORMANCE APPRAISAL VERSUS COMPENSATION REVIEW

In many companies, performance appraisal is combined with the wage-and-salary review process. What, these managers ask, is feedback worth if you don't tie it to what kind of raise someone gets? Combining performance appraisal with wage and salary review may, on the surface, sound like a good idea. Why not pay for performance? What's wrong with reinforcing high performance and sanctioning poor performance by granting or withholding tangible rewards?

There are really two primary issues to be dealt with in this section. The first issue is whether a firm should directly link how well someone does on a performance appraisal to his or her compensation. The second issue is whether doing performance appraisal *at the same time* as pay review dilutes the value of the performance appraisal process.

There are several snags in the seemingly logical approach of directly linking performance appraisals to compensation. First, more than just job performance goes into developing the compensation equation that eventually determines what someone earns. The highest-performing office clerk imaginable, someone who exceeds expectations at every corner, will probably never earn what the least-productive groundwater hydrologist makes. The supply and demand for various types of talent and the resulting demands for particular individuals' services significantly affect what any one individual is worth to a company. Pay is not simply a linear function of performance.

If employees who score well on their performance appraisals get a substantial raise every time, they may end up being paid $15 per hour for a $10-per-hour job, endangering their own long-term job security with the firm. Critics of the argument will say that this issue can be easily overcome by developing specific salary ranges for each position in the company. Then those who peak out in the range won't get paid any more regardless of their performance appraisals. Without getting into a full-blown discussion on compensation, it shouldn't be too hard to imagine the effect of telling someone so definitively that he or she will not earn any more raises because of an arbitrary salary range.

The best argument against combining the wage-and-salary review process with performance appraisal is that it clouds the real purpose of the performance appraisal process—providing specific, constructive verbal and written feedback to the employee. Talking about pay at the same time as reviewing employees' performances creates a scenario in which the only issue of importance to them is whether their raises will meet their expectations. If the raise is acceptable to the employee, any criticism really has little effect. If the raise is not acceptable, the employee will likely be mad or hurt, and the positive effect of any praise will be lost. If the manager waits until the end of the appraisal session to discuss pay, the employee will be likely to be distracted and anxious to get to that subject, again hampering the process of providing meaningful feedback.

Compensation cannot and should not be separated from performance in any company at any position level unless you want to create a bureaucracy that will certainly cause turnover among the highest-performing staff members. However, the performance appraisal session is not the time to make this link. A much better strategy for tying pay to performance will be discussed in Chapter 9.

6.6 PERFORMANCE APPRAISAL INSTRUMENTS

There are practically as many different performance appraisal instruments out there as there are design firms. How does a firm convinced of the benefits of a formal performance appraisal process select the best instrument? Remember, an instrument is simply a tool, a means to an end. Keep in mind the reasons for conducting performance appraisals when selecting or designing the appraisal instrument.

There are two basic types of performance appraisal techniques. They are single-person methods and multiperson methods. Single-person techniques are the most common. They appraise the performance of each employee without directly comparing one employee to another. Multiperson techniques evaluate each employee in the context of his or her performance compared to other employees. The multiperson techniques are likened to the process of grading on a curve. Since multiperson methods are most appropriately used when trying to distribute a wage and salary increase budget, or when deciding who stays and who goes in the event of staffing cuts, the discussion that follows will concentrate on single-person appraisal techniques (see Figure 6.3).

1. Graphic rating scales
2. Forced choice ratings
3. Essay appraisal techniques
4. Performance checklists
5. Critical incident techniques

FIGURE 6.3 Performance appraisal techniques

Single-person techniques include graphic rating scales (the most commonly used in design firms), forced choice ratings, essay appraisal techniques, performance checklists, and critical incident techniques. There are endless variations on each of these techniques.

Graphic rating scales are far and away the most common. Here, the evaluator is required to rate the employee on several types of performance characteristics (for example, punctuality, attitude, and initiative) according to a predetermined performance scale. The scale represents some sort of continuum, ranging from low to high performance for that particular characteristic. Sometimes each position on the scale is defined very specifically: other times each position is merely assigned a general descriptor such as "Poor" or "Excellent." In yet a third case, the scale is simply numerical, ranging perhaps from 1 to 10. In general, explicit ratings, which clearly describe the behavior that goes along with each position on the scale for each characteristic (for example, "Is never late" for "punctuality"), are preferable because they tend to reduce the effect of error or bias in interpreting a merely numerical or generally descriptive rating ("10" or "excellent," for example). Who is to say that three interior design studio heads will all have the same idea of what constitutes a "3," or what is "good" performance in the area of "initiative" (see Figures 6.4, 6.5, and 6.6 for sample performance appraisal forms).

Generally speaking, in addition to requiring appraisers to check the most appropriate position on the scale, most scales of this type provide an opportunity for the appraiser to write comments on any specific performance area. The strength of these systems lies in their convenience of administration, wide-ranging applicability to a number of positions in a firm, and flexibility for the user. Their weakness lies in the tendency of managers to rate most employees higher than they deserve, contributing to less honest feedback than is desirable.

Forced choice methods require the appraiser to choose from a set of descriptive statements about the employee being evaluated. The two to four statements describing employee behavior for each performance category are grouped in such

VH **Employee Performance Appraisal**
Reviewer's Form

Confidentially Route to: _____

Name: _____   Title: _____

Instructions: Study each factor and the description of each degree. Mark the square which most clearly fits the employee's performance. Make comments to explain your evaluation.

Part I: Ability and Application

Initiative - ability to exercise self-reliance and enterprise

- ☐ Grasps situation and goes to work without hesitation
- ☐ Works independently often; seldoms waits for orders
- ☐ Usually waits for instructions; follows others
- ☐ Does only what is specifically instructed to do

Comments: _____

_____

Quality of Work - accuracy and effectiveness of work; freedom from errors

- ☐ Consistently good quality; errors rare
- ☐ Usually good quality; few errors
- ☐ Passable work if closely supervised
- ☐ Frequent errors; cannot be depended upon to be accurate

Comments: _____

_____

Quantity of Work - output of work; performance speed

- ☐ Works consistently and with excellent output
- ☐ Works consistently with above average output
- ☐ Maintains group average output
- ☐ Below average output; slow

Comments: _____

_____

Job Knowledge - technical knowledge of job and industry; ability to apply it

- ☐ Knows job thoughly; doesn't need help
- ☐ Knows job well; seldom needs help
- ☐ Knows job fairly well; requires instructions
- ☐ Little knowledge of job; requires constant help

Comments: _____

_____

Attitude - enthusiasm, cooperativeness, willingness

- ☐ Enthusiastic; outstanding in cooperation; tries new ideas
- ☐ Responsive, cooperates well; meets others more than half-way
- ☐ Usually cooperates; does not usually resist new ideas
- ☐ Uncooperative; resents new ideas; displays little interest

Comments: _____

_____

Dependability - willingness to accept responsibility; to follow through; to meet deadlines

- ☐ Outstanding ability to perform with little supervision; always gets job done
- ☐ Willing and able to accept responsibility; little checking on progress required
- ☐ Usually follows instructions; normal follow-up
- ☐ Refuses or unable to carry responsibility; needs constant follow-up

Comments: _____

_____

Attendance - reliability to be on the job

- ☐ Always can be relied upon to be at work on time; absent only in emergency situations
- ☐ Usually punctual; explained absences occasionally
- ☐ Tardy with reasonable excuses; fairly frequent explained absences
- ☐ Frequent unexplained tardiness and/or absences

Comments: _____

_____

Vanasse Hangen Brustlin, Inc.

FIGURE 6.4   Performance appraisal form (VHB)

Communications Skills - ability to clearly express ideas and thoughts; ability to establish rapport

☐ Outstanding ability to establish rapport and articulate ideas; sensitive to outside clients	☑ Usually is able to express self clearly; few problems internally and with clients	☐ Occasional misunderstandings with others both inside and outside of the company	☐ Frequent misunderstandings and problems with others

Comments:

Leadership - ability to guide, direct others; skill at delegation

☐ Others naturally follow example or direction; obtains good results from others	☑ Willingly assumes guidance of others; is fairly well accepted in this role	☐ Is accepted reluctantly by his group as a guide or example; gets fluctuating results	☐ Shows no aptitude or skill in leadership

Comments:

Creativity - ability to devise improvements, new programs and processes

☐ Consistently comes up with new ideas, figures out new and better ways to do things	☐ Frequently initiates new ideas and programs	☑ Has come up with an occasional good idea	☐ Never comes up with new ideas for products or process improvements

Comments:

Profit Consciousness - bottom line orientation; concern for company dollars

☐ Consistently shows concern for bottom line; guards company resources as own	☑ Frequently stays within budget; usually functions as guardian of company profits	☐ Shows some concern for company profitability; occasional instances showing little concern	☐ Not profit conscious; shows little concern for company finances

Comments:

Planning Skills - Ability to set schedules and anticipate problems

☐ Outstanding planner of projects; meets schedules and deadlines	☑ Has planned successful projects; not consistent in planning	☐ Occasionally plans; planning skills need definite refinement	☐ Does not plan; reacts to crisis; misses deadlines regularly

Comments:

Part II - Advancement Potential

Check applicable sections (more than one section may apply):

☐ Regressing   ☐ Not Suited to Job   ☐ Not likely to advance   ☐ Progressing   ☑ Satisfactory   ☐ Maximum Performance on Job

Review your comments; then set goals for the employee to accomplish between now and the next review period

1.

2.

3.

Time for next review to occur ___1 Year___   Employee's Signature _John H. Landhalt_

Date ___11/17/88___   Note: Employee's signature does not necessarily indicate agreement with the above comments. Is only an acknowledgement that the appraisal occurred.

Supervisor: Complete this section after review meeting.

Employee's reaction to review and suggestions was: (check one)

☐ Appreciation (Completely willing to strive for improvement)   ☑ Interest (Will make an attempt to follow suggestions)   ☐ Disinterest/Satisfied with present status)   ☐ Resentment (Feels review is an imposition)

Conclusions drawn from interview:

Date: ___11/17/88___   Reviewer's Signature: _Mark C. Grey_

FIGURE 6.4   *(Continued)*

GALE ASSOCIATES, INC.
EMPLOYEE PERFORMANCE EVALUATION
EXEMPT

Date_____

EMPLOYEE_____ Date of Hire_____

DIVISION_____ POSITION_____ SUPV._____

TYPE OF REVIEW: ( ) 6-MONTH ( ) ANNUAL ( ) OTHER_____
==

OVERALL PERFORMANCE: ( ) Excellent ( ) Proficient ( ) Qualified
                      ( ) Fair   ( ) Unsatisfactory
==

	E	P	Q	F	U	NA
1. JOB KNOWLEDGE: Employee possesses clear knowledge of the responsibilities and tasks he/she must perform.						
2. PLANNING & ORGANIZING: Ability to plan ahead, schedule and lay out work so as to make most effective use of time.						
3. QUALITY OF WORK: Neatness, thoroughness and accuracy of work.						
4. PRODUCTIVITY: Amount of work produced in comparison to time spent on projects.						
5. TECHNICAL KNOWLEDGE: Extent of basic technical, practical and theoretical knowledge to carry out tasks and to maintain adherence to professional standards of performance.						
6. DEPENDABILITY: Reliability of employee to take initiative and to follow through to completion any assigned tasks and to maintain adherence to professional standards of performance.						
7. JUDGMENT: Ability to draw sound conclusions to accomplish project/company objectives.						
8. COMMUNICATION: Ability to interact verbally or in writing with in-house staff, clients and vendors.						
9. COOPERATION: Willingness and ability to work with and assist others in a constructive manner.						
10. ATTENDANCE AT MEETINGS: Willingness to attend evening meetings (paid or unpaid) and/or participate actively in professional organizations on behalf of the company.						
11. PROJECT MANAGEMENT: Ability to effectively manage and/or be a substantive member of a project team in order to maintain time schedules, budgets and good client relationships.						
12. LEADERSHIP SKILLS: Ability to provide direction and guidance to those working with him/her for maximum efficiency and effectiveness.						
13. SELF-IMPROVEMENT: Employee's drive in terms of desire to attain higher levels of education, technical skill, professional registrations, etc.						

(SEE REVERSE SIDE)

Form #8912

FIGURE 6.5 Performance appraisal form (Gale Associates)

(2)

EMPLOYEE'S STRONG POINTS OF JOB PERFORMANCE: _____
_____
_____

WHAT AREAS ARE OPEN FOR IMPROVEMENT? _____
_____
_____

HOW CAN THIS IMPROVEMENT BE ACHIEVED? WHAT CAN EMPLOYEE DO? WHAT CAN SUPV. DO?
_____
_____
_____
_____

WHAT GOALS OR OBJECTIVES CAN BE ACHIEVED WITHIN THE NEXT 6 MONTHS? _____
_____
_____

WITHIN THE NEXT 12 MONTHS? _____
_____
_____

GENERAL REMARKS, IF ANY: _____
_____
_____
_____

EMPLOYEE REMARKS/SUGGESTIONS: _____
_____
_____
_____
_____

SUPERVISOR: _____ EMPLOYEE: _____
DATE: _____ DATE: _____

DEFINITIONS OF PERFORMANCE RATINGS

E (EXCELLENT)	Outstanding, exceptional - substantially exceeds job requirements, leaving little if anything to be desired.
P (PROFICIENT)	Above expectations - clearly exceeds job requirements.
Q (QUALIFIED)	Normal expectations - satisfactorily meets job expectations - average performance.
F (FAIR)	Minimum expectations, less than satisfactory - barely meets minimum job requirements.
U (UNSATISFACTORY)	Below expectations - requires substantial improvement to meet job requirements.

FIGURE 6.5 *(Continued)*

Employee Performance Appraisal
Professional/Technical

Name _____ Job Title _____

Department_____ Time In Present Position _____

Last Appraisal Date _____ Time Under Appraiser's Supervision _____

Type of Review _____ Probationary _____ Semi-Annual

PART I. JOB PERFORMANCE EVALUATION

Instructions: Check (✔) the appropriate box for each category which best describes the individual's performance. For ratings of Distinguished, Marginal or Unsatisfactory, **comments** must be made.

Distinguished	Commendable	Satisfactory	Marginal	Unsatisfactory
Performance that consistently far exceeds the normal requirements of the job and is clearly outstanding	Performance that consistently exceeds normal requirements and expectancies of the job	Performance that consistently meets the normal requirements and expectancies of the job	Performance that does not consistently meet the normal requirements and expectancies of the job and requires improvement in order to be considered acceptable	Performance that is consistently well below the normal requirements and expectancies of the job and is unacceptable

QUANTITY OF WORK   The volume of work an individual regularly produces in a designated period.

Distinguished	Commendable	Satisfactory	Marginal	Unsatisfactory
☐	☐	☐	☐	☐

Comments _____

QUALITY OF WORK   The accuracy and effectiveness of work that an individual produces in a designated period.

Distinguished	Commendable	Satisfactory	Marginal	Unsatisfactory
☐	☐	☐	☐	☐

Comments _____

JOB KNOWLEDGE   The information, skills and understanding required to perform job duties at a satisfactory level.

Distinguished	Commendable	Satisfactory	Marginal	Unsatisfactory
☐	☐	☐	☐	☐

Comments _____

COOPERATION   The willingness to work toward assigned objectives. Ability to shift priorities when necessary, while working with others and responding to suggestions and criticism.

Distinguished	Commendable	Satisfactory	Marginal	Unsatisfactory
☐	☐	☐	☐	☐

Comments _____

RESPONSIBILITY   The extent of dependability required to do the job with minimum supervision. Also includes the ability to meet schedules and carry out instructions.

Distinguished	Commendable	Satisfactory	Marginal	Unsatisfactory
☐	☐	☐	☐	☐

Comments _____

ATTITUDE   The enthusiasm which an employee demonstrates for the company and profession.

Distinguished	Commendable	Satisfactory	Marginal	Unsatisfactory
☐	☐	☐	☐	☐

Comments _____

INITIATIVE   The motivation and desire to attain goals and achieve desired results.

Distinguished	Commendable	Satisfactory	Marginal	Unsatisfactory
☐	☐	☐	☐	☐

Comments _____

PART II SKILLS PERFORMANCE EVALUATION

Instructions: Give a brief description of the individual's performance as it relates to each of the following areas. Then rate the employee's performance: D-Distinguished, C-Commendable; S-Satisfactory, M-Marginal, U-Unsatisfactory.

1. **TECHNICAL SKILL:** Evaluate the individual's knowledge and skills in the technical requirements of the job and how this knowledge is applied. Give specific accomplishments and achievements.

_____

_____

_____   D___ C___ S___ M___ U___

FIGURE 6.6   Performance appraisal form (Pickering)

2. **DECISION MAKING/PROBLEM SOLVING:** Consider the individual's ability to analyze and evaluate problems and to develop solutions and options in problem solving.

_____

_____

_____ D____ C____ S____ M____ U____

3. **LEADERSHIP/TEAMWORK:** Judge the individual as a leader/teamplayer. Give specific examples of cooperation and motivation demonstrated with individuals as well as groups.

_____

_____

_____ D____ C____ S____ M____ U____

4. **ADMINISTRATION:** Review the individual's work organization, delegation, control and follow up with projects or other related jobs.

_____

_____

_____ D____ C____ S____ M____ U____

5. **INITIATIVE/CREATIVENESS:** Evaluate the individual's ability to act independently as a self starter and to make proposals, develop original ideas and fresh approaches to situations or problems.

_____

_____

_____ D____ C____ S____ M____ U____

PART III. PERFORMANCE PLANS AND ACCOMPLISHMENTS

Instructions: List the employee's objectives, major responsibilities and projects assigned during this performance period, then for each activity listed give the results and output.

List objectives, responsibilities and projects (Key words only)	List performance results (Consider quantity, quality, cost and timeliness)	Comments (Related to performance achieved)

PART IV. DEVELOPMENT REVIEW

Individual's and supervisor's overall assessment plan to help improve job related skills and expand job knowledge. What training and/or action is recommended for development or improvement? Set timetables for ratings of marginal or unsatisfactory.

_____

_____

_____

PART V. OVERALL EVALUATION:

Considering all factors, check the rating which best describes this employee's overall performance during the past period.

Distinguished	Commendable	Satisfactory	Marginal	Unsatisfactory
☐	☐	☐	☐	☐

APPROVALS:

Supervisor's Signature _____

_____
Date

Approved: _____

_____
Date

Approved: _____

_____
Date

_____

_____
Date

Employee's Signature (Verifying that all of the above has been discussed)

EMPLOYEE REMARKS: _____ _____

_____

_____

FIGURE 6.6 *(Continued)*

a way that the appraiser cannot tell what position on the scale they represent. The strength of these systems lies in their tendency to produce lower (and theoretically, more honest) ratings than graphic rating scale techniques. Their disadvantage lies in the fact that they are extremely difficult to design and require completely different descriptions of employee behavior for people in different positions within the firm.

Essay evaluation techniques (see Figure 6.7) are less structured than the two approaches described above. They require appraisers to write about the employee being evaluated. Some essay techniques specify the areas to be covered, while others do not. The strength of this approach lies in the ability of each manager to customize the system to address his or her best needs. Their downfall is the inherent inconsistency built into such a system. Also, the reluctance many technical professionals have to writing tends to result in more delinquent appraisals.

Checklists are yet another possible performance appraisal tool. Checklists comprise statements describing employee performance. In developing the actual performance appraisal, the appraiser checks off any statements that he or she feels apply to the employee. If the item does not apply, it is simply not checked. The items checked are then summed up to provide a specific score for the employee's overall performance.

A variation of this process is the weighted checklist. The only difference is that each type of behavior is given a weighted value that may not count the same as other values toward the employee's overall score. Just as with forced choice scales, the weakness with the checklist approach lies in the difficulty in developing checklists for each position in the firm that all supervisors can agree cover the appropriate and relevant performance categories. Properly designed checklists can be excellent performance appraisal instruments. However, their danger lies in the attempt many technical professionals will make to translate scores on the checklist appraisal into a compensation equation.

Finally, the critical incident technique requires managers be provided with a list of statements describing effective and ineffective behaviors for each employee type. During the period preceding the appraisal, managers check off and write down examples of critical incidents describing that behavior. When the actual appraisal session is held, these become the basis of the discussion. Although a very effective technique, formalizing the critical incident approach as the foundation for performance appraisal in a design firm can be very difficult. The problem lies in developing separate forms and incidents for each performance category, and then getting managers to write down critical incidents throughout the period to be covered by the review.

Whatever performance appraisal instrument or technique you decide to use, don't feel that it has to be complex to be any good. The best systems are simple ones. They should make it easy for the reviewer to stay on schedule with his or her assigned reviews, and they should facilitate clear communication. Firms that do not currently have an appraisal process in place should adopt a simple process first. Just getting managers used to the idea of doing their assigned appraisals is the first step.

Architecture/Planning Associates, Inc. Staff Performance Evaluation
Name of Employee:

Employee No.:

Title: Planner

Labor Category: 6

Department: Urban Planning

Hire Date:

1. List major project assignments during the past year:
2. Please describe the employee's overall performance as indicated by the following tasks on the Planner job description:
   * Prepares reports and presentation materials.
   * Organizes and conducts data collection, analysis, and evaluation.
   * Organizes work efforts for projects and proposals.
   * Participates in meetings and presentations with clients.
   * Helps establish schedule and labor budget for work efforts.
   * Maintains familiarity with firm policies and procedures.
   * Develops skills of sr. planner or project administrator.
   * Adheres to procedures and directions.
   * Contributes to team effort through spirit of cooperation.
3. *Performance factors:* Listed below are various performance factors that can contribute to the individual's effectiveness in his or her position. Please review each factor and make comments on only those specific items that are the employee's strengths and those that are in need of improvement.
   A. *Technical skills:* Consider the individual's level of professional development; how well the individual fulfills the requirements of the position, applies knowledge and stays abreast of new developments. Consider the depth and breadth of the employee's total knowledge for the position.
   B. *Management skills:* Consider the individual's ability to train, develop, and motivate people. How well does the employee delegate duties and direct others to reach common goals? Consider the employee's overall leadership qualities.
   C. *Interpersonal skills:* Consider how well the individual works with others, gains acceptance and cooperation.

FIGURE 6.7   Illustration of essay appraisal format

D. *Decision making/ problem solving:* Consider the employee's ability to effectively analyze problems and make sound, timely decisions. Consider the employee's overall ability to exercise sound judgement.

E. *Planning, organizing and controlling work:* Consider how well the employee plans for both long- and short-range work, handles work schedules and approaches assignments systematically. Are work methods streamlined to increase performance and lower costs?

F. *Timeliness:* Does the individual meet deadlines?

G. *Quality of work:* Consider the quality of work produced—are adequate standards displayed by the employee?

H. *Communication skills:* Consider the individual's ability to foster two-way communications, to disseminate important information to people, and to provide feedback. How well does the employee communicate verbally and in writing?

I. *Initiative/follow-through:* Consider the individual's willingness to assume new and/or additional responsibilities. How well does the employee follow through on assignments? Does the individual capitalize on and maximize potential opportunities?

J. *Adaptability/flexibility:* Consider the individual's ability to adapt to changed circumstances. Is the employee open, positive and responsive to new ideas and suggestions.

K. *Budget control:* How effective is the individual in staying within the budget limits of a project? How effectively does the individual manage budgets internally?

L. *Creativity/original thought:* Consider the employee's ability to think creatively in solving problems and/or generating new ideas.

M. *Effort:* Does the individual exhibit a willingness to work hard to get the job done?

Please write any other comments or observations on this employee's performance:

Reviewers present:

Date:

Notes by:

FIGURE 6.7 *(Continued)*

6.7 THE PERFORMANCE APPRAISAL PROCESS

There are a number of other decisions to be made in designing your performance appraisal process (see Figure 6.8 at end of this section for a sample process). For one thing, policies should be established as to how often and on what schedule staff will be appraised. Once a year probably isn't enough; too much time between appraisals minimizes their effectiveness. Generally speaking, six months is a reasonable interval. While 90 days may be even better, firms that aren't now doing appraisals on a formal basis may want to start with a six-month schedule. Despite the fact that a properly conducted appraisal can be completed in 30 to 45 minutes, managers may still complain that a 90-day schedule takes too much time away from job-chargeable activities.

Whatever the interval between appraisal sessions, they should always be staggered so that managers don't have to do all of them at the same time each year. Otherwise, appraisals receive superficial treatment from harried managers anxious to get them over with.

Notifying managers when appraisals are due is a job best handled by the HR or personnel manager, who should maintain a master schedule on all employees and then police managers who don't stay on schedule. In a typical notification procedure, the HR or personnel manager would send out the P.A. instrument to the employee's immediate supervisor, along with instructions on how to complete and route the appraisal documentation. Also, if the firm uses self-appraisals, the self-evaluation forms should be sent to the employees being appraised.

The decision about whether to use self-appraisals as part of the regular process is a subject of considerable debate. Advocates cite the benefits of finding out if significant communication gaps exist between employees and appraisers. Detractors claim self-appraisals make the process more cumbersome. Most of the more sophisticated performance appraisal systems in use by design firms today do incorporate some sort of self-appraisal. It can be identical to the regular appraisal instrument but printed on paper of a different color, or it can be a completely different instrument.

Many firms that use self-appraisals have found that their use also helps get performance appraisals done on schedule. Evidently, supervisors are more reluctant to disappoint their own employees, who have invested time to complete a self-appraisal, than they are to let down a mere personnel or HR representative.

Firms must also decide who will conduct and provide input to the appraisal sessions. Some firms allow only principals to do appraisals. Others get three or four people involved for each employee. Still others have the employee's immediate supervisor complete the appraisal. The third alternative is preferable. Immediate supervisors should be the ones who do performance appraisals, regardless of whether they are principals. Having immediate supervisors as the primary evaluators empowers them; having someone other than the immediate supervisor do the appraisal *reduces* the power and authority of the supervisor. So, too, does having more than one person sit in on the appraisal discussion, since there is the possibility of creating confusion for the employee if two or more appraisers disagree.

No matter what the process is or who participates in developing the appraisal, each employee should get one and only one appraisal. Any inconsistencies in evaluation input should always be reconciled by the appraiser prior to the actual appraisal session. Nothing is worse than handing an employee a performance appraisal form with five different ratings in each performance category because five different people were consulted on his or her performance.

Another decision to consider when designing your appraisal system is who will see the final performance appraisal documentation after it is reviewed with the employee. It is usually a good idea to circulate performance appraisals through the reporting hierarchy as defined on the corporate organization chart. For example, take the case of a criminal justice facilities architect in one large firm. The appraisal would be completed by the criminal justice studio head. From there it might go to the chief architect, and from there to the firm's director of operations. From the director of operations it might go to the CEO or Managing Partner, and from there to the employee's personnel file.

This routing should, of course, always be handled confidentially in sealed envelopes. Staff members may not want just anyone to see their appraisals. Routing of

Effective March 1, 1989, all employees will have performance appraisals at six-month intervals based on their individual employment anniversary date. The appraisal will be completed by the employee's immediate supervisor some time during the week of the employee's employment anniversary. Additional appraisal sessions can be held at the discretion of the employee's supervisor as long as the scheduled appraisals occur at their normal times.

All new employees will have a performance appraisal within 90 days of starting employment. The employee's next appraisal will take place on his or her six-month employment anniversary, and appraisals will be conducted at six-month intervals based on employment anniversary date thereafter.

Notification of performance appraisals due will be sent to the employee's immediate supervisor by the Human Resources Department on the first of each month. The immediate supervisor will conduct the appraisal session during the week it is scheduled.

Employees will have the opportunity to do a self-evaluation. The employee to be appraised will be sent a copy of the self-evaluation form from Personnel on the first of the month his or her performance appraisal will occur. This completed self-evaluation should be brought to the appraisal meeting.

The performance appraisal is viewed as an opportunity to give the individual constructive feedback to improve performance, as well as an opportunity to reinforce positive behaviors. It is also a chance to determine if any misunderstandings exist between the employee and supervisor.

The same performance appraisal form is used for all employees. It represents a starting place, and individual appraisers may decide to attach additional notes or comments. Managers' supervisors and the human resources manager will be available to the supervisors for assistance in preparing appraisal forms and conducting appraisal meetings.

All managers and employees should understand that the performance appraisal process is completely separate from the wage-and-salary review process. Wage and salary reviews occur four times per year, on January 1, April 1, July 1, and October 1, and/or at the discretion of department managers.

Completed appraisal and self-evaluation forms should be stapled together and routed through the individual's department head (if not coming from the department head) to the appropriate division director or branch manager, to the vice president of the area the employee works in, to the president, and finally to the employee's personnel file in the headquarters office.

FIGURE 6.8 Sample employee performance appraisal process

completed performance appraisals should be clearly spelled out and always handled in a manner consistent with established company policy. Proper routing is essential to realizing one of the chief benefits of performance appraisal, as described at the beginning of this chapter, that is, to identify the firm's high achievers and bring them to the attention of others in the organization.

Finally, it must be determined what type of training will be provided to those responsible for doing performance appraisals. This is critical. Ninety-five percent of firms with a formal P.A. system in place ignore this element in the process. There will be more on training appraisers in Section 6.9.

6.8   THE PERFORMANCE APPRAISAL SESSION

Although no doubt the actual performance appraisal session will vary according to the instrument selected, there are some general guidelines that will apply in almost all cases:

1. Appraisals should be performed carefully, objectively, and honestly. Glowing reports should be given only when deserved. The tendency of some managers to give glowing reviews to all of their staff is sometimes referred to as the "halo effect." Positive reports on mediocre performers are bad for everyone involved—both employees and the company.

2. The performance appraisal session should be nothing to fear, providing the appraiser regularly communicates with the employee regarding how he or she is doing. The appraiser/employee relationship is not unlike a marriage. Spouses who aren't talking have marriage troubles!

3. Any meetings to discuss an individual's performance appraisal should be held privately. Ideally, there should be only two people present at this meeting— the appraiser and the employee. Only when the meeting involves a disciplinary action or termination should you consider having someone else sit in as a witness. Appraisers who do not have private offices should use a conference room or someone else's office.

4. Typical performance appraisal discussions should last a minimum of 20 to 30 minutes, and possibly up to 45 minutes. Discussions lasting longer than that are probably out of control and indicate poor communication between the employee and manager.

5. Managers giving what is a largely negative appraisal should refrain from making personal attacks on the employee. If an employee's performance is substandard, state why it is, giving a full explanation of the appraisal without condemning the employee as a person. If the appraiser is uncertain how to deliver the bad news or if problems with the employee are anticipated, assistance from whoever is in charge of HR (or the appraiser's immediate supervisor) should be sought.

6. The performance appraisal session is an excellent time to establish some specific short-term goals for the employee (six months to a year). Attach extra

sheets to accommodate these goals and objectives if the appraisal instrument doesn't provide enough space. Goals and objectives from the previous P.A. session should be reviewed by the appraiser prior to the appraisal discussion.

7. Appraisers should practice good listening skills and be sensitive to the non-verbal communication cues they might give off, including such things as body language, shuffling papers, tolerating frequent interruptions from others, and so on.

8. Whatever your performance appraisal form or instrument is, it should be signed by both the employee and the reviewer. It is a good idea to print a disclaimer under the space for the employee's signature stating that the employee does not necessarily agree with the appraisal but acknowledges it took place (a sample disclaimer is illustrated in Figures 6.10a and b under the employee's signature). You don't want employees who are terminated for poor performance to deny having been warned. Employees who are unhappy with their reviews may refuse to sign if this disclaimer isn't clearly present.

9. After the review meeting, the employee's reaction to the review should be noted in the appropriate section of the appraisal instrument. Any employee who has an objection to the appraisal should be allowed to attach comments in his or her defense to the appraisal document *before* it is routed, and these should become part of the employee's permanent employment record.

6.9 PERFORMANCE APPRAISAL TRAINING

Unfortunately, training is the most neglected area of the performance appraisal process. Most firms now have some kind of performance appraisal system, yet very few provide any sort of training for its application.

No matter what the system, there are some common threads to the type of training that is required. First, every appraiser and employee to be appraised should be informed of why the company does performance appraisals. Second, every appraiser and employee should be informed of exactly what the company's appraisal process is, how often appraisals occur, who will do them, what happens to the forms afterward, and so forth (see Figure 6.9). To assume that everyone in the company understands the purpose and the process is a mistake.

For example, in many firms with separate performance appraisal and pay review processes, the misconception prevails that appraisals are used simply to determine individuals' raises. This is not the case (see Section 6.5), but as long as managers and employees alike aren't set straight on this point, it will be impossible for them to realize the true purposes and benefits of appraisals.

Every appraiser should be given specific coaching in how to conduct the session, as well as some training on interpersonal communication for supervisors, including listening skills development. Appraisers should be shown examples of the wrong and right way to do appraisals for each of three types of employees: the typical employee (many strengths and a few weaknesses—see Figures 6.10a and 6.10b), the problem employee (so many problems that he or she is one step away from

1. The performance appraisal will occur at six-month intervals based on employees' employment anniversary dates. Individuals are being provided with an opportunity to do a self-evaluation, which will be brought to the appraisal meeting.

2. The performance appraisal form should be completed by the employee's immediate supervisor. Input can be solicited from others the employee interacts with, but use good judgement here—you don't need to consult everyone.

3. Supervisors will be notified by the Human Resources Department of the due dates of appraisals for which they are responsible. Managers are responsible for scheduling and holding appraisal meetings in a timely fashion.

4. Performance appraisals should be treated seriously and carried out carefully, objectively, and honestly. High performers should be reinforced and praised, but glowing reports should be given only when undoubtedly deserved. Give mediocre performers their feedback straight, although when reviewing a negative appraisal with an employee, do not attack the individual personally. If his or her performance is standard, give a full explanation of why it is.

5. The employee and the appraiser should meet privately to compare the employee's self-evaluation with the manager's evaluation. There should be only two people present at this meeting. Any differences in evaluation input should be reconciled by the appraiser prior to the meeting. Managers who do not have offices should use a conference room. The appraiser should spend a minimum of 30 minutes (and possibly up to one hour) with the employee discussing the appraisal.

6. Specific short-term goals should be established (six-months to one year). Extra sheets can be attached to accommodate these goals and objectives, if required.

7. The performance appraisal forms should be signed by the employee and the reviewer. After the review meeting, the employee's reaction to the review should be noted in the appropriate section of the appraisal form.

8. The completed appraisal form and the employee's self-evaluation should be stapled together and routed through the individual's department head (if not coming from the department head) to the appropriate division director/branch manager, then to the vice president of the area the employee works in (if there is one), to the president, and finally to the employee's personnel file.

Any questions on the performance appraisal process should be directed to the human resources manager or Mark Zweig.

FIGURE 6.9 Sample performance appraisal instructions

termination), and the outstanding employee (incredible—no real weaknesses at all). These three employee types represent 95 percent of the cases any appraiser is likely to encounter. Trainers should present the *wrong* way first, then the *right* way. This coaching will be extremely helpful in showing managers how to deal with touchy performance problems, how to reinforce whatever someone has done right, and how to minimize the firm's employment-related liability exposure.

Some firms have used role-playing as a performance appraisal training tool. Managers can take turns playing the role of appraiser and employee in different hypothetical appraisal scenarios. Managers who are not playing appraiser can observe the interaction and make a critique. Although it's time consuming, this technique can be very successful in teaching managers to do appraisals effectively.

VH **Employee Performance Appraisal**
Reviewer's Form   "TYPICAL" EMPLOYEE - WRONG WAY

Name: _John Landreft_   Title: _Civil Engineering Technician_

Instructions: Study each factor and the description of each degree. Mark the square which most clearly fits the employee's performance. Make comments to explain your evaluation.

Part I: Ability and Application

Initiative - ability to exercise self-reliance and enterprise

| ☐ Grasps situation and goes to work without hesitation | ☑ Works independently often; seldoms waits for orders | ☐ Usually waits for instructions; follows others | ☐ Does only what is specifically instructed to do |

Comments:

Quality of Work - accuracy and effectiveness of work; freedom from errors

| ☑ Consistently good quality; errors rare | ☐ Usually good quality; few errors | ☐ Passable work if closely supervised | ☐ Frequent errors; cannot be depended upon to be accurate |

Comments:

Quantity of Work- output of work; performance speed

| ☐ Works consistently and with excellent output | ☐ Works consistently with above average output | ☑ Maintains group average output | ☐ Below average output; slow |

Comments:

Job Knowledge - technical knowledge of job and industry; ability to apply it

| ☐ Knows job throughly; doesn't need help | ☑ Knows job well; seldom needs help | ☐ Knows job fairly well; requires instructions | ☐ Little knowledge of job; requires constant help |

Comments:

Attitude - enthusiasm, cooperativeness, willingness

| ☐ Enthusiastic; outstanding in cooperation; tries new ideas | ☑ Responsive, cooperates well; meets others more than half-way | ☐ Usually cooperates; does not usually resist new ideas | ☐ Uncooperative; resents new ideas; displays little interest |

Comments:

Dependability - willingness to accept responsibility; to follow through; to meet deadlines

| ☐ Outstanding ability to perform with little supervision; always gets job | ☑ Willing and able to accept responsibility; little checking on progress required | ☐ Usually follows instructions; normal follow-up | ☐ Refuses or unable to carry responsibility; needs constant follow-up |

Comments:

Attendance-reliability to be on the job

| ☐ Always can be relied upon to be at work on time; absent only in emergency situations | ☑ Usually can be relied upon to be at work on time; explained absences occasionally | ☐ Comes in late with reasonable excuses; fairly frequent explained absences | ☐ Frequent unexplained lateness and/or absences |

Comments:

Vanasse Hangen Brustlin, Inc.

FIGURE 6.10a Sample wrong way to do performance appraisal for a typical employee

Communications Skills - ability to clearly express ideas and thoughts; ability to establish rapport

☐ Outstanding ability to establish rapport and articulate ideas; sensitive to outside clients
☐ Usually is able to express self clearly; few problems internally and with clients
☐ Occasional misunderstandings with others both inside and outside of the company
☐ Frequent misunderstandings and problems with others

Comments: _____

Leadership - ability to guide, direct others; skill at delegation

☐ Others naturally follow example or direction; obtains good results from others
☐ Willingly assumes guidance of others; is fairly well accepted in this role
☐ Is accepted reluctantly by his group as a guide or example; gets fluctuating results
☐ Shows no aptitude or skill in leadership

Comments: _____

Creativity - ability to devise improvements, new programs, and processes

☐ Consistently comes up with new ideas, figures out new and better ways to do things
☐ Frequently initiates new ideas and programs
☐ Has come up with an occasional good idea
☐ Never comes up with new ideas for products or process improvements

Comments: _____

Profit Consciousness - bottom-line orientation; concern for company dollars

☐ Consistently shows concern for bottom line; guards company resources as own
☐ Frequently stays within budget; usually functions as guardian of company profits
☐ Shows some concern for company profitability; occasional instances showing little concern
☐ Not profit conscious; shows little concern for company finances

Comments: _____

Planning Skills - Ability to set schedules and anticipate problems

☐ Outstanding planner of projects; meets schedules and deadlines
☐ Has planned successful projects; not consistent in planning
☐ Occasionally plans; planning skills need definite refinement
☐ Does not plan; reacts to crisis; misses deadlines regularly

Comments: _____

Part II - Advancement Potential

Check applicable sections (more than one section may apply):

☐ Regressing   ☐ Not Suited to Job   ☐ Not Likely to Advance   ☐ Progressing   ☐ Satisfactory   ☐ Maximum Performance on Job

Review your comments; then set goals for the employee to accomplish between now and the next review period.

1. _____

2. _____

3. _____

Date of next review _____   Employee's Signature _____

Date _____

Note: Employee's signature does <u>not</u> necessarily indicate agreement with the above comments. It is only an acknowledgement that this appraisal occurred.

Supervisor: Complete this section after review meeting.

Employee's reaction to review and suggestions was (check one):

☐ Appreciation (completely willing to strive for improvement)
☐ Interest (will make an attempt to follow suggestions)
☐ Disinterest (sastisfied with present status)
☐ Resentment (feels review is an imposition)

Conclusions drawn from interview: _____

Date: _____   Reviewer's Signature: _____

FIGURE 6.10a   *(Continued)*

VH **Employee Performance Appraisal**
Reviewer's Form "TYPICAL" EMPLOYEE - RIGHT WAY

Confidentially Route to: ___

Name: _John Landraft_   Title: Civil Engineering Technician

Instructions: Study each factor and the description of each degree. Mark the square which most clearly fits the employee's performance. Make comments to explain your evaluation.

Part I: Ability and Application

Initiative - ability to exercise self-reliance and enterprise

☐ Grasps situation and goes to work without hesitation ☑ Works independently often; seldoms waits for orders ☐ Usually waits for instructions; follows others ☐ Does only what is specifically instructed to do

Comments: _Usually jumps right on a new project. Only occasionally needs 'prodding': (Eg: Newbury College Grading plan)_

Quality of Work - accuracy and effectiveness of work; freedom from errors

☑ Consistently good quality; errors rare ☐ Usually good quality; few errors ☐ Passable work if closely supervised ☐ Frequent errors; cannot be depended upon to be accurate

Comments: _John's work is absolutely perfect - sometimes too Perfect Needs to watch budgets, and pay particular attention to Contract reqirements._

Quantity of Work - output of work; performance speed

☐ Works consistently and with excellent output ☐ Works consistently with above average output ☑ Maintains group average output ☐ Below average output; slow

Comments: _Quantity of output is acceptable. Need to be concious of quality - quantity tradeoff, and learn when to turn on / turn off perfectionist tendencies._

Job Knowledge - technical knowledge of job and industry; ability to apply it

☐ Knows job throughly; doesn't need help ☑ Knows job well; seldom needs help ☐ Knows job fairly well; requires instructions ☐ Little knowledge of job; requires constant help

Comments: _Good in water/sewer/pavement. Weakness is drainage. Good Knowledge of both manual and CADD production techniques/processes_

Attitude - enthusiasm, cooperativeness, willingness

☐ Enthusiastic; outstanding in cooperation; tries new ideas ☑ Responsive, cooperates well; meets others more than half-way ☐ Usually cooperates; does not usually resist new ideas ☐ Uncooperative; resents new ideas; displays little interest

Comments: _Always has a cheerful disposition & is a real pleasure to work with._

Dependability - willingness to accept responsibility; to follow through; to meet deadlines

☐ Outstanding ability to perform with little supervision; always gets job ☑ Willing and able to accept responsibility; little checking on progress required ☐ Usually follows instructions; normal follow-up ☐ Refuses or unable to carry responsibility; needs constant follow-up

Comments: _In Most cases can count on for adequate follow through Needs to make sure all redline work is completed._

Attendance-reliability to be on the job

☐ Always can be relied upon to be at work on time; absent only in emergency situations ☑ Usually can be relied upon to be at work on time; explained absences occasionally ☐ Comes in late with reasonable excuses; fairly frequent explained absences ☐ Frequent unexplained lateness and/or absences

Comments: _Average attendance. Not excessive use of sick leave._

Vanasse Hangen Brustlin, Inc.

FIGURE 6.10b Sample right way to do performance appraisal for a typical employee

Communications Skills - ability to clearly express ideas and thoughts; ability to establish rapport

- ☐ Outstanding ability to establish rapport and articulate ideas; sensitive to outside clients
- ☑ Usually is able to express self clearly; few problems internally and with clients
- ☐ Occasional misunderstandings with others both inside and outside of the company
- ☐ Frequent misunderstandings and problems with others

Comments: Good verbal communicator. Greatest weakness lies in not fully explaining why things need to be done when working with drafters. Too much "Just do it."

Leadership - ability to guide, direct others; skill at delegation

- ☐ Others naturally follow example or direction; obtains good results from others
- ☑ Willingly assumes guidance of others; is fairly well accepted in this role
- ☐ Is accepted reluctantly by his group as a guide or example; gets fluctuating results
- ☐ Shows no aptitude or skill in leadership

Comments: John does a good job of taking the bull by the horns when given the opportunity to supervise drafters, although has had only limited exposure to the role. Leadership is a latent talent of John's.

Creativity - ability to devise improvements, new programs and processes

- ☐ Consistently comes up with new ideas, figures out new and better ways to do things
- ☐ Frequently initiates new ideas and programs
- ☑ Has come up with an occasional good idea
- ☐ Never comes up with new ideas for products or process improvements

Comments: Occasionally comes up with new ways to organize production on jobs. Would like to see more initiation of new ideas.

Profit Consciousness - bottom line orientation; concern for company dollars

- ☐ Consistently shows concern for bottom line; guards company resources as own
- ☑ Frequently stays within budget; usually functions as guardian of company profits
- ☐ Shows some concern for company profitability; occasional instances showing little concern
- ☐ Not profit conscious; shows little concern for company finances

Comments: Consistently stays within budget for his part of project. Would like to see John significantly beat budgets everyonce in a while — I know he can do it.

Planning Skills - Ability to set schedules and anticipate problems

- ☐ Outstanding planner of projects; meets schedules and deadlines
- ☑ Has planned successful projects; not consistent in planning
- ☐ Occasionally plans; planning skills need definite refinement
- ☐ Does not plan; reacts to crisis; misses deadlines regularly

Comments: Generally plans work effort verywell. Occasional Oversights (I.e. Burger Works (Framingham) site plan.

Part II - Advancement Potential

Check applicable sections (more than one section may apply):

- ☐ Regressing
- ☐ Not Suited to Job
- ☐ Not likely to advance
- ☑ Progressing
- ☑ Satisfactory
- ☐ Maximum Performance on Job

Review your comments; then set goals for the employee to accomplish between now and the next review period

1. Be more proactive in seeking out the info. You need to do your job.
2. Demonstrate understanding of quality-quantity tradeoff- all clients don't want the samething
3. Improve knowledge of drainage calculations.

Time for next review to occur ___90 Days___ Employee's Signature ___John H. Landsoft___

Date ___11/17/88___

Note: Employee's signature does not necessarily indicate agreement with the above comments. It is only an acknowledgement that this appraisal occurred.

Supervisor: Complete this section after review meeting.

Employee's reaction to review and suggestions was: (check one)

- ☑ Appreciation (Completely willing to strive for improvement)
- ☐ Interest (Will make an attempt to follow suggestions)
- ☐ Disinterest/Satisfied with present status)
- ☐ Resentment (Feels review is an imposition)

Conclusions drawn from interview: Review went well. John appears to have a good understanding of his strengths & Weaknesses.

Date: ___11/17/88___   Reviewer's Signature: ___Mark C Snow___

FIGURE 6.10b   *(Continued)*

Finally, if you have a self-appraisal process, employees should be trained in how to use it appropriately by being shown good and bad examples of completed *self-appraisal* forms. Again, showing specific examples of the right and wrong way to do the self-appraisal is extremely effective in communicating how the process should be handled. This can probably be accomplished in a simple 15-minute meeting with groups of no more than 30 people (see Figure 6.11).

To make sure this training isn't forgotten, give all trainees copies of appropriate training materials to take back to their desks for future review. This material should be revised periodically and recirculated so its message on how to do effective appraisals is not forgotten.

1. As part of the regular MZ&A performance appraisal process, each employee is asked to fill out a self-appraisal prior to meeting with his or her appraiser. Attached is the self-appraisal form.

2. Your appraisal session will occur some time this month, and you will be contacted soon by the individual responsible for your appraisal to schedule a 30-minute to one-hour meeting with you. Please have your self-appraisal form completed for this meeting and bring it along with you.

3. When completing the self-appraisal, study each factor carefully and mark the square that most clearly fits your position. Also, in the comments section please give specific examples to illustrate your rating, whenever possible.   .

4. The purpose of the MZ&A performance appraisal system is to provide you with specific feedback, both good and bad, on how you are doing in the eyes of the company. It is not to set salaries. This does not mean, however, that performance and salary aren't related—they are.

5. We ask that you complete a self-appraisal to help us identify where we have failed in our efforts to provide you with the best possible feedback and guidance. Our goal is to develop a complete mutual understanding between you and the company as to how you are doing at your job.

6. Ideally, this performance appraisal discussion should be a meeting with no surprises. It will be just that if you and your supervisor have been in contact all along. Please take this self-appraisal seriously and in the spirit of cooperation that was intended.

Should you have any questions on the review process, please address them to the human resources manager or company president. Thank you.

FIGURE 6.11 Sample self-appraisal instructions

6.10 PITFALLS OF PERFORMANCE APPRAISAL

The potential of the performance appraisal process to enhance HR management is considerable. However, the process can also backfire. Sometimes, despite the best intentions of management, performance appraisal not only fails miserably in fulfilling its objectives, but creates altogether new problems with morale, productivity, and liability. Some of the reasons for this are:

1. Managers who are poor communicators can demotivate good people. For example, performance appraisers are often instructed to identify relative weaknesses or areas for improvement in *every* person appraised, even their best performers. Assuming that 80 percent of a firm's staff is basically competent, the potential for demotivating good people through the P.A. process is significant. This potential is multiplied when no training is provided to appraisers.

2. Performance appraisals can be used against the firm in law suits from employees who have been terminated or passed over for promotion. If the employee terminated or passed over for promotion has had nothing but outstanding reviews that do not convey major shortcomings (halo effect), then these reviews may be used as evidence that the employee should not have been fired or laid off, or that the employee should have been promoted over someone else who may have simply had a more honest appraiser.

3. Most companies have policies to do performance appraisals on a particular schedule. The problem comes from firm managements that don't force appraisers to stay on track. Typically, the worst offenders are managers at the *top* of the organization, who thereby set the bad example for everyone else. Not doing appraisals when scheduled creates all kinds of anxiety for the employees affected. They may assume that something is wrong, that their supervisors are unhappy with them, that they are about to be let go, and so on. In addition to hurting productivity, this anxiety can lead a good employee to look for another job. Not doing appraisals when scheduled also has an adverse effect on management's credibility.

4. Improperly trained managers can create false expectations of good things to come, some of which they may not be able to follow through with. This can happen at times other than performance appraisal as well, but when these "promises" are put in writing, their effect on morale and liability becomes greater. Common examples of this include a supervisor promising a raise or promotion that the supervisor alone is not empowered to give. When the raise or promotion is not granted, the employee becomes bitter and demotivated, whereas if the expectation had never been created, there would not be a problem. Again, just as with appraisals not performed on schedule, failing to follow through on promises compromises management's credibility.

5. Managers may put off dealing with personnel-related problems until the scheduled performance appraisal session, allowing trouble to get out of hand. Design firm managers who despise confrontation may seize on any semilegitimate excuse to procrastinate dealing with a staff problem.

6. Technical people functioning as managers frequently bastardize the company's performance appraisal instrument or process, turning it into a nightmare of checkmarks, multiple opinions on performance, redefined scales, and so forth. The final result is usually an appraisal clear as mud to the employee being appraised.

7. Some firms adopt performance appraisal systems so complex and time consuming that they are doomed to failure from the start. For example, a New

York A/E firm required both the appraiser and the employee being appraised to fill out over 10 pages of forms. Developed by a leading design industry management consultant, this complex appraisal system literally required the firm to shut down for two days each year just to do appraisals.

6.11 CONCLUSION

The two major benefits of performance appraisal are that it can be a motivational tool and that it helps minimize employment-related liability.

Design firms need to pay more attention to performance appraisal. Too many principals don't know what P.A. is, why it's important, or how to do it. Often, little or no training is provided. Design professionals are reluctant to dole out criticism and praise, which results in many late appraisals.

Firms would be wise to spend the time and money necessary to develop a formal performance appraisal process. Those that don't develop any formal appraisal process often end up in a lawsuit.

7

TRAINING

"If you think education is expensive, try ignorance."

—Derek Bok

7.1 INTRODUCTION

Design firms everywhere tout their commitment to training. Yet the average design firm spends only 0.4 percent of its total revenues to train staff (PSMJ Financial Statistics Survey, 1988).

Occasions arise daily in design firms that point out the need for training—even if that investment is minimal compared to what other industries spend: A top designer is promoted to a project management position and proceeds to alienate everyone he or she comes in contact with. Inexperienced staff are hired to do asbestos inspections when experienced staff are needed. Principals are frustrated by an architectural studio manager's inability to produce projects within budget constraints. A young project manager's fee collection letter goes out to the firm's best client, who calls the company president to chew him or her out. A newly hired engineer quits after three months on the job because of poor supervision. The firm invests $750,000 in state-of-the-art CADD, and the CADD work stations sit unused six months later.

In a typical design project, when the budget gets tight, the first thing to go—rightly or not—is the landscaping. It's the same with training in a design firm: When firms feel budget pressures, training is the first thing to get cut. But, are profits low because the firm spends too much, or because staff are inadequately trained to perform their roles? Or is the company not making good use of the money it does spend on training? The answer is probably a combination of all three factors.

Of course, simply allocating more money for training isn't the answer. If firms are to get their money's worth from the training budget, they will need to ask the right questions and weigh the alternatives. What training is needed? How can it best be provided? Who should participate? What will it cost? How can a company make the best use of its own resources? What are some of the alternatives to outside seminars? What are the leading firms doing to train staff? How does a firm get the biggest impact for the money it spends?

7.2   WHAT IS TRAINING?

Training is a systematic process of changing behavior or attitudes of employees to improve the organization's effectiveness. It is usually accomplished by providing learning experiences or educational opportunities to staff members. Learning is not an end in itself; training should improve job performance. In addition to improving job-related skills, training experiences can also be a significant motivator. In one study of the motivations of professionals, the chance to grow and learn was fourth on the list of important motivating factors.

Since training involves learning, certain principles of learning theory apply to job-related training for design and other technical professionals. In abbreviated form, these principles are:

1. All human beings can learn, even if not at the same rate.
2. To learn, individuals must be motivated.
3. Learning is an active process and is stimulated by involving the senses.
4. The quality of learning is improved through guidance.
5. The process of learning requires time to assimilate, accept, and apply what has been learned.
6. Learning methods should be varied to combat boredom.
7. Learners need to understand the purpose of what they are learning.
8. Learning should be reinforced with specific and understandable rewards.
9. Standards of performance should be set for the learner in order to provide goals that when achieved afford a sense of accomplishment and satisfaction to the learner.
10. Different individuals will be more receptive to learning at different times.

These 10 learning principles should be applied to the design of any firm's training program.

7.3   HOW MOST DESIGN FIRMS HANDLE TRAINING

Most companies in the A/E/P business handle training on a catch-as-catch-can basis. Take the following example. Roberta, a project manager in a New York interiors firm goes to a building products trade show. The next thing you know, her name gets on a mailing list, initiating a barrage of junk mail promoting all kinds of seminars. One day, she gets a promotion piece for a two-day seminar entitled *How to Turn Project Managers into Principals*, to be held in a pleasant East Coast vacation spot. She turns in a request to attend the seminar to the higher-ups in the firm. Given its title, they figure the seminar is worth gambling $795, so they send in the registration fee and make $600 worth of airline and hotel reservations.

By the time the company is through sending Roberta to this seminar, it will have spent $800 for registration, $600 for air travel and lodging, another $150 for a rental car, and $90 on meals and tips. Two complete days of Roberta's time, totaling $1360 (16 hours at her $85 per hour billing rate), are revenues the firm forgoes as a result of the seminar. Roberta's company is out a total of $3,000 for sending her to this seminar.

If Roberta works in a 40-person company doing $3,000,000 in annual revenues, 0.4 percent of total revenues (the average percentage of total revenues spent on training in a design firm) equals $12,000. This means that the company, if in line with the rest of the industry, would be spending 25 percent of its total training budget for one member of its 40-person staff to attend a single two-day seminar without her or the company knowing anything ahead of time about the quality or content of the seminar.

What happens after the seminar? Nothing. Roberta brings back a three-ring binder of seminar materials and sticks it on her cluttered office bookshelf. When asked about the trip, she raves about the great sailing conditions that weekend and says the program was okay, although it seemed to be aimed more at architects and consulting engineers than interiors people.

Consider next the case of the firm that decided to spend its training dollars on once-a-week brown bag lunches. Because there was no clear agreement as to what kind of training was desirable and because no one was assigned the responsibility for finding speakers and audio or video tapes, the whole program died by the fourth week. Employees who were first enthusiastic about the company president's announcement of a firm-wide training program now had one more reason to grumble about how their employer never follows through on anything.

When training is approached haphazardly, money and time are wasted. What could have been a significant performance enhancer and a relatively inexpensive motivator neither enhances performance nor increases motivation. In some cases, poor management of the training process even backfires completely and leads to staff demotivation.

7.4 GETTING STARTED WITH A TRAINING PROGRAM

Design firms don't *have* to rely on outside seminars. They are not restricted to approving requests from staff members who get promotional flyers in the mail. A design firm can take control of its training investment, but it must thoroughly rethink the way things have been done.

Just as with the hiring process, centralization and standardization are the keys to making order out of training chaos. Start by assigning one person to coordinate and manage the entire company training effort for both technical and nontechnical training. If you have a personnel or human resources person, use him or her. If not, pick someone who is detail oriented, has an interest in training, and has shown the ability to stick with a long-term project and see it through to fruition. This person is the *training coordinator.*

Provide the training coordinator with a budget for all training, including planned expenditures for outside and in-house seminars, audio and video tapes, self-instruction materials, and staff time for individuals who participate in or conduct training sessions of any kind. Staff time is particularly important because it is typically the largest single component in a design firm's training budget. Although this top-down approach to budgeting for training has its disadvantages, at least someone will be making sure that the company's money is going where it's best spent.

If you do nothing else with your training program, at least take the following step: As soon as the training coordinator has been identified, immediately start forwarding to him or her all seminar information and other training-related promotional materials that come into the firm. These promotional brochures and fliers should all be classified according to some predetermined scheme and stored in a file cabinet or in large three-ring binders with proper dividers. After six months or so, you will have accumulated a wealth of material on what training is available and who is offering it. This will help when the company must judge whether the program an employee asks to attend is the best or most cost effective. These training files are also a good place to look for a source to fill a particular type of training need.

The firm should also require anyone who attends company-sponsored training provided by an outside source to write an evaluation of the course. This evaluation should be attached to the seminar or program brochure and filed along with the rest of the training literature. The next time someone from the firm considers attending the same program, they'll find specific feedback from a known participant.

In addition to determining what sources of training are available, the firm must also get a handle on its overall training needs—in other words, determine what skills are lacking and how many individuals need training in those areas. The training coordinator will first have to thoroughly review the job descriptions for each and every position in the firm. Properly structured job descriptions will identify the skills needed to accomplish the duties and fulfill the responsibilities of each position in the firm (see Section 12.3 in Chapter 12). Meanwhile, supervisors at all levels should assess how well the skills of specific individuals they supervise compare with the skills needed to fulfill the requirements of the individuals' job descriptions.

Once this data is assembled, mid- and top-level managers should meet to review the needs identified and discuss the training program. Provided with the right data, these decision makers will be able to develop a bottom-up, needs-based budget that is far more ideal than the common way to handle a training budget. The point is to assess overall training needs and establish priorities within the constraints of the budget: A big job no doubt, but manageable—and necessary if a firm really wants to make staff training a significant priority.

After the firm's training needs have been inventoried and prioritized, make an effort to identify all in-house training resources. The results will be surprising. Most design firms have employees with skills the firm is completely unaware of. One firm had a CADD operator, David, who had earned a master's degree in communications prior to getting his drafting certificate. He had even taught courses in public speaking and presentations. All this was, of course, unknown to his employers until they sent out a questionnaire to identify skills and interests in conducting in-house training. It was then that David stepped forward. It turned out he had gone into the CADD field only because of his inability to earn the kind of money he felt he needed to support his family. David eventually put several seminars together for the firm on his own time, which were used for a variety of purposes. And, he was thrilled to be able to put his communications education to further use.

Clearly, a training assistance questionnaire (see Figure 7.1) is a simple and easy way to identify in-house capabilities and interests in training. It is particularly effective in identifying technical training resources, but, as in David's case, it may reveal nontechnical training resources, as well. For many design professionals, just having the opportunity to show others what they know is a real motivator.

Once a staff member comes forth and expresses interest in conducting training, determine the number of people he or she will have to train, the length and format of the program, and when it will be conducted. If possible, a master schedule of all in-house training should be prepared a year in advance.

Generally speaking, if there is an in-house resource person available to teach a course, you ought to try that person. Exceptions might be cases where you know your volunteer's poor communication skills would jeopardize the project, or where the person has such poor credibility with other employees that the message wouldn't be well received.

One question that frequently comes up is whether training should be conducted on the company's or the individual's time. There is no clear-cut answer. Certainly, it depends on the type of training. Generally, if the training is required by the company, it ought to be at the company's expense. On the other hand, when dealing with salaried professionals, it may not be too much to ask for them to participate in an occasional early evening or Saturday session, or to read and study on their own time.

In short, if the training is totally optional and if the employee is going through the training to improve his or her own career opportunities, it may not be a bad idea to train the employee on his or her own time. However, if the company feels that the training would improve individuals' on-the-job performance (one of the best reasons for training), try to provide it during regular working hours.

To provide control over the training process, the training coordinator should be the person who reviews actual expenditures versus budgeted expenditures for staff training. The training coordinator should regularly report at principal/manager meetings on the status of the firm's training program and what has been achieved.

Jorgensen Design Group is in the process of developing a company-wide training program for all staff. This program will include both technical and nontechnical training.

Part of this program will rely on in-house expertise to conduct seminars or courses. We want to identify staff members who have a particular area of expertise of strength who could design and conduct a course on some specific topic. If you would be willing to help, please answer the following questions:

A. Title or topic of seminar(s) or course(s) that you would be willing to design and conduct for other staff:

Course 1: _____

Course 2: _____

B. Proposed time required to conduct course or seminar (in hours):

Course 1: _____

Course 2: _____

C. Please write any additional comments you may have regarding training at Jorgensen Design Group:

_____

_____

_____

_____

_____

_____

D. Name and title: _____

Please return completed questionnaires by May 15 to Mike Lenox in the San Diego office. Thank you for your help.

FIGURE 7.1 Sample in-house training assistance questionnaire

More often than not, the training coordinator has to encourage managers to use their training budgets. Money allocated but not spent may not be in the company's best interests.

Employees who go through any company-sponsored training (beyond viewing a video or listening to a tape on their own) should have that fact indicated in a special section of their personnel file. The company's training coordinator should make sure this information is not lost. During the course of the year, those who go through a major training effort of some type should get recognition for it, especially when personal sacrifices were involved.

One architectural firm's CEO calls the whole firm together each time they graduate a class from their in-house Intergraph CADD training program. He makes a big fuss over the graduates and presents each one with a special certificate of completion. Even if your firm doesn't want to go to that much trouble, you should at least publish an end-of-year list of who went through what type of training during the year, and put it in the company newsletter or up on the company bulletin boards.

One last point: It is strongly recommended that you develop a mandatory training program for anyone who will function as a project manager. Ideally, anyone who becomes a project manager will already have had this training, but if you are forced to put someone into a project management role *before* he or she goes through the training, make sure it takes place within a reasonable time period—say, six months. Face it—this sort of contingency is the norm, not the exception, in light of today's shortage of project management talent. Project management will always be the most critical training need, since any design firm is only as successful as the sum of its performance on all of its projects.

A project management training program should cover how the company processes a project; how to open a job number; what the company's policies are on charging time to projects; what contract forms are used and when; who in the firm has contracting authority (meaning who can commit the firm); and what are the invoicing procedures, the project–filing procedures, and the project close-out procedures. It should include instruction in how to prepare project budgets, fee estimates, and project schedules for projects of the size and type the firm typically gets involved in.

Project management training should also include instruction in how to properly write letters, memos, and reports as well as how to practice good listening and note-taking skills. Presentation skills should be covered. The basic principles of supervision should be taught, since just about all project managers will have to supervise the work of others. Finally, project managers in design firms should know how to negotiate fees and how to dress properly.

7.5 OUTSIDE SEMINARS

There's no need to rely completely on in-house training and disregard the wealth of professional training available for our industry from outside providers. As discussed in Section 7.4, the keys to getting your money's worth from outside seminars are centralizing all information on programs and providers, and requiring evaluations from all who attend. In addition, there are a few other points to make regarding outside seminars.

First, if at all possible, avoid sending people out of town for training. Travel adds greatly to the time and expense required for attendance at a seminar. Even if a local date for a particular program is not listed in the promotional literature, call the seminar company to find out if it will be offered in your area in the near future. If not, look for other sources of the same training who might provide it locally.

Second, if you do have to send someone out of town, try to make it somewhere that he or she can accomplish two or more goals on the trip. This might include calling on an old client who is headquartered in the area. It could mean calling on a potential new client the firm has targeted. It could also simply involve combining the trip with other opportunities to get further training. This is one of the major benefits of the education programs offered by some of the industry's larger trade shows, many of which offer several hundred seminars on an incredible number of topics over a single two- or three-day period.

Third, if you are unhappy with a particular seminar someone attends, call or write the seminar provider to complain. Most reputable organizations will be glad to refund your registration fee or at least give you a credit toward another training program. Sometimes seminar providers switch speakers, and you could end up with someone who is not really qualified to be conducting the session. Complain! Also, don't send 47 people to the same seminar if you aren't sure it is a good one. There is too much risk. Send one or two of your staffers as test cases first, then send everybody else if you like.

Fourth, consider asking those who attend outside seminars to share what they've learned by conducting their own in-house programs. This practice has several benefits: You make the best use of your training dollars by getting wider coverage of the topic without any additional registration or travel expenses. Also, when people who attended the outside seminar come back and relay the course material to the others in the firm, they learn the material better themselves. In addition, after such a program, other employees will expect the staffer who conducted their in-house seminar to practice what he or she has preached. Hopefully, he or she will strive to live up to these expectations.

Finally, don't count on any single one- or two-day seminar to be a panacea. It's unfortunate that some seminar providers feel they must oversell their programs, but don't let a copywriter's promises give you unrealistic expectations for long-term behavior change in an individual who attends just one seminar. Remember, training must be ongoing to be effective. It may take three seminars on the same topic before the material starts to stick.

7.6   IN-HOUSE SEMINARS

Beyond the discussion in Section 7.4 of things like administering the in-house training assistance questionnaire and making best use of existing staff resources, there are a few other key points regarding in-house seminars.

Most outside training providers will be willing to present their program at your location. This can save you a lot if you have a number of people you'd like to run through the program. For the cost of sending one staffer to a $1500 outside seminar, a firm may be able to bring the seminar provider in-house and run 20 staffers through the training. In many cases, an in-house presentation allows you to customize the program for your firm's needs. The need for customization may be acute for programs in project management, liability reduction, or performance appraisal training.

What is the best time to conduct in-house training sessions? People are most alert in the mornings, although that may also be when they are most productive in terms of their job-chargeable activities. Some firms find that morning or all-day sessions on a Saturday work well. Others find that employees don't like having to attend on a weekend because they regard the weekends as their own time. The same holds true for evening sessions, although there is generally more resistance to an evening session than there is to a Saturday session, since most design professionals are anxious to get home to their families at the end of the day. Ask the people and the managers responsible for them what they think is best.

7.7 AUDIO AND VIDEO TAPES

Audio and video tapes are one of the least expensive training vehicles available to a design firm. Just about every firm has some. Make an inventory of exactly what tapes your company has and send the list out to everyone in the firm. Tapes should be stored where anyone with an interest can get to them. If you have a technical resource library, it would be the ideal place to keep these tapes. Require individuals who use the tapes to check them out, so you don't lose track of them. This check-out procedure also allows you to keep track of who is using the tapes, giving you an indication of who on your staff is most interested in self-improvement.

Video tapes on all kinds of interesting topics are becoming more available, and you don't always have to buy them. Plenty of tapes are available to borrow or rent at prices ranging from nothing to $50 for two days. Your public and local university libraries, as well as some of the larger industrial firms' private libraries are a few good sources for videos on a wide variety of topics. Put a VCR and a 19" to 25" monitor in the conference room or employee break room so these videos can be viewed easily. Most firms should have a VCR for marketing presentation purposes, anyway.

A few specific points on audio cassettes: Just about every national conference is taped, and the tapes are made available for purchase by the sponsor of the event. These tapes can be a low-cost alternative to sending several people to a conference for two or three days. Get the firm to invest $100 in a "boom box" audio cassette player. Play the cassettes at brown bag lunches open to everyone in the firm or department. Also, every time your firm buys or leases a new company vehicle, make sure it has a cassette player so that an employee traveling on company business can make good use of the time by getting in some training.

Here's an example of what can go wrong with a design firm's audio and video tape resources. One A/E firm had all of its tapes in the hands of the person who headed up the project management group. He was rarely in his office, and no one knew exactly what tapes the firm owned. It didn't take company management very long to figure out why they weren't being used.

7.8   SELF-INSTRUCTION MATERIALS

Any time someone checks out an audio cassette, videotape, or book on some subject and uses it, he or she is going through self-instruction. Making self-instruction materials widely available to your staff is one of the most cost-effective training opportunities at your disposal.

Self-instruction programs for the architectural and professional engineering examinations are available from a number of sources, typically for around $150. They usually include a practice exam that can be sent off for scoring, so their value is limited to one-time, one-person use.

Interactive computer programs for CADD and other computer software training are also becoming more common. Many design firms have found that a successful formula for developing CADD skills is to require staffers to go through a self-instruction tutorial for 8 to 80 hours before they move on to more advanced and formal training provided by in-house or external classroom and experience-based sessions. This way, employees show they are serious about wanting to learn the skill before the company makes a major training investment in them.

7.9   TUITION REIMBURSEMENT

Just about all major design firms have some sort of tuition reimbursement program or policy. These plans typically help pay for a certain amount of job-relevant continuing education for staffers. (*Note*: Any contributions from the company are considered taxable income by the IRS at the time of this writing, and should be reported on the employee's *W-2* form.)

Most of these plans either specify the schools that employees can be reimbursed for attending, or they set some maximum dollar contribution because even a single class at a prestigious private university or college can cost thousands. Most tuition reimbursement plans set a limit of either three or six hours per semester. Some of these plans reimburse employees at the time of registration; others at the time grades are reported; and still others pay a portion up front, and the balance upon successful completion. Also, more firms are requiring employees to achieve a grade *B* or better in order to receive reimbursement. The logic is, "Why pay for mediocrity?"

7.10   ON-THE-JOB TRAINING

On-the-job training (OJT) is often referred to as the "school of hard knocks." All design firms rely on OJT at one time or another. Whenever anyone is shown how to do anything related to work, that constitutes on-the-job training. It may be as informal as giving a trainee an assignment or project of a sort he or she has not done before and letting the trainee ask any questions required to get it done. It consists of an experienced professional giving a little advanced coaching to someone who has less expertise in that particular area. Some on-the-job training is formalized as a company-sponsored co-op or internship program. Alternatively, it could be a formal training program for new graduates that provides exposure to all aspects of their discipline.

Of course, design firms will never be able to structure all the opportunities for on-the-job training experiences. As a result, most on-the-job training happens to the employees who most aggressively and ambitiously seek it out.

7.11   CO-OP PROGRAMS

Co-op programs are formalized on-the-job training for students who want to supplement their educations with real-life work experience. Though other industries have had them for years, many design firms are just beginning to realize the benefits of a formal co-op program. Firms as small as five people can develop one, and certainly all large firms can and should have one (see Figure 7.2).

1. Co-ops are a good source of long-term employees upon graduation.
2. Hiring a co-op as a full-time employee is generally less risky than hiring a new graduate who has not co-oped.
3. Co-ops allow a firm to have human resource continuity in junior-level positions.
4. Co-ops allow firms to staff lower-level openings with higher-potential people.
5. Successful co-op programs can benefit a design firm's other recruitment efforts.

FIGURE 7.2   Co-op program benefits

A co-op program is not a quick fix to a design firm's staffing woes. It requires a long-term perspective and the dedication of someone in the firm who is committed to the goals and benefits of the program. Co-op programs have several significant benefits for design firms who establish them:

1. *Co-ops are a good source of long-term employees upon graduation.* Firms that have a co-op student in-house for three or four consecutive terms know exactly what that person's capabilities are. By the same token, the co-op

knows exactly what to expect from his or her first full-time work experience in the design firm. Realistic expectations on both sides means that hiring a co-op as a full-time employee is generally less risky than hiring a new graduate without co-op experience. In fact, the turnover rate in the first two years of full-time employment for design professionals with co-op experience is half what it is for those without.

2. *Unlike summer internships, co-op programs allow a firm human resource continuity.* The true co-op program is distinguished from a summer internship program by the fact that co-op students work and attend classes on alternating semesters. This means that the co-op student will take longer to get a degree than the student who does not co-op—typically five or five and one-half years to get a standard four-year degree. It also means that the company who staffs its co-op slots on a continuous basis will always have someone of any particular skill level in the position. This is critical. For a co-op program to be seen as a benefit to the technical people who use this human resource, someone has to be in the program at all times. Firms must plan for co-op vacancies well in advance and aggressively recruit co-op students for each succeeding work term.

3. *Co-op programs allow firms to staff lower-level openings with higher potential people.* Because co-ops are individuals who are pursuing their professional degrees, they are, as a class, probably more intelligent and ambitious than those filling lower-level posts on a permanent basis. As a result, co-ops are known to be quick studies who learn new tasks easily and pursue new learning experiences with a zeal not always found in career technicians.

4. *A successful co-op program can benefit a design firm's other recruitment efforts.* A successful co-op program garners publicity. Universities offering co-op programs usually have awards for co-op employers who provide the best co-op experiences. The relationships formed with the universities through a co-op program often prove valuable in identifying the school's best new graduates, even among those who haven't been through the co-op program. The co-op recruitment fairs that many schools hold are also frequently attended by nonco-op students as well, helping companies make their recruitment budgets go farther.

For a co-op program to be all that it can be, certain steps should be taken (see Figure 7.3).

1. *Select the best and the brightest students for your co-op program.* Just as with new graduates, your risk is lower when you select the best students. Most co-op programs have minimum grade point average requirements around 2.8 on a 4.0 scale, anyway. Making your grade requirements tougher (3.0 or higher) is probably a good idea. Also, as with all other positions, make sure you recruit only those who have good communication skills as well as good grades.

1. Select the best and the brightest students for your co-op program.

2. Assign one person the responsibility for the firm's co-op program.

3. Design a progressive co-op experience that gives students some real learning opportunities beyond just drafting or making blueprints.

4. Require that new co-op students have had at least *some* graphics training.

5. Staff all co-op openings on a continuous basis.

6. Develop co-op recruitment materials to use when recruiting co-op students.

7. Determine salary or hourly rate ranges for co-ops in advance, and provide this information to potential co-op students.

8. Debrief co-ops after each work term.

9. Educate managers and other staffers as to why you have established a co-op program.

10. Promote your co-op program's successes through press releases, articles in the company newsletter, and articles in the local and college newspapers.

11. Stick with your co-op program once you start it.

FIGURE 7.3   Co-op program steps

2. *Assign one person the responsibility for the firm's co-op program.* Like so many of the other programs and processes recommended in this text, if a co-op program is to be successful, it must be run by one person who is totally committed to it. This may be the HR manager, if you have one, or it could be a technical professional who was once a co-op and is sensitive to both the needs of the company and co-op students.

3. *Design a progressive co-op experience that gives students some real learning opportunities beyond just drafting or making blueprints.* Most design firms fail in their co-op programs because they have students back for two, three, or four terms to do the same thing every time. This is probably the biggest single gripe of co-op students who have worked in A/E/P firms. The best co-op programs are those where students are rotated into different areas of the firm. Students can start out drafting, working on a field survey crew, counting cars, or making prints, but they should be exposed to *all* areas within their discipline, if possible (see Figure 7.4).

4. *Require that new co-op students have had at least some graphics training.* Although ideally, the co-op will be doing more than drafting later on in the co-op experience, drafting is a good first-term experience that all co-ops should go through. Beyond that, having some appreciation for what has to be done in drafting and how long various tasks take will make for a better future architect or engineer.

5. *Staff all co-op openings on a continuous basis.* If the technical people who use your co-op talent are to see these people as a resource, they have to be able to count on having someone at that desk or station all the time, even if it's not the same person. This means that companies with co-op programs

A/E/P Associates, Inc.
Civil Engineering Co-op Program

A. Work Assignments:

First Co-op Term: Assignment to civil engineering department. Master basic drafting skills, do data entry, plus do whatever else is assigned.

Second Co-op Term: Assignment to surveying department. Get experience as floating crew member and survey technician, performing duties including deed research and plat calculations.

Third Co-op Term: Assignment to civil engineering department. Assume junior design responsibilities, including calculating street and water and sewer grades and performing alignment calculations, etc.

Fourth Co-op Term: Assume higher level design responsibilities in civil engineering department. Write specifications. Prepare cost estimates. Possibly rotate into structural engineering, traffic engineering, hydraulics/hydrology group, or construction administration.

B. Co-op Compensation (Based on individual abilities and progression):

First Co-op Term: $7.25 to $8.00 per hour

Second Co-op Term: $7.75 to $8.75 per hour

Third Co-op Term: $8.75 to $9.75 per hour

Fourth Co-op Term: $9.75 to $11.00 per hour

FIGURE 7.4   Sample co-op program for civil engineers

have to consider their needs beyond the immediate semester, communicate with the schools they work with, and see to it that co-ops are hired to fill vacancies created by those returning to school. Again, this is a major failing of co-op programs in A/E/P firms. The program falters when positions are not staffed continuously.

6. *Develop co-op recruitment materials.* These should be designed specifically for co-op students and should include a description of your program, the kinds of work experiences the co-op could expect, the salary ranges for co-ops at various stages in the program, and anything else that would be helpful in recruiting, such as testimonials from current or past co-op students. Also, firms should design some graphic materials illustrating the types of projects the firm does for use on a portable display of some type that can be carted around to co-op fairs. Some firms even have videotapes or slide shows they use at co-op fairs. The competition from private industry for engineering co-ops in particular is fierce. Firms without impressive recruitment materials are often out-recruited by the large electronics and aerospace firms who go all out.

7. *Determine salary or hourly rate ranges for co-ops in advance, and provide this information to potential co-op students.* Co-ops should get raises each succeeding term. Depending on the co-op's technical specialty, where the

student is in his or her education process, the level of the co-op's interpersonal skills, and the wage scale of the geographical locale, starting co-op hourly pay rates range from $6.00 to $9.00 per hour. By the end of a four-term co-op experience, these people should be making roughly $2000 or $3000 less than they could make on a full-time salaried basis after graduation. This is one case where the general rule to avoid publishing salary ranges goes out the window. Most students are on a tight budget and need to know exactly what they will be making in order to evaluate multiple opportunities and compare co-oping with staying in school. Again, the big companies provide this data. To compete, you will, too.

8. *Debrief co-ops after each work term.* Although most schools with co-op programs require their students to evaluate their co-op employers, you should take the time yourself to talk with each student returning to school. Ask what they liked and didn't like about the program. Find out how the students think you could make your program better. Get ammunition to use when developing your student testimonials.

9. *Educate managers and other staffers as to why you have established a co-op program.* More than one co-op program in a design firm has failed to get off the ground because management assumes that everyone understands what the program is, why the company started the program, and what its goals are. Old-line technical people, particularly designers and technicians, all too often expect co-ops to have drafting or other technical skills that they don't yet have. They compare a co-op at a certain hourly rate to other nondegreed people who may have more actual work experience, and decide that co-ops are a waste of time. If these people know what the company's goals are in the co-op program and have some understanding of what the total experience will be, they may be more understanding. Experience will also show that having a successful co-op program over time will eliminate most of this problem.

10. *Promote your co-op program's successes through press releases, articles in the company newsletter, and articles in the local and college newspapers.* Nothing will do your co-op program more good than promotion (see Figure 7.5). Again, use testimonials from students in your articles and press releases.

11. *Stick with the co-op program once you start it.* After you have taken the time to get organized, design and promote your co-op program, and educate your staffers, it would be a real waste to let it die. Firms with the best co-op programs hire co-ops in good times and bad. They make adjustments in other staff areas if they must to keep their co-op program rolling. To kill off your co-op program by neglecting to recruit students or to put it on hold because of tough times may hurt your relationship with the colleges or universities that you deal with, hampering your ability to recruit the best students. Likewise, you do not want to throw a wrench in the plans of a co-op student in the middle of his or her education process by deciding at the last minute not to have him or her back.

FORT WORTH CO-OP PROGRAM
OFF THE GROUND AND RUNNING

In August, 1985, the Fort Worth office of Carter & Burgess instituted a formalized engineering co-op program in concert with Texas A&M University and the University of Texas at Arlington. We now have a total of seven co-ops, six in Civil and one in MEP.

Students can be admitted to the program after completing a minimum of 45 hours in an accredited engineering program, completing at least one semester of engineering graphics, meeting certain grade standards, and displaying excellent communication skills.

The co-op program is structured whereby students work a semester, go to school a semester, come back to work for a second semester, etc., until they are finished with school.

In the civil program, co-ops start their first term as junior drafters and doing whatever else they are capable of. Next, they either go to the Survey Department for their second term and work as a survey technician and "floater" on a field crew, or they work their second term in the Civil Department assuming progressively complex design functions as they are capable. By the third term, if they have not worked in Surveying yet, they will then do so. If they have worked in survey, they will then go back to Civil to work on more complex design and drafting. If the individual works a fourth term, he or she would be performing more complex design assignments as well as getting exposure to construction administration, hydrology/hydraulics, etc., as opportunities for learning in those areas present themselves.

Co-ops currently enrolled in the program are:

o   Mike Erion, Senior - Civil Engineering, UTA. Mike will be returning for his third co-op term with the company in January of 1987. He was selected outstanding civil engineering student at UTA in both his sophomore and junior years.

o   Marci Davis, Senior - Civil Engineering, UTA. Marci has just returned from having a baby, and is currently working in her second official term as a co-op in the Surveying Department.

o   Susan Spore, Junior - Civil Engineering, UTA. Susan has just returned for her second co-op term and is currently working in the Civil Department.

o   Gage Muckleroy, Junior - Civil Engineering, Texas A&M. Gage will be returning for his second co-op term in January of 1987.

o   David Wagner, Senior - Civil Engineering, Texas A&M. David will be returning for his second co-op term in January of 1987.

MCZ 9/26/86

FIGURE 7.5   Sample public relations article on co-op program

o   Andy Miller, Junior - Electrical Engineering, UTA.   Andy will be returning for his second co-op term in the summer of 1987.

o   John Reynolds, Junior - Civil Engineering, Texas A&M.   John has just started his first co-op term in the Civil Department.

According to Gerald Lemons, Vice President and Civil Department Manager, he "believes our experience thus far with the co-op program has been very positive,' is "impressed with the quality and character of the co-ops, and believes the program is doing exactly what we hoped it would." He concluded by saying that "we look forward to hiring our first graduate engineer in the Civil Department that has gone through the co-op program here at Carter & Burgess."

FIGURE 7.5   *(Continued)*

The issue of appropriate fringe benefits for co-ops needs to be resolved. Some companies provide co-ops the same benefits they give any other regular employee. Some even pay co-ops' tuition and fees during terms they are not working. A few firms even provide housing for co-ops while on a work term. More often, design firms simply provide whatever is required by law in addition to granting paid holidays.

Often firms who develop a co-op program come to the realization that it is an excellent model to use for a formal on-the-job training program for newly graduated professionals without co-op experience. These firms simply concentrate the co-op experience into a shorter time frame. After all, a new graduate should be able to do more than a first term co-op who still has most of his or her education to complete. Also, the new grad doesn't need to go back and forth to school on alternating semesters.

7.12   INTERNSHIP OR SUMMER WORK PROGRAMS

Many design firms use internship or summer work programs instead of or as a supplement to more formalized co-op programs. Some firms attempt to treat these summer work experiences just like a co-op program, but there are a number of important distinctions.

While summer internships provide some of the benefits of a co-op program, they don't provide the continuous, human resource supply that co-op programs do. For many firms, the workload is no greater in the summer than any other time, making it difficult to use the intern. Also, since summer interns are only with the firm for three months at most, it can be difficult to find out what their capabilities really are.

On the other hand, a summer internship does give the student some exposure to what it's like to work in a design office, which may prove valuable to him or her in the long run. It also keeps the firm involved with the school that offers the program, although not to the same extent as a more formal co-op program. Another important advantage of internships is that students may be willing to work for free just to get some experience, whereas co-ops are always paid in some fashion.

Summer internships are better than nothing but probably not as worthwhile as formal co-op programs for providing serious on-the-job training. Summer internships may be a good supplement to a co-op program, and they may work out particularly well in small firms that can't afford a co-op program.

7.13 CONCLUSION

Design firms spend only 0.4 percent of their total revenues training staff. Designers are promoted to management positions and inexperienced people are hired to do work when experienced staff are what's needed. Firms invest money in CADD, and the workstations are unused. Communication and morale problems resulting from poor supervision abound. In a typical design firm, training is the first thing to get cut when budget pressures mount.

If firms are to make the most of their training budgets, they need to know what training is needed, how it can best be provided, who should participate, what it will cost, what in-house resources are available, and what the alternatives to relying on outside seminars are. Audio and video tapes, self-instruction programs, tuition reimbursement programs, and on-the-job training—including co-op programs and summer internships—are valuable components of a design firm's overall training effort.

8

CAREER DEVELOPMENT

If you want a place in the sun, prepare to put up with a few blisters.

—Abigail Van Buren

8.1 INTRODUCTION

Self-sacrifice no doubt plays a critical role in career development for design professionals, but it is not all there is to the career development process. Design firm management also needs to play an active role and invest in staff.

It's not without good reason that architects and engineers, like lawyers and doctors, are called professionals. A profession isn't merely a job or an occupation. It is a career-long journey toward greater mastery of one's discipline and greater responsibility in the profession. Professional registration is an important early milestone in this career development. Becoming an owner or partner in a firm is the ultimate milestone and the goal for most design professionals. In between, the typical professional has many miles to cover, and these steps are marked by many smaller milestones. There is no need to force people to grope along the course blindly with no guide and no road map. Design firms owe it to themselves and to the profession to listen to, advise, guide, and lead those who have shown a willingness to learn and follow. The career development process is a way of formalizing this commitment and putting it into action.

8.2 WHAT IS CAREER DEVELOPMENT?

Too many design firms fail to identify and accommodate the real needs and aspirations of staff members, to remove the actual or perceived roadblocks to their careers, and to encourage them to maximize their fullest career potentials. The result is increased turnover, poor morale, and decreased effectiveness. Given the critical role of a design firm's human resource assets and the work, risk, and expense associated with hiring new staffers, these issues need to be addressed for *all* employees in the enterprise. This includes design professionals, technicians, and support staff.

In simplest terms, a career development process is a formalized rap session between management and staff. It provides for communication and feedback that break down the walls between people in the firm. It identifies opportunities and gets problems into the open. It is the perfect antidote to the tendency of principals to isolate themselves and lose touch with the pulse of their own firms. Specifically, career development meetings have three distinct, yet inextricably linked, purposes:

First, by sharing perspectives, you establish congruence between the goals and expectations of the firm and the employee. You may be counting on one of your promising young engineers or architects to develop into a project manager, only to find out that he or she wants to pursue a purely technical career.

Second, employees can identify problems that are keeping them from doing their jobs, hindering their productivity, or making them think about quitting. At the least, you will be able to nip problems in the bud before they reach a crisis and it is too late to solve them except by firing someone or having someone quit. At best, you will be able to eliminate the roadblocks and demotivators that keep staff from self-actualizing and reaching their potential.

Finally, if a grievance is unearthed during this process, and neither the situation in the firm nor the mindset of the people involved can be changed, just getting the problem into the open, showing the employee that management is interested, and allowing him or her to let off steam may have a therapeutic effect.

Design firms need to establish a process of talking with all employees regularly, identifying their unique needs, tapping into their insights, and either addressing their concerns or explaining why they cannot be addressed. You can't expect employees to do this for themselves. Unfortunately for the design profession, it is usually only the most aggressive staffers who get a hearing. When management concentrates only on reacting to crises, it is at the expense of those who don't make their goals and aspirations widely known, who aren't good at office politics, and who aren't prone to voice their complaints. As long as they keep to themselves, they don't seem to be a problem—at least not in the short term.

Career development's focus is long term. It involves assessing the employee's particular strengths and weaknesses, his or her long- and short-term goals, and how all of that meshes with the firm's needs and plans. Of course, it requires the motivation, interest, and commitment of the employee to do what is necessary to advance within the organization and profession. Above all, don't confuse career development with performance appraisal; the focus of career development is *not* to evaluate employees but to unlock their potential.

8.3   THE CAREER DEVELOPMENT MEETING PROCESS

One way to address the individual career development needs of all employees in an A/E/P firm is through an ongoing process of regular career development meetings.

In one firm, for example, an annual career development meeting is held between a representative of senior company management or some objective third party who serves as an interviewer and each employee in the firm. In some large, multi-discipline firms, the assignment of individuals to be interviewed is split up among a number of the firm's principals. Each principal should interview employees he or she does not normally oversee.

The career development meeting is typically held outside the office in some nonthreatening environment. People tend to open up more outside of their regular work surroundings. They can relax without being preoccupied by fears of others overhearing the discussion, which may keep some things from coming out. The employee should always be assured at the beginning of the discussion that any comments he or she makes will not result in repercussions. Why are witnesses before a grand jury promised immunity? Because it is impossible to get full value from the testimony as long as there is fear of recrimination. Also, those conducting the interviews will need to practice good interviewing skills just as they would in any other interview situation. Often, these career development discussions are held over breakfast or lunch at a quiet restaurant.

The purpose of the career development meeting is to focus on the long-range career plans and concerns of the employee in a nonevaluative, two-way discussion format. The interviewer uses a pre-established set of questions. One example has been provided (see Figure 8.1). You may want to come up with your own interview questions. For these career development meetings, the interviewer takes copious and accurate notes. Tape recorders may inhibit interviewees and slow production of the notes. Lap-top computers, too, can be intimidating. At the conclusion of the meeting, the interviewer either prepares the notes for distribution or dictates them for compilation by a trusted word processor or secretary. The completed discussion notes are then sent to the interviewee for any changes required to ensure accuracy and intent.

1. What do you like about the company? What do you like about your position?
2. What do you not like about the company? What do you not like about your position?
3. What are your greatest strengths? What are your greatest weaknesses?
4. If you were CEO or president of this firm, what, if anything, would you do differently?
5. What are your goals? (Allow the employee to use any time frames he or she pleases.)
6. What are you doing to further your goals?
7. How can the company help you achieve your goals?
8. How is the company hindering you from achieving your goals?
9. Do you have any other questions, concerns, or comments that you would like to go on the record?

FIGURE 8.1 Questions to ask in career development meetings

The final draft of the discussion notes is copied and distributed in confidence to the CEO; the appropriate division, branch, or department director or manager; the employee's immediate supervisor; the employee interviewed; and finally, to the employee's confidential personnel file. To protect interviewees from nosey third parties, these reports should either be hand carried to those on the distribution list or sealed in an envelope and routed.

Meetings should take no longer than an hour and a half, and the notes should take no more than an hour to prepare. That means that the total process should not exceed a total of four man-hours staff time per meeting.

Once a month, a career development committee comprising two or three top management staff members and the HR director (or person responsible for the HR function) meet to determine what actions will be taken by the company to either resolve the employees' concerns or inform them of why their concerns cannot be addressed. Also determined at the meeting is who specifically has responsibility for following through with actions to be taken and explanations to be given. At each succeeding meeting of the career development committee, the actions taken and explanations given are reviewed to make sure nothing falls between the cracks.

8.4   BENEFITS OF THE CAREER DEVELOPMENT PROCESS

A formal career development process yields many benefits for a design firm. For one, it can aid a firm's efforts to reduce turnover, because the employees develop a sense that the company really cares about them as individuals. Compared to an average cost of $6000 to replace just one professional—not including downtime, training, and the opportunity cost associated with a key vacancy (all far more than $6000)—the investment required to go through this process for each person in the firm seems minimal.

Career development meetings also help identify the issues and set the priorities for the firm's overall HR management program. Firms that want to embark on a new path in HR management often find that interviewing all employees through a process similar to that outlined here is a good place to start.

Paying attention to career development also leads to significantly improved morale. When a serious effort is made to develop realistic expectations on the part of each staff member, they are less likely to be disappointed. Soliciting employees' perceptions of their own strengths and weaknesses often leads to a more critical self-evaluation and less tendency to blame problems on management. What's more, just giving employees the opportunity to unload while someone listens and takes notes can have a cathartic benefit, even if nothing else comes of it.

The career development process sensitizes management to the organizational and personnel issues it faces. Hearing loud and clear what specific individuals have to say about the firm makes it difficult for management to bury its face in the sand. Hand in hand with this awareness comes the opportunity to identify staff concerns before they erupt and to defuse trouble before it's too late to do anything.

Last but certainly not least, a regular career development interview and follow-up process differentiates the company from its competitors. It not only helps staffers achieve their potential; it can also benefit the firm's recruitment efforts to attract new staff members, who will be impressed that a firm goes to the time and expense to conduct individual discussions not related to performance appraisal. They will appreciate that a formal vehicle is there for them to communicate their goals, aspirations, and concerns to the highest level of management. The firm can also highlight its career development process in its public relations and marketing efforts. *Clients* like dealing with design firms they think are progressive and well managed.

Still, nay-sayers disparage the process of career development interviews, saying that no employee will be honest and say what his or her real concerns are for fear of reprisals. Skeptics may add that the process should be reserved for professionals only, or they will say the whole idea is just another overhead activity that wastes valuable staff time and costs the firm for a lot of expensive meals. These objections don't stand up under scrutiny. First of all, most firms that start a career development process are amazed at how open and honest their people are. If anything, managers may at first be shocked at how much they have been missing and may even find themselves wishing for a little less candor, at least until they come to see the long-term value of opening up communication channels between management and staff. This goes for nonprofessional staffers as well, who are in many ways equally essential to the success of the firm and some of whom may even become the firm's future professionals. Everyone has insights that can benefit management.

Finally, when you weigh the many benefits of the process (see Figure 8.2) against its relatively low per-head price-tag, it's well worth it. When it comes to producing quality work, the old adage goes, "You never have time to do it right, but you always have time to do it over." The same applies to career development. The savings in reduced staff turnover *alone* can justify the implementation of this process.

1. *Reduces turnover:* Average cost of $6000 to replace one professional, not including downtime, training, and the opportunity cost associated with not having someone in a position (all far more than $6000).
2. *Improves morale:* Attitudes improve through development of more realistic expectations. Functions as employee catharsis, if nothing else.
3. *Improves management:* Management becomes sensitized quickly to issues it faces. The best process known to identify internal management problems. Management may learn about potential problems before they fester.
4. *Helps keep HR management program on track:* The feedback that comes from the process is a good vehicle for determining ongoing HR management priorities.
5. *Differentiates the company:* Progressive HR management not only benefits staff; it can also benefit company management if used in recruitment of new staff and in marketing or public relations efforts.

FIGURE 8.2   Benefits of a formal career development meeting process

8.5   PITFALLS OF THE CAREER DEVELOPMENT PROCESS

In spite of the best intentions, a formal career development meeting program can backfire if not handled with care. As with most new management initiatives, the initial enthusiasm quickly wanes when the day-to-day drudgery of following through sets in.

Too many firms embark on the course of holding regular career development meetings and then fail to talk to everyone in the company as initially scheduled. Lack of commitment and follow through in any HR program severely damages management's credibility with staff and undermines employee morale, which is the complete opposite of the program's intended effect.

The same can be said for firms who identify a specific issue or concern in a career development meeting and then fail to address the problem or neglect to tell the employee honestly and privately why it can't. Poor follow-through is probably the number one cause of failure in the career development process. Although the cathartic benefits mentioned earlier are real, they won't last if the firm never takes any action.

8.6   SAMPLE REPORTS

Because every firm is different and because it is nearly impossible to catalog all the issues that might arise in career development meetings, the bulk of this chapter is devoted to some real-life cases illustrating the general flavor and course of these dialogues, as well as how some actual firms catalogued the problems that were uncovered. The names and places have all been changed to protect the individuals and companies involved, but all other details of the original interview notes are present.

Notice how the interviewer has recorded in very specific detail what was said, including misuse of the language. These interview notes should include plenty of direct quotes and paraphrasing, and should always be attached to a specific employee by name. Experience will show you that having direct quotes as opposed to vague interpretations lends greater impact to the employee's commentary. It also helps reduce the need for employee corrections and clarifications after the notes are prepared.

Notice, too, how the issues to be addressed have been quickly summarized by the interviewer at the end of each set of interview notes. This summary is used to determine the actions to be taken or the explanations to be given by the career development committee. Each one was dealt with separately.

Perhaps these cases should have been placed at the beginning of this text. The comments of the interviewees are *so* typical of the human resource management issues design firms of all types and sizes are facing. Most problems aren't new; they have been confronted and solved by others before us.

Sample Career Development Meeting Reports

Case 1   Billy Ray Smith is a 28-year-old degreed mechanical engineer working in a two-year-old branch office of a 200-person engineering/architectural firm. Prior to joining the company, he worked in his family's mechanical contracting business and for a local consulting engineering office.

To: Billy Ray Smith's personnel file
From: Mark C. Zweig
Subject: Career Development Meeting
Date: September 14, 1981

I. Likes

A. Billy Ray likes the freedom and responsibility he has working for Altwell/Rubenstein. He has worked for several other firms, and although he had freedom and responsibility for his designs, he did not have the involvement he has with us in hiring, firing, client contact, fee negotiation, and the like.

B. Billy Ray is having the most fun and making the most money he has had in his four years of working in the consulting engineering field.

C. Billy Ray feels that we have great potential to have a first class team there in Peoria. He feels good that, at the age of 28 and soon to be registered, he will be in a leadership position in a growing, aggressive company.

D. Billy Ray feels that his goals are congruent with those of the firm. He is glad that we want a hard-hitting, aggressive, quality staff of engineers.

E. Billy Ray is glad Bill Cantwell has moved to Peoria. He stated that Bill is definitely not a "milktoast" kind of guy.

F. Billy Ray also stated that he was glad he worked with the group that he did—a group that can take criticism and learn from each other. He respects the other people that he works with.

G. Billy Ray is glad that Tim is very accessible. He feels that he is very well informed, and knows exactly where the branch stands on profits and cash flow due to his involvement in the branch operations.

H. Tim Anderson is very optimistic. Billy Ray likes that quality and indicated he thought Tim was very capable as a manager and good at dealing with people.

II. Dislikes Billy Ray has no major dislikes. Some of his minor complaints include:

A. Billy Ray does not like not getting paid only on the first and fifteenth of the month. He stated that it plays havoc with his personal budget. He indicated that sometimes he gets paid on the 5th or 6th of the month because of the mail. He stated that it's tough to maintain his family budget and keep his creditors satisfied when he gets paid on an erratic schedule.

B. To go along with A above, Billy Ray indicated that he did not feel that they in Peoria are very well served by the finance and accounting department. He said billing is a major hassle every month. He gave an example, that being the Hall High School re-roofing job. He stated that they had negotiated some very favorable hourly rates for their time and had supplied these rates to the finance and accounting office in writing. He went on to say that finance and accounting had called them after that point at least six times to get those rates over the telephone and that he and Tim spent too much time doing those kinds of things. He also indicated that another problem they have is with the computer printouts they receive from the F&A office. Billy Ray said they are never correct. He expressed concern that the F&A function was not operating with the same level of professionalism as the rest of the company. He said they are not responsive. Another example Billy Ray used to illustrate his complaints was that of an aerial photograph they had taken by a local contractor. It bothered Billy Ray because he felt it would hurt the firm's credibility in the Peoria local market, which they are fighting so dearly to establish, over an unnecessary delay in paying a relatively small invoice.

III. If Billy Ray were company president: He would strengthen the firm's capabilities in finance and accounting. He would also strengthen our experience level in mechanical engineering in Chicago. As a mechanical engineer, Billy Ray is concerned that there is no one other than Richard Breier whom he can call on to solve a problem. He was not aware of Rod Barker in our Carbondale, Illinois, office. Billy Ray also expressed concern that the SMPE (structural-mechanical-plumbing-electrical) branch, particularly the MP portion of the branch, had poor morale. He stated that on one occasion he worked in the Chicago office for a whole day, and the mechanical department was gone by 4:30 or 5:00. Billy Ray felt that was evidence of poor morale in that department. Billy Ray stated that he thought part of the problem was in having someone like Mark Polson as branch manager of the SMPE branch. He went on to say that, although Mark is a good man, he doesn't have the experience, the technical expertise, the stock, or the clout to manage a Breier.

Billy Ray feels that we need to straighten out the "flagship." He would feel better if operations were smoother in Chicago than they are, and if we had greater capabilities in the mechanical area than we do. He doesn't want to see us hang our hat on one man. He went on to say that if we really want to implement our quality assurance program (which is a great idea), we need more than Richard. He stated Richard has his own projects. Billy Ray also said he would like to have someone here in Chicago who had the time that he could call on to question his equipment selection, his calculations, and so forth. Billy Ray said he wants to be proud of the home team in Chicago and to feel like they in Peoria are an extension of a "crack crew." Instead, he feels that they are going to be the "crack crew" there in Peoria, and it's tough to go out in good conscience and sell our 200-man company when they'll end up as being solely responsible for getting the work completed properly and on time there in Peoria.

IV. Billy Ray's goals

A. *Short-term*
1. To get registration as a professional engineer in the state of Illinois. He is taking the test this month.
2. To get more involved in marketing, client relations, fee negotiations, and management.
3. To get more experience. He felt this would come about as a result of getting more projects like Newman Technology Research Labs, and some of the others they have going.
4. To be happy.

B. *Long-term*
1. Three to five years from now, Billy Ray would like to be in Peoria making good money and, if not the head mogul, to be one of the head moguls of the mechanical department.
2. Three to five years from now, he would like to be very involved in marketing, but also to still be doing some actual design work.
3. More than anything else, he would love to prove to his friends, past associates and competition that we, Altwell/Rubenstein, are a good company and have proven ourselves successful in Peoria.

V. Billy Ray feels that we, as a company, can help him to achieve his goals

by moving ahead and doing the things we say we are going to do. He said that if they don't get done, it would be better to have never brought them up. Two of the things in particular that he mentioned were the Deferred Merit Incentive Bonus Program and the options to buy stock in the firm.

VI. Some of Billy Ray's additional suggestions

A. Billy Ray is concerned about our buying the firm of H.G. Associates. He does not want to see the Peoria office lose the good architectural clients they have just because we own an architectural firm. He went on to say that if we do go "A" and "E" both, we should do it fast, we should do it in a big way, and we should do it right. Otherwise, he feels that our architectural clients will cut us off.

VII. Recommendations of reviewer (M. Zweig) of action to be taken

A. Thoroughly review the performance of the finance and accounting office. Determine what action, if any, needs to be taken to improve the service we provide in that area to the Peoria branch.
B. Start payroll for those on a salary basis a day or two early so that the checks will be ready on the first or sixteenth of the month. Perhaps by doing so it will make it easier to get the other checks done on the first and the sixteenth or shortly thereafter. By the other checks, I am referring to those checks for people who work on an hourly or hourly-salary basis.

C. Establish a company policy as to how we pay invoices. It is the function of the financial manager of the company to do what is necessary to see to it that funds are available to pay for those invoices on whatever time schedule we have established in our policy.

D. Determine exactly what our plans are as it relates to H.G. Associates, and when possible, inform division managers who in turn can inform branch managers as to what those plans are.

E. Publish our policies on the D.M.I.B. plan and stock purchase.

Copies to: Billy Ray Smith
Isaac Wilson
Tim Anderson
Dick Simpson

Case 2   Bob Wilson is a 27-year-old technician working in the asbestos abatement section of a large engineering/architectural firm. He has a four-year engineering technology degree and has worked for the company in their headquarters office for several years.

To: Bob Wilson's Personnel File
From: Mark Zweig
Subject: Career Development Meeting
Date: June 6, 1983

I. Likes

A. Bob likes working in the specialized areas that he has. He started in SSES, and he's now into asbestos. He feels that there's a good mixture of office and field work.

B. Bob likes to work independently and is glad no one "breathes down his back." He likes working for Burt Godsey and Willard Thomas, and with the others in his group.

II. Dislikes

A. Bob feels that sometimes "high-tech" gets slighted. He doesn't like working with three other people in one cubicle and says it's just too cramped to work effectively.

B. He feels that there needs to be more equity in pay in his group. He cited a specific example of Don Kipp compared to Rich Kyle. He doesn't want to see Rich's pay reduced, but he feels it's tough on Don because he's making considerably less for essentially the same job. He also indicated that if this is the case in his group, it is likely to be occurring in other areas of the firm.

C. Bob doesn't understand how the business office can close itself off from the rest of the company for half a day. He feels their needs should be serviced when they need them serviced. Sometimes, it's difficult to wait until they open. Bob feels that if they can get us any time they need to, why can't we get them? Bob also stated that there is probably a good explanation for this being the case.

III. **If Bob were company president:** He would realize that things don't change overnight. He feels that these development meetings are good as long as people give us honest feedback. Bob says all he would try to do is find out what people feel and want, and try to meet their needs. If he couldn't give them what they wanted, he would explain why that was the case.

IV. **Bob does not have clearly defined career goals.** He feels that asbestos will be good for at least five years, but realizes he'll have to have other skills beyond what he has now because asbestos work will eventually decline.

It has been indicated to Bob that one day he might be put in charge of all field work (asbestos related). He would be interested in that position when the company feels he's ready for it. He wants to do something "worthwhile."

V. **According to Bob, we as a company need to** give more incentive in the form of limited stock options and profit sharing to those in the same category as he is. He feels that he won't be satisfied 20 years from now to still be working on an hourly basis. For now, that's fine.

VI. **Other suggestions Bob had for us**

A. To expand our effort to fill positions from the inside when possible.
B. To paint a realistic picture of what someone could expect when hiring new employees. To not "blue-sky" new people only to disappoint them later.
C. To not hire people unless we absolutely need them. Bob cited an example of someone who was hired during SSES who went out and made a long-term commitment to finance a new truck and then got laid off due to lack of work only two or three months later.
D. To strive to reward performance on a timely basis.

VII. **Recommendations of reviewer (M. Zweig) of action to be taken**

A. Look into the space situation for the asbestos technicians to see if additional space is needed on a long-term basis or if the current situation is temporary. If temporary, consider the possibility of using some available space in the Mechanical Engineering Department.
B. Give Don Kipp a performance and salary review.
C. Examine the business office's hours of availability and see if they cannot be expanded.
D. Have Burt Godsey get together with Bob Wilson for the purpose of developing alternative career paths for Bob Wilson.
E. Make sure that our new search/interviewing/hiring procedures are followed through on.

MCZ/tdc
Copies to: Bob Wilson
          Frank Kent
          Burt Godsey
          Sue Willard

Case 3   Katie Stewart is a 37-year-old woman working as a receptionist/
switchboard operator for a mid-sized architecture and interiors firm. Her
previous experience was mostly sales oriented, and she had no previous
design firm experience.

To: Katie Stewart's Personnel File
From: Mark Zweig
Subject: Career Development Meeting
Date: October 2, 1984

I. Likes

    A. Katie likes working for ABCD, Inc. She likes "just about everything"
about the firm.

    B. Katie likes being able to "deal with the public" as she does in her position.
She enjoys meeting and talking with a variety of different people and
having some diversity in her activity.

    C. Katie likes the "principal stockholders" and finds them good people who
set good examples.

    D. Katie likes the idea of our "career development meetings," and feels that
they will be very beneficial.

II. Dislikes

    A. Katie feels her job would be better if she didn't have such a difficult
time trying to get company cars for those who ask her to find them. She
said that Dave Sanders, Irwin Westmeyer, and the other principals are
always cooperative and willing to part with their cars if they aren't using
them. Some of the others, however, are almost always uncooperative and
unwilling to let anyone else in the firm use their car. She went on to say
that she dreads calling Jim Butler to "beg" for the use of his car, and that
he is particularly uncooperative.

    B. Katie suggested we maintain our company cars better than we do and that
if so many weren't out of order, she would have an easier time finding a
car when she has to.

    C. Katie dislikes people being rude to her and calling her a "bitch" when
she has a slight frown or isn't all smiles. She said that she realizes it's
part of the job to be smiling and to project a positive impression, and
she does that. But she doesn't like the way people treat her when they

are under pressure and they aren't in good moods. According to Katie, then it's okay for them to be rude to her.

D. Katie feels that the raises she has received in her two and one-half years have been mediocre. She stated that she realizes it may be the position she works in and that we just can't pay more for someone to fill that position.

E. Katie stated that if she has peaked in terms of earnings because of the position she is in, she would like to be moved to a different position. She mentioned that she has a number of skills which aren't being utilized. She said that she was told when she came to work for the firm that we "promote from within," and that she would have a number of opportunities in the company. She went on to say that since she has been with the firm she has not had any options presented to her.

F. Katie didn't like being excluded from training on the Lanier Word Processor when all other secretarial and financial personnel went through the training.

G. Katie said that the phone system is not adequate for our needs and that people are often waiting to get an outside line.

III. If Katie were company president: She would make every effort to see to it that everyone in the firm is treated fairly.

IV. Goals: Katie has no well-defined goals at this point. She feels she has had to "squelch" herself because six months after she came to work here, she developed the feeling that she would not be promoted. She again reaffirmed that she likes her job, but thought that it would get old some time and that we wouldn't want an "old lady" in her position, anyway.

V. We, as a company, can help Katie in several ways

A. Tell her what she needs to do to advance beyond her current position and earnings.

B. Give her some options to learn new things, to try a different position if we have one available matching her skills.

C. If we aren't even going to give her an option beyond her current position, she would like to know that.

VI. Additional suggestions from Katie Stewart

A. When people who have company cars leave town, they should do as Terry Jackson does and leave their company cars here at the office so others can use them if need be.

B. Katie would like to be kept better informed by the others she works with. She feels she would be able to do a better job if others would buzz her and tell her when someone is coming in to see them, when we are having a meeting in a conference room, and when a group of people will be touring the facility.

VII. Recommendations of reviewer (M. Zweig) of action to be taken

A. Inform those people who consistently refuse to let others use their company car that they could lose it if they aren't more cooperative. This warning should come from the president.

B. Ask those who have company cars and leave town to make an effort when possible to leave them available for use when they are gone.

C. Increase the number of company cars in operation.

D. Assign the responsibility of monitoring maintenance of company cars to one person. This person will check mileages, oil changes, and the like and keep a service record on every car we own. This person could remind those who need to get their cars in for service to get them in, to get their tires rotated, to clean their vehicles, to get their transmission fluid changed, and so on.

E. Determine if there are alternative career paths for Katie to follow with the company. If not, tell her so. If there are (and there should be), make her aware of what they are and what she needs to do to advance to the next position.

F. Follow up on where we stand with the phone system, and determine just exactly what our options are.

G. Send Katie to Lanier school if that is consistent with her desired career path.

MCZ/int

Copies to: Katie Stewart
           Irwin Westmeyer
           Mary Tyler
           Dave Sanders

Case 4   Jack Bartlett is a senior civil engineer working in a 60-man civil engineering department. He is in his early 40s, and had been with the firm about four years at the time of this meeting.

Career Development Meeting
Employee: Jack Bartlett
Interviewer: Mark C. Zweig
Date: June 2, 1985

I. Likes

A. Jack thinks Hamilton & Associates is a progressive company. He likes the size of the firm and the atmosphere here.

B. Jack is really extremely happy about the change we have made to the team concept. He said that if he had a concern with our organization before, that was it.

C. Jack said the company is concerned about the clients' best interests, and he likes that.

D. Jack said that here we show concern over the employees' comments and try to respond. He thinks there is legitimate concern for the employees.

E. Jack likes the library.

F. Jack likes the prestige he gets from working at Hamilton & Associates. He said the firm is well respected and its name carries weight. He said as an individual working for the firm, it carries over to him.

G. Jack said he feels comfortable in the position he is in now, although he said "he is too comfortable sometimes." He likes the location of his cubicle in the Civil Department as it relates to his neighbors.

H. Jack said that most likes, until they are taken away, you don't fully appreciate—that you take them for granted. He said he has many other likes about the company.

II. Dislikes

A. Jack said at this point in time, he is much happier with our organization than he used to be. He said two months ago, before the new team concept was put into effect, he had a major dislike. He said that he wished we had adopted the team format two years ago.

B. Jack said he has been a little bit unhappy and a little bit bored with his job. He said he wants something that is "perhaps a little more challenging."

C. Jack said he doesn't really understand his role within the organization. He "doesn't understand what he's supposed to be doing in order to advance and what positions are available." Jack thinks maybe with the team organization it will change, and career ladders will be better defined. He asked, "Is the next step up team leader?" and "What is a senior project manager?" Jack thinks that the firm is trying a lot of things right now and feels these things will be clarified when we get "some of these other things out of our hair."

D. Jack doesn't see from his position where the firm is growing. His interest is in growing with the firm, and that he doesn't see that happening right now. Jack said he sees more people but doesn't see where they are going. Jack doesn't see standing still as a benefit to himself. He said for him to grow, someone would either have to "die, get fired, or whatever." Jack said he wants to advance because we're "growing so much, it's embarrassing, because we can support 57 teams, or because we're opening a new office somewhere and need to staff it."

III. When asked if he were company president, what, if anything, he would do differently, Jack Bartlett said:

A. According to Jack, a firm this size needs a strategic plan, a philosophy, to know where we are going. He said that people like him would feel much more secure if we had a philosophy, a plan, and knew what we were trying to do. Jack thinks that this would give the atmosphere here more stability. He raised the questions: "How do we get past a downturn in the economy?" "What do we do when the business cycle changes?" "Do we have any contingency plans?" "Have we thought about acquiring a smaller firm?" "Has anyone given any in-depth thought to these things?" Jack said he would feel a lot more secure if these options would be considered in advance, so if and when they occur we can take action. Jack said that he's not sure if Mr. Hansen has these things done or not. At Jack's level, he can't see it. Jack said all this may have already been done, and "they're just holding it close to their chest." Jack went on to say that also knowing the firm's course of action will enable him to tailor his goals to those of the organization. He "doesn't think the firm will change their goals to meet his," and that he is a lot more flexible than the firm is.

B. Jack went on to say that if he were company president, he would not be delegating this strategic planning to a committee. He would be doing it himself and would get assistance from the financial director, marketing director, chairman of the board, and others as needed, but he'd be making the decisions. Jack thinks there's less risk and better quality of decisions from the president than from a committee.

IV. Goals

A. Jack said he would like to move into more of a managerial position but doesn't really know how. He said there is conflict between what a senior project manager is and what a team leader is. He raised the question, "Is a team leader only an administrative role?" Jack said he can't pick up a lot of uniformity between what the team leaders are doing. He went on to say that he would also like to know what a project manager is under the team concept. He said right now he is "kind of groping in the dark," trying to figure out where he can go in the firm. Jack said the team organization has not been around very long, and maybe that will come in time. He doesn't expect to get all his questions answered immediately.

B. Jack said his personal goals are to "make so much money, it's embarrassing!" He wants to retire at 60 and live comfortably off of his investments. His family goals are to get his daughters through college and buy a house.

V. When asked what he is doing to achieve his goals, Jack Bartlett said that he is going to night school pursuing his MBA at the University of Arizona. He will be graduating in August.

VI. When asked what we, as a company, could do to help him achieve his goals, Jack Bartlett stated:

A. One of the major things that we have already done is support his educational experience. Jack said there is no way he could have done it without that support.

B. Jack said that after taking the Simmons examination seeing the words of Dr. Simmons (a psychologist) saying "Jack wouldn't be a good manager," it was a real blow to his ego. He said he learned from this experience greatly. Afterward, he said there were the two management courses that the company provided to him and others here, and those got him excited. Jack said that he was "like a drowning guy who saw a rope." He said the educational experience that the company provided for him was really good and gave him the opportunity to learn a great deal about management in a controlled environment where his mistakes would not affect a lot of other people adversely.

VII. When asked what opportunities he perceived existed for the firm, Jack Bartlett said:

A. The biggest opportunity for the firm would be an expansion geographically. He said we have our little market here in Tucson, but we need to go beyond these geographical limits. Jack said he is interested in Phoenix and other major growth areas, wherever they are.

B. Jack said that he thinks that the company's growth is the only way he will be able to grow. He said that if we don't grow, he doesn't.

VIII. When asked what threats he perceived existed to the firm, Jack Bartlett said:

A. The adoption of a "no growth policy" by the city of Tucson, be it either formally or informally.

B. Competition from other firms.

C. A downturn in the economic cycle. Jack said we are on about a five-year cycle, and it looks to him in about 18 months we'll have another downturn. Jack said we need someone to look at how we will treat that, that is, develop contingency plans, and the like.

IX. Additional comments and suggestions from Jack Bartlett

A. Jack said there has to be a better way than word of mouth to retrieve data on previous jobs. We have no good way to quickly and efficiently retrieve standard details, for example. We have drawers, but they are not user friendly, they're in no particular order, they are not filed chronologically, and Jack thinks it's a problem. He thinks it may be good to divide the drawer space among the various teams, and then the team would have the responsibility for maintaining those drawers. He thinks that this would improve neatness and accessibility, and that they could set up typical drawers per town, per type of project, and so on. Jack went on to say that going through employees to find this information is fine but they leave and then you lose it. Jack gave an example of a job that he did for Richton Hills, that he had to come up with all new details for this project. He said that after the job was submitted, he found the standard detail sheet for Richton Hills in a drawer. He went on to say that both of these jobs were done by the same PIC!

B. Jack feels that we need flow charts on how to administer a job through a particular city. He thinks the team concept may accomplish this, and that even an informal flow chart would help. Jack went on to say that we can retrieve the information we need with our present system, it's just "time consuming as hell." He said that these jobs don't require a senior man to be doing clerical work, and there has been a great deal of discussion regarding this subject, but no effective action has been taken to solve it. Jack went on to say he thinks it needs to come down from the top, that it could be done on a team-by-team basis, but we need it department-wide. Jack said that this is particularly a problem with new employees who need access to historical data on projects without having to go from person to person until they discover someone who was familiar with the project. He said that the new guy doesn't know where things are. He said we run people all over looking for "the last job we did for Richton Hills," for example. Jack said to give the new guy a chance to start from "zero" as opposed to "minus one." Jack said we need to explain not only the formal organization but also the informal organization to new people.

C. Jack's main complaint in the above is that there is not a quick, efficient method to retrieve historical information on jobs for "the guy who has been here less than four years."

MCZ/spl

Copies to: Dale N. Hansen
William T. Bosworth
Jarvish Pradhan
Larry Thompson
Dick Dietrich
Jack Bartlett
Jack Bartlett's personnel file

Issues to be resolved: Jack Bartlett

1. Jack wants more challenge in his work.
2. Jack does not understand where he fits into the organization and what it will take for him to advance to the next step, whatever that is.
3. Jack doesn't see the firm growing and is concerned that if it isn't, his opportunities are limited.
4. Jack feels we need a strategic business plan.
5. Jack would like to become a manager. He does not know if the team leader's position is only an administrative role.
6. Jack would like to see us open branch offices.
7. Jack would like us to have a better way to retrieve data on previous jobs.

8. Jack feels we need to define the process to get projects through a particular municipality.

Case 5   Winston Hardcastle is an articulate, 31-year-old planner/architect who has worked for the same old-line, well-established 300-man A/E/P firm since graduation from college.

Career Development Meeting
Employee: Winston Hardcastle
Interviewer: Mark C. Zweig
Date: January 13, 1989

I. Likes

A. *With respect to the company*
1. Winston feels the company is a good, strong organization. "We are secure and a good size."
2. Winston said there are possibilities for advancement here, "although when you hit a brick wall, you really hit a brick wall." Winston said that benefit-wise, we appear to be excellent. He added that there have been some positive, dramatic changes in the last few months in our benefits that he appreciates.
3. Winston said one of the most positive things happening here is there appears to be a "much more positive approach to employee growth."
4. Winston said we have some "very good people in the organization, one of our greatest strengths."
5. Winston said "environmentally, we have some positive people and positive situations," although he doesn't feel that way about the building itself.
6. Winston said there are "several intangibles that are difficult to list specifically." He said people "seem to have confidence in you and want you to take initiative." He said "they are supportive in terms of providing both positive and negative criticism."
7. Winston said "it's good we have a profit-sharing program, but it isn't real solid due to profits fluctuating."
8. Winston said that the company has a good image, that to come from The Arch/Eng Consortium means something. He gets immediate respect from clients. He thinks that's something that comes from having good people who want to do a good job, do a good job, and are rewarded for it.

B. *With respect to his position*
1. Winston enjoys doing the type of work he does, although he would like more of it.
2. Winston feels that Lionel (his department head) has a positive esteem for him and the feeling is likewise.

3. Winston thinks the principals have given him opportunities to do the best job he can do. That is one of the greatest motivators to him. He feels there have been distinct rewards tied to that and it is much appreciated. Winston said that's a positive approach to bringing someone along. "Label-wise," he's at an architect/planner II position, but "responsibility-wise," he does much more than that. Winston thinks that's great. He feels people come to him to get things done before they go to someone else.

4. Winston enjoys working with the other professionals in similar fields and feels that it's a great learning opportunity. He also feels he gets respect from other people outside of the firm, clients and competitors both (such as Joe Dutton, Bill Ester, Rich Bonivan, for example.)

5. Winston "feels there's a niche at The Arch/Eng Consortium for him."

6. Winston's work "is fun," and he gets "pumped up and excited about it."

II. Dislikes

A. *With respect to the company*

1. Winston said the company is "slow to react on some key issues." There are and have been problems being able to hire and keep good people. It "seems at times we don't react until it's too late." Winston feels that has been addressed now, but in the past, we lost some good people.

2. Winston feels the profit-sharing program is "not a viable long-term investment option." He would like to see something more positive than our existing profit-sharing program.

3. Winston said that ownership transition is a big question. He asked, "what does it take to become a stockholder?" "What are the magic ingredients?" And, "At what point do those individuals who management feels have potential to become stockholders get informed of that?" He feels there should be "fail-safe points, perhaps a certain age or career point, that if you reach it and you aren't yet a stockholder, you will be informed that it's not likely to happen." Winston said if he hits 35 and is not an owner, all he could hope to be would be a senior architect/planner or associate. He asked, "Would the company plan on keeping him around thirty years longer in spite of that?" He understood that from Brett Bonsignore approximately one year ago that there are criteria for ownership here. He asked, "What are they?" "How effective are they?" And, "Are they used in all situations?"

4. Winston feels there should be some equality in levels. We've gone through so many transitions, project managers, senior project managers, studio leaders, and the like, that before we make any changes in the future there needs to be more forethought.

5. Winston added that the company needs to have some sort of club membership downtown so that the client and the project manager can

go out if they happen to be in the middle of a city council meeting, for example, and a principal is not around.

B. *Regarding his position with the firm*

1. Winston has no dislikes about his position in particular because he does whatever he likes. One thing that is a concern are the "limits of the position." Winston said that Lionel lets him take a job and run. The question for Winston is, "how far do you take it?" He said that as it is now, the planner II position is "somewhat nebulous." He said it is a "quasi-senior planner position with the majority of the planner II's." He asked, "At what point do you become a senior planner?" He feels that there are arbitrary limits at this point in time, and that if someone is not doing the job and they are in the position, then they should not remain in the position. Winston thinks our job descriptions are "a little arbitrary and need to be reviewed."

2. Winston said it is not the position that has problems, but it is the working relationships people have with their superiors. He said, "If you have a good relationship with your superior, that individual will let you go as far as you can." He said "it's when you have problems with that relationship that it can hold you back." He said, "as it is now, there are opportunities and it's more or less up to you to take advantage of them."

3. Winston said that one thing he does have a little concern about, with respect to the architect/planner II position, is the role he has in marketing with his responsibilities in project management and as a designer he has real limits on how much marketing he can do. Winston thinks it's good to get someone like him involved in marketing, but it's a little difficult to handle all of those roles effectively and do everything well. Winston said "and then you get into collecting bills, etcetera," and that he "doesn't understand at what point the client manager comes in." Winston said there is a "potential for burnout if there aren't opportunities to slow down."

III. When asked if he were company president, what, if anything, would he do differently, Winston Hardcastle said:

A. First of all, he would define the roles clearly at each level of management in an attempt to get some uniformity in management and in the manner in which we process our projects.

B. Winston said he would get all the principals and project managers more involved in getting work and in getting the job done. Some of our PICs are more business developers and others are more project managers. There are some PICs who sell the job and then get out of your way if there's no problem and help you when there is; whereas there are others who get the project and then get involved into the details of the job, and then when they aren't here, you have a lack of communication problem. Winston said that there is a third type, those that do absolutely no marketing, do all the design work themselves, and you, in effect, are a technician. He said you may have a project manager's title but you have no control over what's happening on the job. He said we need better definition of the role of the PIC. There has been an evolutionary process, and many of these guys got into the position with no formal training. He said it's "kind of like you can't teach an old dog new tricks." He said we "need a training program for principals and key people who will be future principals." He said we need to let those people know what the guidelines are and what is expected of them, and five years later, if they aren't doing it, you cut them loose. Winston said that the "higher people get, the harder it is to move them out." He said the future of the company depends on our having a good staff with good management skills, and as president of the company, he would see to it that was the case. Winston thinks that "most people have good technical skills but are weaker in management skills, and that we need a program that keeps the good people in the system."

C. Winston said there also needs to be an understanding of how people grow. "Not everyone will be a principal, but even if a technician, you need to be able to grow responsibility-wise and financially." Winston thinks that we need a dual career path. He doesn't think we want to develop people who are nondegreed and become super-specialists because if you take them out of that environment (specialty), "how valuable are they?" He said there also needs to be a means of recognizing and supporting those people so your competition doesn't steal them. The way to do that, as he sees it, is to develop a means for bringing them along and giving them some type of title or position that will allow them to feel "they have accomplished something, that they have arrived." He said that we have these kinds of people on-board now. He doesn't believe we should penalize people for not having a degree in engineering or planning, but in the future, the emphasis should be on degreed and registered personnel and away from the nondegreed designer. Winston said that he believes in the next 10 years, the super designers will accept the fact that they are doing a good job and will get good bonuses but it takes more to be a "principal." "How do you tell someone that and still keep them onboard?" We need to get the Kermit Stillers, Fritz Ernsts, and Larry Lieberts more involved—they are aggressive, motivated and have 30+ years to work and grow here.

D. Winston said another fallacy is that "you can't get rid of stockholders." "You need to be able to do that just like you can with anyone else." If he were president, maybe he would look into the possibility of another kind of stock without voting rights that converts after a certain amount of time to regular stock with voting rights. He said we "need to take advantage of the young professionals" and that they are "a good aggressive group." He said we need young aggressive owners in this competitive marketplace. Winston said that The Arch/Eng Consortium is a good, conservative company, yet we can't be so conservative that we don't take a few chances. He said "some of us young people are pretty conservative and we are responsible, but feel like we can take a few risks." Winston feels there is some hesitance to make decisions because of the competition and the fact that we have 300+ people and their families to be responsible for, but he feels while we are being so careful, "we're losing a good share of our marketplace." He feels that same complacency over the last few years is why we don't have work now.

E. Winston feels the working environment is very important in that we tend to ignore "the setting." Winston said he feels that we need to develop a good positive physical work environment, and that way, a lot of the nonphysical things would be affected such as developing a more positive attitude toward the firm on the part of the employees. With respect to location, Winston thinks "we need to look at where our roots are before we move out somewhere else." He did say, however, "on the other hand, we need to look at what our competition has and what our clients expect of us as a leading edge design firm, too."

IV. Goals

A. *Short-term (one year):* Winston wants to become a more essential part of the architecture/planning group. He wants to improve professionally, and does not want to be held back (by himself) by "minor inconsequential situations and conditions."

B. *Mid-term (one to three years):* Winston wants to become a senior architect/planner. He wants to help influence changes and become more critical in the decision-making and management processes of the firm. He feels like he's doing exactly what a senior architect/planner should do but does not feel we have a distinct separation between architect planner II and senior architect planner. Winston thinks there needs to be some steps or means that he can grade himself by for advancement—this is a problem at all levels. He "did not even know when he became an architect/planner II," and we need "a better means of distinguishing roles."

C. *Long-term (four to five years):* Winston expects to be a senior architect/planner, at least in an associate's position, and working very diligently towards ownership. Winston thinks he needs to develop the management skills, and continue to grow professionally, identifying his shortcomings and improving on those, and becoming well-respected by fellow professionals within his field and the community.

V. When asked what Winston is doing to achieve his goals, he said:

A. He is "starting at the basics and becoming even more competent and continuing to learn new things." He may attempt to continue his education with a business degree.

B. Winston said he is "trying to interact more with the decision makers in the company, to get a better understanding of how and why things operate the way they do." Winston said if he has any suggestions, he makes them.

C. Winston said he is "developing a more diverse client and project base."

D. Winston said he is trying to "work better with his fellow architects and planners, and maintain good communications with each of his fellow employees."

VI. When asked what we, as a company, could do to help him achieve his goals, Winston said:

A. Other than the things he had already pointed out, "it's hard to say." He said the people he works with have always been open in attempting to help him. He has always gotten questions answered, and even if he did not get the answers he wanted, he "got answers."

B. Winston said that one thing that would be helpful would be a better attempt to bring him along in management skills. He thinks if he is a better manager and designer, it will help the company as a whole, as well as the people he works with directly. Winston said he thinks the company has been "pretty open-minded."

C. Another thing he would like to see is that there be a little bit more responsiveness to the changes in the professional practice. He said we "used to be able to do things on gut instinct but now we need more professional support." He said we need to look at what our needs are personnel-wise, and perhaps get individuals with better backgrounds in certain specialties. He said in the past, we have reacted to crises and are usually six months behind in getting the staff we need because it's difficult to locate the person and bring them on quickly. He said we need to target not just our marketing needs but our personnel needs with at least six months to one year advance planning. He went on to say that "as planners, we need the best traffic people, the best urban signage people, etcetera, and that we can't always count on resources (expertise) from outside sources when we need them."

VII. When asked what opportunities he perceived existed for The Arch/Eng Consortium, Winston said:

A. If The Arch/Eng Consortium thinks positively and aggressively, we can get back into the role of "the best firm." He said that we are good in Roberts County, that we're the biggest and can respond the quickest, but that doesn't make us the best. We need to look at the quality of our clients and our projects. We need to diversify our client base and if we do that, with the size firm we are, the facilities we have, and the possibilities we have, we could be "one of the strongest architecture and planning firms in more than just the northeast." Winston said we need to develop good staff and take care of them, which goes hand-in-hand with more profit. Then we can get more and better people, have better benefits, and so on.

B. Winston said we have the opportunity to become more civic oriented. If The Arch/Eng Consortium principals would get more involved with community affairs, it would help. We've got to get more and more involved with who the decision makers are so that whenever they need help they can look to us for guidance.

C. Winston thinks The Arch/Eng Consortium has the opportunity to go into new areas and new fields we've never been into before. He said if we had mechanical and electrical capabilities, it would help architecture, structural, site planning, and landscape architecture.

D. Winston said we should increase our vacation benefits. He would like to see three weeks after 7 years, and perhaps four weeks after 15 years.

E. Winston said we need to clear up the situation on what exactly is job chargeable in certain situations.

F. Winston said the greatest opportunity is to "continue to provide opportunities for our people to grow, and if we do that, there is no limit to our opportunities as a firm." Winston said we will probably "never be the biggest, but we can be the best."

VIII. When asked what threats he perceived to exist to The Arch/Eng Consortium, Winston said:

A. Not moving fast enough on critical issues is a serious threat.

B. Not addressing the potential of our competition is a threat.

IX. Additional comments from Winston Hardcastle

Winston said one thing he is concerned about with respect to our salary situation is that the department head has a certain budget he has to stay within. Winston said he is concerned about keeping all of our people current salary-wise, and if the department head has X budget, he will probably try to take care of everybody first. Winston is concerned if we aren't careful, it could hurt the performers and they could fall behind and then we would have to make "special adjustments" that, according to him, cause problems.

MCZ/jla

Copies to: Harvey Wolters
James Alison
Lionel Chastain
Durward Davis
Winston Hardcastle
Winston Hardcastle's personnel file

Issues to be Resolved: Winston Hardcastle

1. Winston would like to see an improved profit-sharing program.

2. Winston would like to know what the requirements are to become a stockholder.

3. Winston would like to know what it means to be an associate.

4. Winston would like for the firm to have a corporate membership at a downtown club.

5. Winston would like clarification on the distinction between the role of PIC and project manager.

6. Winston would like to see the company move to better physical space.

7. Winston would like us to provide more management education.

8. Winston would like to see the firm's principals more involved in community and civic activities.

9. Winston would like us to re-examine our vacation policy.

10. Winston would like further explanation on time charging.

Case 6   Paul Thornbusch is a 41-year-old draftsman working in the headquarters office of a large multidiscipline firm. Although he still holds the title of Chief Draftsman, due to organizational changes, he no longer heads a drafting pool. He has been with the firm for 20 years.

Career Development Meeting
Employee: Paul Thornbusch
Interviewer: Mark C. Zweig
Date: July 2, 1987

I. Likes

A. Paul said he has always liked the company. He said that what he likes particularly is the quality of the product that this firm has turned out. He said he learned about JR&A while working at the city of Austin. He said he had friends with the firm and knew several other people, including Susan Labowitz and John Russell. He had wanted to get into a private firm, and although it took him a while to get into JR&A, he knew it was what he wanted. He took a cut in pay to come to work for the firm. According to Paul, "this firm has always been a family-oriented company and were particularly so back when we were so small."

B. Paul likes the fact that JR&A is a growing firm. We may not be growing physically but are knowledge-wise. What he was referring to specifically is the CADD, the computers, and the like. "JR&A is not afraid to try new techniques," and he thinks "it is an innovative company."

C. Paul said he likes the people in management—"those that run our company." He said they are "not so much better than you that they won't come to your home or invite you to theirs." Also, according to Paul, management participates in our sporting events and firm functions. "You can talk over your problems with anybody in management in this company."

D. With respect to his position, Paul said he is quite proud of it and has worked hard to achieve what he has. He tries to do his best job. He likes his job not just as draftsman, but the aspects of working with the people, ordering supplies, handling outside reproduction, and the like. Paul feels he can save the company money by being selective in what we buy and who we buy from, both equipment-wise and reproduction-wise.

E. Paul likes being able to work with the job right from the very beginning and be involved in the planning and production of it all the way through completion.

F. Paul appreciates the fact that people in the company and on his team will come to him and ask his advice and opinion. He is also proud to be named to the office and workstation committee for the new building.

II. Dislikes

A. There is still a lack of communications, even though we have tried to improve it. He said he has "lately mentioned things to those in a management level, they say it will get done, but it doesn't." Paul said it might not be their fault, but there has been no follow-through with additional communication as to why it hasn't been done.

B. Paul would like to see more promotion from within the company. If someone is capable of doing the job, let him have the chance before "going and getting someone off the street."

C. Paul doesn't have a lot of dislikes, but when a decision is supposed to be made to do something, he would like to either see a decision made or get some additional communication.

D. Paul said he likes our company-wide meetings, but thinks that the bi-monthly meetings should happen monthly. He added there is too much hearsay with the staggered meetings.

E. Paul said physically, he needs a little more room. That applies not just to himself but to others in his department as well. He said it is not necessarily a fault of management that we are simply short on space.

III. When asked if he were company president, what, if anything, he would do differently, Paul Thornbusch said:

A. He is not sure he would make any changes. He would do the things that he previously mentioned in this interview. He would perhaps mingle throughout the company a little more. He knows Mr. Russell is busy, but if he was in his shoes, he would try to get out a little more because people are afraid of him. He would let people know he is "no one to be afraid of."

B. Paul went on to say that if he were company president, he would try to stay on top of the financial condition of the firm. He would start earlier than the end of the year as it relates to our collections, and get his people trained to get money out of our clients a little earlier than right before Christmas.

C. Paul said all in all, "the president's job is a tough job to have!"

IV. Goals

A. Paul said he is not sure if it is possible, but he would like to become an associate in the firm. He saw information in a newsletter a couple of years ago that listed the criteria to become an associate. He is not sure if that's possible without a degree, but what he saw were somewhere between three to five requirements, and none of them led him to believe he needed a degree to become an associate. Paul would like to accomplish this goal as soon as possible. He said he does have client contacts, does have a feel for how to get a job out, can estimate fees, and so on; and those were some of the qualifications mentioned in the newsletter article.

B. Paul said he wants to be "the best at his job that there is." If he sees a way to improve himself, he wants to "attack that, learn it, master it, and be the kind of person the company is glad to have, to keep, and to promote should we decide to promote someone." Paul said he knows it will take dedication and a person who has sacrificed and will continue to sacrifice for the company. He wants to be the best his position will allow him to be.

C. Paul would like to continue his education. He has "toyed with the idea but wants to get his kids taken care of first." He would probably pursue something in civil line.

V. What Paul is doing to achieve his goals

A. Paul is trying to get more involved in company matters.

B. Paul is trying to help in any way he can for the company to advance; that is, he is trying to promote the company outside, and if he sees an opportunity for the firm, "put the sales pitch on them."

C. Paul is trying to dress better, look good, and put forth a good image for the company in the eyes of our clients. He is trying to be as professional as possible.

D. Paul has made a conscious effort over the last several years to improve his attitude. He used to get upset with all the revisions and changes, but now he puts that aside and does whatever it takes to get his job out. He felt he had really improved in this area.

VI. When asked what we, as a company, could do to help Paul achieve his goals, he said:

A. We should conduct more frequent interviews with him. We need to "talk with him." We need more meetings like this one if we want to find out what he wants and what he can expect from the company. Paul said, in general, we need "more communication with him."

B. Paul said we already have a program of tuition subsidizing.

C. He is not sure if it is possible, but if not an overpowering task, he would like to see us start a credit union.

D. Paul said he is not sure there is anything else the company can do that we aren't doing to help him with his goals. We are large now and just have to be resigned to the fact that we can't be as personal with each of the employees, it just takes too much time and manpower to do so.

VII. When asked what opportunities he sees for the firm, Paul Thornbusch said:

A. Paul sees us being able, with our advanced technology, to branch out into unlimited opportunities job-wise.

B. Paul sees us growing considerably and becoming one of the "super-companies" in the area. Paul said there is a lot of competition, but by maintaining a quality staff, we can do it. Paul said we need to maintain our quality. He said we have always been known as a "quality company," and if we can retain staff and produce good quality at a reasonable price, we will have a lot of clients and also have a lot of our old former clients and staff coming back to us.

C. Paul thinks the decision to get into a new facility and get everyone under one roof will help us do a better job for the client, and "that's what it's all about."

VIII. When asked what threats to the firm he perceived, he said:

A. "Training employees and having them leave us." This happens because of salary, because of promises made that weren't kept, and the like. Paul said that happy employees are not necessarily the best, but it is a more remote possibility that someone who is unhappy at his job is going to do his best work. Paul said we need to keep people involved in the company. He said losing people to another firm means a loss of revenue and a loss of service. Paul said that people who leave also occasionally take clients with them. According to Paul, if we don't follow through with our new technology, new building and facility, and constantly improve our equipment (staying up with modern trends), it will hurt our success—the client will go where he can get the job done faster and cheaper.

B. Paul said a potential solution to this problem is to give people more opportunity to advance, more in-house training in the disciplines and in the use of our equipment. He thinks our brown bag lunches are nice, although they seem to have slacked off somewhat. He said we could use guest speakers to inform us about new products, services, and the like. Paul said there are also people in our office who could pass things on. He said that we have also lost people to other firms because we would not let them use the CADD system.

IX. There were no additional comments or suggestions from Paul Thornbusch.

MCZ/cnt
Enclosure

Copies to: John Russell
Ward Samuels
Jerry Andrews
Bernard Wetjen
Susan Labowitz
Richard Fontbonne
Paul Thornbusch
Paul Thornbusch's personnel file

Issues to be resolved: Paul Thornbusch

1. Paul feels we have a lack of communications. Paul said he would like to see decisions made or get additional communication.
2. Paul would like to see more promotion from within the company.
3. Paul thinks our bi-monthly meetings should be held monthly.
4. Paul could use more physical work space.
5. Paul would like us to have a collection policy that is ongoing so we don't just start trying to get money out of our clients right before Christmas.
6. Paul would like to become an associate in the firm. He does not know what the requirements are.
7. Paul wants to eventually continue his education. (Perhaps we should encourage him actively to do this and develop a schedule that would allow him to do this.)
8. Paul would like us to have a credit union.
9. Paul would like us to start up our brown bag lunch program again.

8.7 CONCLUSION

Design firm management needs to play an active role in the career development of each staff member. Design firms owe it to themselves and their staffs to listen, advise, guide, and lead those who show a willingness to learn. A career development process formalizes this commitment and puts it into action.

Many firms don't make a sincere effort to identify the needs and aspirations of their staff members, remove their career roadblocks, and encourage them to maximize their potentials. This results in turnover, and morale and performance problems. A career development process provides for communication and feedback, identifying problems and opportunities for management to either act on or explain.

Career development meetings share three distinct purposes. First, they establish congruence between the goals and expectations of the firm and the employee. Second, they allow employees to identify their problems, helping management deal with these issues before they turn into crises. Third, they can provide a catharsis for frustrated employees.

9

COMPENSATION

Money is good for bribing yourself through the inconveniences of life.
—Gottfried Reinhardt

9.1 INTRODUCTION

A design firm's greatest single expense is its payroll, so it's amazing that the overall compensation picture in a design firm rarely gets the scrutiny it deserves. The crisis management orientation of so many firms often results in the squeaky wheel getting all the grease. In other words, he or she who complains the loudest gets the biggest rewards.

From most employees' point-of-view, compensation is a necessity of life. As hard as it may be for many design firm principals to believe, there are some people—even professionals—who work only for a paycheck. For others, compensation represents much more than what they can buy with it. To them, compensation is a measure of their value, something that gives them a sense that they are appreciated by the company. They derive personal satisfaction from what they earn.

Obviously, people's expectations of compensation, as well as their actual compensation, vary greatly depending on position in the firm, length of time with the company, performance, stock ownership, market for services in the discipline, and many other factors. Further, the amount of compensation the firm can afford to provide is definitely limited by the amount of work it sells, the fees it produces, and the efficiency with which it performs for its clients. The challenge for design firm management is to administer compensation wisely, to cut up the compensation pie fairly enough to adequately support and reward all of its employees.

Every day, design firm management is liable to face any one of an overwhelming array of compensation-related issues. How do you reward high performers significantly more than low performers? How do you decide who gets overtime pay and at what rate? How do you deal with salary compression (when more experienced staff make close to what new staffers earn)? How do you react to someone who asks for or demands higher pay? How do you deal with employees who have reached their peak earnings? How do you determine incentive compensation? How do you cope with rising costs for benefits (which, once given, are extremely difficult to take away)? How do you keep compensation data out of the hands of employees who see it everywhere—on project reports, proposals, and billing rate schedules?

Dealing effectively with these issues requires an appreciation for the whole compensation puzzle. It means looking at each case in perspective, realizing that each piece of the puzzle affects every other piece and that each employee's compensation is linked to every other employee's.

9.2 COMPENSATION OVERVIEW

Unfortunately, as the following examples will illustrate, the way compensation issues are handled in most design firms flies in the face of all logic and common sense.

Take the example of Harold, a registered architect with 20 years experience in higher-education facilities projects. Harold has been with his company for the last 10 years, only the second firm he ever worked for. He left his last firm because there was no possibility of becoming a principal: It was a small office, and the heir apparent to the throne was the founder's only son.

In spite of the fact that Harold's present employer never did any better than break even on a higher-education project, the firm's principals were committed to doing the work for the glory and perceived prestige associated with it. No one would argue that Harold was a talented designer, but his performance as a project manager would have to be termed less than stellar. Nevertheless, Harold was made an associate of the firm three years after joining it, partly out of the guilt the firm's principals felt for not making him a partner, and partly from Harold's persistent complaints about how he should be rewarded as the firm's top higher-education designer.

Every year the ritual was the same. Each time they sat down with Harold at annual review time to discuss his performance and salary, they offered him a raise. Each time, Harold squawked about how he deserved more, how he left a great job to join the company, and how if not for him the firm wouldn't have any higher-education projects to work on. After each annual meeting to discuss his performance and pay, Harold politicked with any principals who would lend a sympathetic ear, saying how he had two kids in school, how his mortgage was killing him, how his health had suffered from all the long hours he worked, and how he had sacrificed everything for the company. Each year, the principals would decide to give him another $1000 or $2000 just to shut him up.

The firm finally woke up the year there was no bonus money to distribute among the partners. Harold had gotten to the point where he earned a salary of $60,000 per year, while some of the less senior owners with comparable experience and job responsibilities were only earning $50,000. Because the firm had in the past always more than made up for it with bonus money for the partners, this was never a major issue. But this year, one of the more aggressive and boisterous junior partners, a 40-year-old architect who had brought in over $3 million in profitable design contracts to the firm that year, screamed bloody murder. It was Harold or him that had to go. He just wasn't going to put up with this nonsense any longer, and he was probably right. Harold was a good designer but didn't really make any money for the firm. Although he was probably well worth a $45,000 salary as a designer, he couldn't justify himself at $60,000. He was overpaid because he complained so much, and the firm's management just didn't have the guts to say no.

Or take the situation of Gina, a young electrical engineer who graduated *summa cum laude* from Penn State's A/E program with a specialization in lighting design and illumination. Gina was hired right out of school to join a 20-person, Houston-based consulting engineering firm that specialized in high-rise glamor projects. She had worked over the summers while in college with a New-York based A/E firm, and although they wanted her full time upon graduation, she really didn't want to work in Manhattan.

In the two-year period she worked for this Houston firm, Gina's performance was outstanding. She maintained an average utilization rate of 92 percent and never had a complaint on any of her work. The first year there, she got the standard 6 percent salary increase that just about everyone else got. The second year, thanks to the depressed Texas economy, she only got 3 percent. Firm management thought this would satisfy her because she was one of only four in the company who got any raise at all, and after all, Texas was going through some tough times.

Because Gina wasn't a complainer, the company never realized that she was seriously disappointed with her first-year raise of 6 percent. She knew she was talented and had worked hard. When one of her friends, who had gone to work for a St. Louis firm upon graduation, called up to brag about the 15 percent raise and $2000 bonus he got after his first year, Gina looked at her own situation and felt cheated. Wanting to give her employers the benefit of the doubt and wary of looking like a job hopper, she waited through her second year only to fare even worse.

By the end of the second year, Gina's salary was $27,500, more than her employer had ever paid someone with her experience. Imagine their surprise when, two weeks into her third year of employment with the company, she told them she was leaving for a job that paid $35,000 at a firm across town. They ended up paying $40,000 for her replacement, a fellow with six years' experience and no license who turned out to be a complete dud.

These cases are typical of the way compensation is treated in design firms. They are symptoms of the real problem: Design firms haven't looked at the overall compensation picture and addressed all of its components in a systematic way. Your firm's payroll is its biggest and most omnipresent liability—one that must be met month in and month out as long as the firm is in existence. The total compensation the firm provides is composed of all the paychecks, benefits, bonuses, and perquisites paid to all the individuals who are part of the company.

Each individual's total compensation is made up of several distinct components. There is the base salary or hourly wage that a person receives. There is overtime pay for some people, paid either at straight time or at time and a half. There is the bonus or incentive compensation that some people working in design firms receive on top of their base pay. Then there is the whole issue of fringe benefits, which often make up 30 percent or more of an employee's basic earnings and include such things as medical and life insurance, profit sharing/401(k) contributions, vacation and sick leave, and mandatory benefits, such as the employer's portion of FICA tax.

In short, compensation for individuals in design firms is made up of four components:

1. Base salary or hourly rate of pay.
2. Overtime compensation, if paid at all.
3. Bonus or incentive compensation, if paid at all.
4. Fringe benefits.

Each of these variables has to be carefully considered for every individual in the firm. The compensation package for each individual should be designed so that:

1. Comparable individuals are treated similarly. This means that when experience, education, and interpersonal skills are roughly equivalent, compensation packages will be, too. There should not be any differences based on sex, race, or handicap status.
2. The firm can attract the best possible people for any position opening. If the compensation package the firm can offer is insufficient to hire anyone but the dregs in any job category, the firm won't be able to attract staff.
3. Once hired, individuals do not leave the company because of poor compensation. Total compensation should be sufficient to retain staff and keep turnover down. The firm should not be in a position of making counteroffers to staff members who are leaving because they aren't paid fairly.
4. Compensation is not so high that the marketplace for services keeps the firm from selling individuals' time profitably. There is in most cases only so much a firm can charge for a particular type of talent.
5. The compensation mix gives the firm and the individuals in it the greatest benefits at the lowest cost. This requires a clear understanding of employees' wants and needs and a willingness to consider departing from the firm's traditional method of compensating staff.

9.3   MONEY AS A MOTIVATOR

Everyone knows money is a prime motivator. Used properly, it can motivate design professionals to ever higher levels of performance. But money as a motivator in a design firm environment is something far more complex than a magic carrot. Used indiscriminately, it can actually destroy morale, productivity, and profitability.

First, not everyone who works in a design firm has the same needs or is at the same station in life. For those in the earlier stages of their careers, money is likely to be much more important. For someone just coming out of school, there are many needs that require money. The person who has just graduated probably needs to buy a car, find a place to live, buy furniture, buy appropriate work clothes, and so on. And the dual-career family with a new house and growing family is bound to be feeling even more increased financial pressures. Money is probably more important to them than it is to the 54-year-old architect who has owned his home for the past 20 years and whose kids have already been through college. He is more likely to be thinking about downscaling his personal overhead and moving to a smaller house. He almost certainly is not experiencing the growing financial needs of his counterpart 20 years younger with a young family.

Second, overestimating the value of compensation as a motivator too often leads managers to pay insufficient attention to other, often more important motivational factors—for example, keeping staffers informed of what is going on in the company, letting people complete what they start, providing new learning experiences, and so on. An inordinate reliance on money as a motivator frequently backfires. Money may keep people in a job they wouldn't stay in otherwise, but it won't cause them to perform well if the other ingredients aren't there. It's easy to see why managers make this mistake. It may be easier to throw a little more money at a problem than to deal with the real issues, especially when the person who grants the rewards is not solely responsible for controling the rest of the firm's environment. This practice of throwing money at discontented staffers can result in some salaries getting out of proportion with others and with what the company can charge for labor in the open market.

Third, the motivational effect of increases in compensation, at least the way those increases are usually granted in a design firm environment, is short-lived. Although no one would argue that an increase in pay can provide a boost, it is quickly forgotten. Most people's overhead increases correspondingly according to their income, and within a very short time the extra compensation is already accounted for. Also, in all too many design firms, the way increases in pay are determined is unclear. What are the criteria? How much can someone who is a high performer expect to get? Is it clear that if a particular employee does *A*, he or she will get *B*? The motivational effect of a raise is diminished by the uncertainty of what the firm really expects in exchange.

This last point is the real problem in most design firms. While money is almost universally hailed as a great motivator, rewards are distributed in such a way that little or no potential motivational benefits are realized. Take the example of Brian, a 35-year-old mechanical/electrical project manager in a large multidiscipline firm. Clearly recognized as one of the firm's top achievers, Brian earns a salary of $58,000, a good wage by almost anyone's standards. Over a five-year period, his increases have averaged 9 percent per annum. When he compares his raise to everyone else in his department (as a PM he has access to all salaries), however, he sees that other people who are not high performers received raises as good or just slightly less than his in most years. He can only conclude that, while he is paid well for what he does, the firm really doesn't recognize performance. Although firm management thinks they have done extremely well for Brian and that the generous raises are reinforcing his high performance, in fact the overall raise policy is sending a very different message. When at Christmas time the firm distributes bonuses across the board based on a percentage of base salary, once again Brian is not recognized significantly above the others, and the result is not motivation but *demotivation*. Meanwhile, the firm's management believes it has a strong incentive compensation program.

The bottom line to this discussion is that, while money can be a powerful motivator, its effect is usually short-lived and varies greatly from one employee to another. Firms need to establish policies that adequately discriminate between high and low performers. They need to understand where people are in their careers and personal lives to structure their compensation. Firms should strive to compensate people fairly, while at the same time paying more attention to the other factors that motivate design professionals and don't erode the firm's long-term ability to compete. A difficult task with no clear-cut answers, but nevertheless an important one.

9.4 EXEMPT VERSUS NONEXEMPT EMPLOYEES

Anyone who determines compensation in a design firm must understand the difference between exempt and nonexempt employees and how to classify each. In simplest terms, exempt employees are exempt from laws requiring the payment of overtime compensation. Nonexempt employees, on the other hand, must receive overtime pay at time and a half for any hours over 40 in a given week. Strict legal requirements make classifying employees as one or the other the necessary starting point in any compensation plan.

Design firms are notorious for ignoring the laws created by the Fair Labor Standards Act (FLSA) of 1938 (as amended) and frequently compensate those who should be classified as nonexempt as if they were exempt. State laws also exist on this subject and should be consulted to make sure people are being compensated legally.

The Fair Labor Standards Act contains provisions and standards concerning overtime pay and recordkeeping. The basic requirements of the Act apply to employees engaged in or producing goods and services for interstate commerce; to employees in certain other enterprises, including state and local governments; and of key importance to readers of this text, to design firms. The Act is administered by the U.S. Department of Labor's Wage and Hour Division, and compliance is also enforced by the Office of Federal Contract Compliance Programs (OFCCP), which periodically audits firms holding or about to receive federal government service contracts.

Unless specifically exempted, employees covered by the Act must receive overtime pay for hours worked in excess of 40 per week at a rate not less than one and one-half times their regular rates of pay. There is no limitation in the Act on the number of hours employees may work in any given work week. They may work as many hours as their employer sees fit, as long as they are paid in accordance with the Act's requirements. The Act does not require overtime pay for hours worked beyond eight per day in any one day, or for work on weekends or holidays, as long as the weekly total does not exceed 40 hours.

A basic rule: Bona fide executive, administrative, and professional employees are exempt from the minimum wage and overtime requirements of the Act, assuming they meet the tests set for each category. Whether employees are exempt depends on two things: their duties and responsibilities and their salary paid. Figure 9.1 contains an excerpt from the Wage and Hour Division publication spelling out these tests. Read this excerpt carefully, because it is critical that anyone responsible for a compensation program thoroughly understand these distinctions.

The following is excerpted from WH (Wage & Hour Division) Publication 1363 (Reprinted December 1983). Clauses that don't apply to design firms have been omitted:

Executive Employees

In order for an employee to be exempt as a bona fide executive, *all* of the following tests must be met:

1. The employee's primary duty must be management of the enterprise, or of a customarily recognized department or subdivision; and

2. The employee must customarily and regularly direct the work of at least two or more employees therein; and

3. Must have the authority to hire and fire, or recommend hiring and firing; or whose recommendation on these and other actions affecting employees is given particular weight; and

4. Must customarily and regularly exercise discretionary powers; and

5. Must devote no more than 20 percent (less than 40 percent if employed by a retail or service establishment) of his or her hours worked to activities not directly and closely related to the managerial duties; and

6. Must be paid on a salary basis at a rate of at least $155 a week (or $130 a week in Puerto Rico, Virgin Islands and American Samoa) exclusive of board, lodging or other facilities.

FIGURE 9.1 Classification tests for executive, professional, and administrative employees

The percentage tests on nonexempt work would not apply in the case of an employee who is in sole charge of an independent establishment or a physically separated branch establishment, or who owns at least a 20 percent interest in the enterprise where employed.

A determination of whether an employee has management as the primary duty must be based on all the facts in a particular case. In the ordinary case, it may be taken as a rule of thumb that primary duty means the major part, or over 50 percent of the employee's time. Time alone, however is not the sole test, and in situations where the employee does not spend over 50 percent of the time in management duties, the employee nevertheless might have management as the primary duty if the other pertinent factors support such a conclusion.

The exemption is applicable to employees employed in a bona fide executive capacity and does not include employees in training to become executives and not actually performing the duties of an executive.

Administrative Employees

In order for an employee to be employed in a bona fide administrative capacity, all the following tests must be met:

1. The employee's duty must be responsible office or non-manual work directly related to the management policies or general business operations of the employer or the employer's customers; and

2. The employee must customarily and regularly exercise discretion and independent judgement, as distinguished from using skills and following procedures, and must have the authority to make important decisions; and

3. The employee must:

   A. Regularly assist a proprietor or a bona fide executive of administrative employee; or

   B. Perform work under only general supervision along specialized or technical lines requiring special training, experience or knowledge; or

   C. Execute under only general supervision special assignments; and

4. The employee must not spend more than 20 percent of the time worked in the workweek (less than 40 percent if employed by a retail or service establishment) on nonexempt work—that is, work not directly and closely related to the administrative duties, and

5. The employee must be paid on a salary or fee basis at a rate of not less than $155 per week (with exceptions as noted above for executive employees).

The percentage limitations on nonexempt work do not apply to an administrative employee who is paid on a salary or fee basis of at least $250 a week ($200 per week in Puerto Rico, the Virgin Islands, or American Samoa) exclusive of board,

FIGURE 9.1 *(Continued)*

lodging, or other facilities. The employee will be exempt if the primary duty consists of responsible office or non-manual work directly related to management policies or general business operations.

The employees for whom exemption is sought under the term "administrative" have extremely diverse functions and a wide variety of titles. The exempt or nonexempt status of any particular employee must be determined on the basis of whether the duties, responsibilities and salary meet all the requirements of the appropriate section of the regulations and a title alone is worth little or no assistance in making this determination (the interpretation of the regulations in WH publication 1363 clearly excludes private secretaries from being exempt.)

Professional Employees

This exemption includes the learned, the artistic, and the teaching professions.
Except as otherwise noted below, a professional employee must meet all these test to be exempt:

1. The primary duty must be either:

    A. Work requiring knowledge of an advanced type in a field of science or learn-ing, customarily obtained by a prolonged course of specialized instruction and study; or

    B. Work that is original and creative in character in a recognized field or artis-tic endeavor and the result of which depends primarily on the employee's invention, imagination, or talent; and

2. The employee must consistently exercise discretion and judgement; and

3. Must do work that is predominantly intellectual and varied, as distinguished from routine or mechanical duties, and

4. Must not spend more than 20 percent of the time worked in the workweek on activities not essentially a part of and necessarily incident to the professional duties, and

5. Must be paid on a salary or fee basis at a rate of not less than $170 a week (or $150 a week in Puerto Rico, the Virgin Islands and American Samoa) exclusive of board, lodging, or other facilities.

The 20-percent test on nonexempt work does not apply to a professional employee who is paid on a salary or fee basis at a rate of at least $250 a week ($200 a week in Puerto Rico, Virgin Islands, and American Samoa) exclusive of board, lodging or other facilities, provided:

The employee's primary duty consists of work requiring knowledge of an advanced type in a field of science or learning; or

The primary duty is artistic work that requires invention, imagination, or talent in a recognized field of artistic endeavor.

FIGURE 9.1 *(Continued)*

One of the conditions for being considered a professional employee is to work in a profession requiring a prolonged course of study. For the purpose of this text, the professions that meet the requirement for a prolonged course of study include architecture, engineering, and various types of chemical and biological sciences, among others. The typical symbol of the professional training is the appropriate academic degree or registration. In order to be considered a professional, an employee must be engaged in work predominantly intellectual and varied in character as opposed to routine mental, manual, mechanical, or physical work. Technicians who have only limited opportunity for the exercise of independent discretion and judgment, usually performing their duties under the supervision of a more highly qualified employee, are not exempt.

Typically in a design firm setting, all registered professionals should be treated as exempt, although designers, technicians, and degreed professionals in training should not. If design firms err, it is usually in attempting to treat senior designers and technicians, field survey crew members, and secretaries or word processors as exempt when they shouldn't be.

Firms found to be violating the Fair Labor Standards Act may be held liable for back wages (in terms of overtime premium that should have been paid) and back taxes, with penalties. Typically, it is either the securing of a new government contract or the allegedly unfair dismissal or treatment of a disgruntled employee that results in an audit, although the Department of Labor (DOL) claims to make periodic audits on a random basis. Firms having any question on exempt or nonexempt status of a particular employee or class of employee should contact their local DOL office or experienced legal counsel for clarification. A word of caution: the rules and their interpretations, as can be seen from the excerpts included in this chapter, are not always crystal clear.

9.5 WAGE AND SALARY STRUCTURES

Design firms should generally seek to classify as *exempt* everyone who can legally be classified as such under the definitions of the Fair Labor Standards Act as outlined in Figure 9.1. This allows the firm maximum flexibility in structuring its compensation plan.

Exempt employees should be paid on a salary basis; and nonexempt employees, on an hourly basis (with a few exceptions that will be covered in Section 9.7). The three basic variables affecting a staffer's salary or hourly rate (see Figure 9.2) are the market value of services (how much the company can bill the employees's time for), the individual's performance relative to others in the firm, and the minimum rate the company would have to pay to get someone of comparable background or qualifications (the "price floor" for a given type of talent).

The problem of determining starting salaries was addressed in Chapter 4. Now the issue becomes how best to make adjustments in those salaries to reflect an individual's value to the firm over time, to meet the individual's needs and wants as far as possible, and to yield the maximum motivational benefit that compensation increases can provide.

1. Market value for services
2. Individual's performance relative to others
3. Price floor for individuals of comparable qualifications

FIGURE 9.2   Variables affecting base pay

Firms must pay as much or as little as necessary to keep employees from becoming demotivated or seeking employment elsewhere, to maintain fairness by keeping in line salaries of comparable performers in comparable positions, and to keep company labor costs in check. It's not just a matter of paying for performance. A firm could have the best-performing shop-drawing file clerk in the world and probably not ever be able to pay that person what they would have to pay the worst-performing groundwater hydrologist. Basic pay should be based on the employee's *value* to the firm.

Some firms have rigid job classifications with set salary ranges for all of their employees. This provides managers with guidelines and gives the firm a certain comfort level that it has a handle on the whole issue of pay. Unfortunately, this type of structure does not accommodate the special needs of some individuals in the firm, and it may create certain barriers to hiring and keeping the best people over the long haul.

Certain employees may be working in particular specialties or geographic areas where the demand for their skills far outstrips their availability. In these cases, set salary or hourly pay ranges quickly become out of date. In other cases, individuals are discovered who, based on their particular talents or lack of talents, either deserve more or less than the published ranges would permit. Not many high performers are comfortable working in such a stratified environment. The best people, even if not at the salary limit their position classification allows, simply don't like the idea of there being a constraint on what they can earn. For these reasons, it is not recommended that design firms establish fixed salary ranges.

On the other hand, there is nothing wrong with publishing position salary ranges for purposes of internal management or service pricing—all firms should have this data readily available to whoever really needs it. It is not a good idea, however, to widely distribute salary or hourly rate data. It will certainly fall into the wrong hands, and those who discover themselves at or near the bottom of their respective classification are bound to become dissatisfied. Studies on this subject confirm that the more data on pay that is available to employees, the more likely they are to be dissatisfied with what they earn.

These recommendations are based on the assumption that a firm is starting with salaries or hourly rates that are currently accomplishing these goals. Before any firm embarks on a new wage and salary review process or administration program, inequities should be addressed through special adjustments for those who are earning less than they should and terminations or reassignments of position or responsibility for those who are earning more than they should (more on this in Section 9.8). Only then can a design firm reasonably expect to establish a successful new process for distributing salary adjustments or hourly rate increases.

Any discussion of salary structures also calls for an important liability alert. Be very sensitive to any inequalities in compensation for white males compared to minorities and women in equivalent positions. Try listing all members of a given job classification with their corresponding rates of pay. There should be no discrimination that would be apparent to an auditor, judge, or jury. If the lowest-paid members of any particular job classification happen to be minorities or women, you've got serious potential liability exposure.

Finally, there are a number of resources available to firms who want to see how their salaries or hourly pay rates stack up compared to other firms in this business (see Figure 9.3). These surveys should be used with caution! Some firms get the idea that no one can earn more than what a published salary survey says people in that job category should earn. Conversely, there have been cases of A/E/P firms getting hold of one of these surveys and making wholesale adjustments in pay to bring their people in line. Neither of these courses is recommended.

There are so many variables that go into the base rate compensation equation that no survey should be your sole guide. Huge disparities exist in the earnings of individuals doing essentially the same job for different companies. No survey will address all of the variables in any specific case. Also, firms that have a goal of acquiring the best staff possible need to seriously consider whether this can be achieved by paying only average or median salaries as quoted in the surveys. On the other hand, salary surveys do satisfy managers' natural curiosity about what others in the industry are paying for particular types of talent. They are only one indicator of what someone should actually earn, however.

9.6 WAGE AND SALARY REVIEW PROCESS

Assuming that everyone is paid properly to start with, that no discrimination exists, and that no job market-related adjustments are needed, the compensation issue usually boils down to raises—how much to give and to whom. The following discussion outlines one proven process for handling wage and salary review. No system is fool-proof, but this one is flexible enough to be applied to almost any design firm setting, large or small.

It starts at the first of the year with the creation of a budget for wage and salary increases. This budget is something every firm needs, regardless of how they want to handle wage and salary increases. At the time this text was written, most design firms had annual raise budgets in the range of 5 to 7 percent of total salaries. This range has held pretty constant throughout most of the 1980s, although during the high-inflation years in the mid-70s to early 80s, wage and salary increase budgets were as high as 12 to 15 percent in some firms. Wage and salary increase budgets rarely surpass the inflation rate, since if they were consistently higher, design firms would quickly price their services out of the market.

Firms that don't set wage and salary increase budgets usually end up spending more than they need to. It's easy to get carried away with granting rewards when there aren't any constraints. And, to attempt to deal with that issue by setting constraints on individual raises is not advisable. Exceptions will always come up,

Architecture

Salary Report For AIA Firms. Office of Research and Planning, AIA Press, American Institute of Architects. 9 Jay Gould Court, Waldorf, Maryland 20601 (800) 242-4140

Architectural Salary Survey. D. Dietrich Associates, P.O. Box 511, Phoenixville, Pennsylvania 19460-9988 (800)654-8258

Architectural Management Salary Survey. D. Dietrich Associates, P.O. Box 511, Phoenixville, Pennsylvania 19460-9988 (800)654-8258

Architectural Drafting and Design Salary Survey. D. Dietrich Associates, P.O. Box 511, Phoenixville, Pennsylvania 19460-9988 (800)654-8258

Engineering

Income and Salary Survey. National Society of Professional Engineers. Orders Department, 1420 King Street, Alexandria, Virginia 22314 (703)684-2882

Engineering Salary Survey. D. Dietrich Associates, P.O. Box 511, Phoenixville, Pennsylvania 19460-9988 (800)654-8258

Executive Engineering Compensation Survey. D. Dietrich Associates, P.O. Box 511, Phoenixville, Pennsylvania 19460-9988 (800)654-8258

Drafting and Design Salary Survey. D. Dietrich Associates, P.O. Box 511, Phoenixville, Pennsylvania 19460-9988 (800)654-8258

Landscape Architecture

National Salary Survey of Landscape Architects. American Society of Landscape Architects. L.A. Bookstore, P.O. Box 6525, Ithaca, New York 14851 (607)277-2211

Interior Design

Contract Compensation Survey. Contract Magazine. Gralle Publications, 1515 Broadway, New York, New York 10036 (212)869-1300

Scientific Staff

Scientific Salary Survey. D. Dietrich Associates, P.O. Box 511, Phoenixville, Pennsylvania 19460-9988 (800)654-8258

Lab Technician Salary Survey. D. Dietrich Associates, P.O. Box 511, Phoenixville, Pennsylvania 19460-9988 (800)654-8258

Marketing Staff

Marketing Salary and Expense Survey. Society For Marketing Professional Services, 99 Canal Center Plaza, Ste. 320, Alexandria, Virginia 22314 (800)292-7677

Support Staff

Support Services Salary Survey. D. Dietrich Associates, P.O. Box 511, Phoenixville, Pennsylvania 19460-9988 (800)654-8258

All Design Firms

Incentive Compensation Survey For Design/Professional Firms. Professional Services Management Association, 1213 Prince Street, Alexandria, Virginia 22314 (703)684-3993

PSMJ Executive Management Salary Survey. Practice Management Associates, Ltd. 10 Midland Avenue, Newton, Massachusetts 02158 (617)965-0055

Executive Compensation Analysis of Professional Service Firms. D. Dietrich Associates, P.O. Box 511, Phoenixville, Pennsylvania 19460-9988 (800)654-8258

Non-Cash Benefits Survey. D. Dietrich Associates, P.O. Box 511, Phoenixville, Pennsylvania 19460-9988 (800)654-8258

FIGURE 9.3 Salary surveys available on the design industry

and if not made in the context of the firm-wide budget, they'll increase the total cost of raises beyond what was planned for.

Next, firms need to decide how often they want to review wages and salaries. Some A/E/P companies do this only once per year; others do it twice per year. Still others do it four or more times per year.

A schedule of conducting salary reviews only once per year is probably not frequent enough for most design firm staffers. To go a whole year without even being considered for a raise is a lot to ask, especially for young professionals. This becomes even more of a problem for employees who do not receive a raise or adjustment during the review cycle. Even if they address the performance or other issues that kept them from getting a raise the last go-around, under a once-per-year adjustment schedule they will have to wait an entire year before being considered for a raise and before receiving any tangible reinforcement for their improved performance.

A schedule of reviewing basic compensation every six months makes far more sense. Critics will say this costs the firm more money. But it doesn't have to. The firm shouldn't give out more raises in total if it reviews salaries every six months than it would on a 12-month schedule, as long as a budget is set and stuck to. By looking at pay every six months, the company is also more likely to be able to keep up with the earnings expectations of its highest achievers, who will no doubt be receiving invitations from other firms and recruiters on a continuous basis.

Suppose late in the year the firm falls on harder times than expected. With a once-per-year schedule, it might be too late to adjust the budget by the time the year's poor financial performance became apparent. On a twice-per-year schedule, the firm doesn't have to use the entire wage and salary increase budget initially set out. Last but not least, if there is any motivational value to salary increases, the firm that has two opportunities per year to grant raises will get twice the motivational effect for the same expense.

Finally, *when* should the pay review process be conducted? Should everyone be looked at simultaneously, or should the pay reviews be staggered (as performance appraisals often are), based on employees' anniversary dates or some other schedule? Experience with the process will prove that unless you have a very small firm or group to deal with, you're better off looking at everyone at the same time. Critics of this approach will say it encourages people to talk about and compare what they make. Even if that is the case, its advantages far outweigh its disadvantages:

1. It makes sticking with the budget easier.
2. It makes the comparison process easier.
3. It minimizes the likelihood that a particular employee will fall through the cracks and be forgotten at pay review time.
4. It makes it easier to keep the company's hourly billing rate schedule current.
5. It is easier to administer.

Once the budget is set and the frequency of pay reviews established, the next question is how to distribute the budget to those managers who will be deciding or making recommendations for individual rate changes. In small firms or firms with one person setting everyone's salary, this isn't a big issue. It becomes much more difficult in larger firms with multiple departments or branches of varying size.

In these cases, the firm's CEO or chief operating officer (with the input and recommendations of whoever is in charge of the HR function) should make the decision as to how the budget is split between branches, divisions, or departments. In firms that are arranged in divisions or branches, it may be sufficient to give the division heads or branch managers a lump sum budget and allow them to distribute it as they see fit.

But what about a firm that has one group of 50 employees in a traditional discipline area with an average age of 45, and another group of only six employees in a hot new specialty service area, with an average age of 29? The percentage-increase budget probably can't be equal for both groups. First, in any group of 50, there are probably enough marginal employees whose salaries go into calculating the overall budget to ensure that adequate money will be available for those who really deserve it. Second, hot service areas' salaries may be going up more quickly than those in mature service areas. For example, in some environmental service areas, 15-percent increase budgets in recent years have not been uncommon. Finally, younger people early in their careers expect their earnings to grow at a faster rate than do their older counterparts. This has always been the case—it is at the beginning of one's career that learning typically occurs at the fastest pace, and one's value to the firm and earnings grow accordingly.

This is where the CEO (or COO) and HR person have to put their best judgment to the test in distributing the wage and salary increase budget. Everyone will think that his or her own group deserves the most. In any case, it's usually best to reserve a certain portion of the overall raise budget for contingencies or unanticipated special requests for increases.

After the budgets are set up, you must make the individual decisions on who gets what, if anything, in the way of a raise. Generally speaking, raises should be largely determined by employees' immediate supervisors. The more knowledgeable the person setting the raise is about the employee's performance, the better. In some firms, all salary changes are made by principals, who may be four or more levels away from the person whose salary they are setting. This is probably not the best way to go, even though principals understandably don't want their money to be squandered. That's why the budget-setting and distribution process is so important—it ensures that, overall, things won't get out of hand.

Just as with performance appraisals, specific training and instructions should be given to all managers who participate in the process of setting salaries (see Figure 9.4 below).

1. The total amount of all of your raises should not exceed $_____. The total of all your raises cannot exceed this amount. Nonexempt staff members' raises should be based on what they would earn working 40 hours per week.
2. Rank order all of your staff members in terms of their value to you. Work with your subgroup leaders as necessary. Group your employees into the top third, middle

FIGURE 9.4 Sample instructions for managers for a wage and salary review process

third, and bottom third, with the top group being employees you would keep if you had to let go the rest of your staff. Keep this ranking confidential.

3. Distribute 65 percent of your budget to the staff members in the top third, and 35 percent to the group in the middle third. The bottom third should not receive any raises.

4. Studies have shown that, typically, high achievers expect annual increases in the range of 10 to 15 percent of their base salary. Also, those who are in the early stages of their careers expect their earnings to rise at a faster rate than more senior staff members. Everyone does not have to get a raise each review cycle. It is not in the firm's best interests to reward poor performance with a salary increase. The number of those receiving large raises or adjustments should be roughly equivalent to the number of those receiving no raises or adjustments.

5. Do not discuss any raises that you have recommended with your employees prior to approval from the wage and salary review committee.

6. After your recommendations have been approved, call in each of your employees individually to let them know what, if anything, they received in the way of a raise and when it will take effect.

FIGURE 9.4 *(Continued)*

Next, all managers with a budget to allocate should rank their staffs, putting at the top of the list those staffers they would least like to lose and at the bottom of the list, the people less critical to their operation. A simple comparison matrix may be helpful in this process. It allows managers to make one-on-one comparisons of each of their staff members, tabulate the results, and come up with a rank ordering. For managers with larger departments or groups, subgroup managers or team leaders should be consulted as necessary. The final comparison matrix should be kept confidential, and *never* shown to any employee!

Once employees are ranked, group them into the top third, middle third, and bottom third. Sixty-five percent of the budget for the entire group should be distributed to the top third. The second third should be given 35 percent of the budget. Those in the bottom third should receive nothing. Some firms even take a more radical approach to budget distribution; they give as much as 75 percent to the top third and only 25 percent to the second third. This is what this text terms a *value-based* wage and salary review process.

To many readers, this budget distribution may seem unduly harsh. Some people prefer to take care of everyone first with a cost-of-living increase and then give what's left over to their best people. The problem with this approach is that it does not significantly reward the best people over those who are marginal. Let's take a typical 6-percent increase budget. If the cost of living rose 4.8 percent over the year, that leaves only 1.2 percent of the total budget for allocation to the best people. In this scenario, you're likely to end up with your worst people getting 5 percent raises and your best people getting 6 to 8 percent, at *most*. This 1 to 3 percent differential is not likely to be enough to satisfy your highest achievers. Studies have shown that high achievers expect 10 to 15 percent annual increases, good times and bad.

**Sample Value Comparison Matrix
for Wage & Salary Review Process**

	Jeff	Becky	Ed	Lamar	Jean	Harry	Pete	Scores:	
Becky	Jeff							Lamar	7
								Pete	5
								Ed	4
Ed	Ed	Becky							
								Jean	3
								Dave	3
Lamar	Lamar	Lamar	Lamar					Becky	3
								Harry	2
Jean	Jean	Jean	Ed	Lamar				Jeff	1
Harry	Harry	Becky	Harry	Lamar	Jean				
Pete	Pete	Pete	Ed	Lamar	Pete	Pete			
Dave	Dave	Becky	Ed	Lamar	Dave	Dave	Pete		
	Jeff	**Becky**	**Ed**	**Lamar**	**Jean**	**Harry**	**Pete**		

FIGURE 9.5   Sample value comparison matrix for a wage and salary review process

The value-based wage and salary review process runs counter to the tendency of many design firms to try to take care of everyone first, then go on to the high achievers and most valuable people. The problem with that approach is that if you try to take care of everyone in the company first, there won't be enough left over for those who are doing an outstanding job. Companies using this approach eventually end up running off their best people because they are taking care of the needs of their weakest team members *first*. This is one more illustration of the significant differences between the human resources and human relations schools of management thought (see Chapter 1). In order for the value-based wage and salary review process to work as intended, the human resources philosophy has to be accepted and endorsed by all key management personnel who participate in setting salaries.

The preliminary raise numbers developed should then be passed along to either the firm's CEO or a wage and salary (W&S) committee comprising a number of the firm's top managers and the HR director (if there is one). After confirming that each manager has followed the required process, this group should then either approve the manager's recommendations or send them back with appropriate comments or questions.

Generally speaking, the CEO or W&S committee should make as few changes as possible in the managers' recommendations. Putting reward power in the hands of immediate supervisors will give them a tool that can help in their efforts to control their staffs. Constantly second-guessing your first- and second-line supervisors will demotivate them and contribute to their feelings of powerlessness.

On the other hand, having a check and balance before final salary changes are made can help guide an inexperienced (or irrational) manager. It can also provide some means for reconciling differences that may crop up in essentially equal people in unrelated or different areas of the company (see Figure 9.7 for a summary of the process's benefits).

Each employee whose pay is reviewed under the firm's wage and salary review process should be taken aside and told what, if anything, he or she will receive in the way of a pay increase. This is an important step. Some companies grant pay increases and then don't even tell their people what they are. The employee simply notices that the paycheck has gotten bigger, which only serves to reinforce the misconception that increases are automatic and not tied to performance. This kind

Wage & Salary Increase
Sample Budget Distribution

6 month budget = 3.5% of salaries = $11,060

Total salaries of employees in group = $316,000

All employees:		Raise Budget	x		Amount for Group	
Jeff	50,000	$11,060	x	.65	=	$7,189
Becky	23,000	$11,060	x	.35	=	$3,871
Ed	37,500					
Lamar	60,000					
Jean	55,000					
Harry	27,500					
Pete	21,000					
Dave	42,000					
	$316,000					

Top 1/3	Salary	Raise	New Salary	%Increase
Lamar	$60,000	$2,993	$62,993	4.9%
Pete	$21,000	2,250	23,250	10.7%
Ed	$37,500	2,000	39,500	5.3%

Total for top 1/3 = $7,189

Middle 1/3				
Jean	$55,000	$1,921	$56,921	3.5%
Dave	42,000	1,200	43,200	2.9%
Becky	23,000	750	23,750	3.3%

Total for middle 1/3 = $3,871

FIGURE 9.6   Sample wage and salary increase budget distribution

of impersonal treatment is sure to give employees the idea that the firm doesn't really care about its people.

A few more points with respect to basic compensation: First, firms should recognize that there are circumstances that call for granting special increases or making adjustments to base pay between normal review times. For example, some firms like to give an increase at the time a professional earns his or her registration. Others do it when someone is promoted. Still others may find the employment market for certain kinds of talent gets so heated that outside pressures require the firm to make some adjustments just to keep up. There is nothing wrong with allowing exceptions in such cases as long as management does it for good reasons and doesn't let the situation get so far out of hand that it makes the normal pay review process a joke. In any event, this is one more reason why firm management should probably keep a small percentage of the normal wage and salary increase budget in reserve to handle these situations without blowing the overall firm-wide budget for wage and salary increases.

One issue that many firms find hard to deal with is when a valued employee complains about his or her raise, or when the employee asks for or demands more money at some other time. Low-paying firms are in this predicament constantly, but even some of the best-paying firms find themselves in this situation occasionally. The firm should always hear out employees' complaints to get all of their justification for why they feel they deserve more money. The problem lies in the fact that if the firm makes it a regular practice to meet such demands they are reinforcing employee complaints. The solution is that if there are inequities in pay that need addressing, they should be taken care of *before* the employee complains. However, if the firm is paying what they feel is fair, then they should not give in to employees' demands. It's that simple.

Although no one likes to deliver bad news, it may be necessary at times. The firm should believe that it is a good place to work, that it pays fairly, and that compensation is only one part of the total employment experience and opportunity that it provides the employee. If this is true and can be clearly communicated, most employees will realize it and quit griping. If not, the firm ought to address those issues anyway, in consideration for all of its staff.

1. Wages and salaries of individuals are set by those who are most able to evaluate their performance—their immediate supervisors.
2. Managers are in control of the reward system. They need to be if they are to be held accountable for the performance of their staffs.
3. Management knows what it will be spending on raises before actually going through the wage and salary review process.
4. The people the firm could least afford to lose will be taken care of first, and those the firm would not mind losing will be taken care of last.
5. The individual managers must inform each employee of his or her raise (or lack of raise), ensuring that the full potential of the salary review process to provide tangible feedback on job performance will be realized.

FIGURE 9.7 Benefits of value-based wage and salary review process

Finally, there is the issue of salary freezes and salary reductions. Some design firms, when feeling the pinch of hard times, have resorted to pay freezes and/or salary reductions across the board. Neither of these alternatives is advised. Pay freezes will simply tell your best staff members that they can't expect to do any better with your company. You may as well suggest they quit and go to work somewhere else where that constraint doesn't exist.

The same applies to pay cuts. Firms that opt for a reduced work week and corresponding across-the-board pay cuts have problems retaining key staff. Morale suffers and productivity declines at the time it is most needed. If cuts in pay are taken, they should be taken by the firm's owners and not by the staff. Principals who take visible pay cuts during times of crisis will be more than repaid in sustained morale and future loyalty from their staff. In the early 1980s, one Tennessee A/E firm had all of its principals take pay cuts of as much as 40 percent in one year, and yet still granted raises as high as 30 percent to some staffers over the following 18-month period. They got through the tough times and today are an incredibly successful firm.

Some companies elect to make selective pay cuts during tough times or when they are unhappy with a particular staff member's performance. These rarely ever accomplish what they are intended to. Instead of motivating an employee to work harder or do better, pay cuts tend to discourage and demotivate. If there are employees who can't justify their current base pay, they should probably be let go. A pay cut simply turns unproductive employees into unproductive and unhappy employees, whose bad attitudes and complaining act like a cancer in overall staff morale.

In conclusion, you're better off to let people go or make cuts elsewhere in the firm's overhead to save money than to freeze or cut the pay of existing staff. The only possible exception to this is in the area of principals' salaries, where cuts may in fact boost firm morale and performance.

9.7 OVERTIME COMPENSATION

The laws spelled out in the Fair Labor Standards Act establish the differences between exempt and nonexempt employees (described in Section 9.4). As stated earlier, design firms should try to classify as *exempt* everyone that they legally can. That way the firm doesn't have any legal obligation to pay overtime to the employee.

Nonexempt employees are required by law to receive time and a half pay for all hours worked over 40 in a week. Firms who want to stay legal really don't have any alternative. Therefore, the issue of overtime really revolves around whether design firms should pay overtime compensation in any form to employees who can be legitimately classified as exempt from overtime.

Firms that do want to compensate exempt employees for overtime have a number of options:

1. Treating all exempt employees exactly as they do nonexempt employees, giving them overtime pay at the rate of 1.5 times their normal hourly rate.

2. Treating exempt employees as salaried, with the exception of paying overtime hours at the employee's normal hourly rate for all hours over 40. Other variations of this kind of compensation program used by some design firms include paying straight time for all hours over 45 or paying overtime for all *billable* hours over 40 in a week.

3. Creating two classes of exempt employees, those who get overtime (OT) compensation at a straight-time rate, and those who are strictly salaried. Often firms adopting this approach will put senior technicians and junior professionals in the category that gets straight-time OT and place all other senior professionals in a straight salary situation. Some who do this are walking a fine line with respect to violating the laws governing overtime.

4. Granting exempt employees compensatory time for all hours worked over 40 in a given week. By giving compensatory, or "comp" time, the firm is granting time off in the future above and beyond the employee's normal vacation allowance. (*Note*: Some design firms have tried to deal with nonexempt employees in this fashion, something that in just about every case is illegal, including cases where the employee agrees to it in writing. If you are handling overtime for nonexempt people in this fashion, consult your attorney.)

But is overtime for exempt staff a good idea? Advocates of paying some sort of compensation to exempt staff maintain that:

1. It's the only fair way to pay people.
2. It can be a significant motivator.
3. The company's overhead has been charged out in the first 40 hours, so why not?
4. The company can't legitimately bill clients for overtime hours worked if they aren't paying employees for them.
5. It helps the company in its recruitment efforts.

Those who are opposed to paying overtime to exempt staff maintain that:

1. It encourages inefficiency because people get paid to work longer hours than they would need to otherwise.
2. It is difficult to police.
3. It can be a demotivator to staffers who don't abuse the system when they see others who "get their bonus on the installment plan."
4. It promotes a blue collar work ethic; that is, it encourages employees to do *only* what they get paid for.
5. In the case of firms paying comp time, the firm may accumulate a huge liability that it doesn't really have a handle on.

There are no doubt some very successful firms, both large and small, that pay overtime to exempt staff. But consider the following case of one real-life firm that paid straight time to all exempt staffers.

The firm was a 250-person, multidiscipline company with three offices, whose volume had declined from $18.5 million one year to a projected $15 million for the current year. Staff had peaked at 341 two years before, and declines were attributed to a combination of forced and voluntary reductions. Meanwhile, utilization rates were hovering around 65 percent for the entire company, while management knew a 70 percent rate was needed to achieve modest 15 percent profit goals. All salaried (exempt) employees with exception of principals received straight-time OT. Nonexempt employees received 1.5 OT pay. Still, management didn't view this as a problem, since OT was considered largely billable on the firm's cost-plus contracts, where it was reimbursed anyway. The bonus pool was based on profits. Bonuses were paid to all employees on a purely discretionary basis. In the past, some employees had received up to 25 percent of base pay in bonus.

The firm had 14 principals, all with technical backgrounds. The financial manager had no prior experience in the A/E/P industry. A reporter rather than a results affecter, he was not someone who wanted to rock the boat. He projected overtime compensation to be only $150,000 for the year that was almost over. While the HR director worried about a potential bonus pool decline of 70 to 100 percent due to low profits, he regularly heard reports from demoralized staffers of others abusing the company's overtime payment policy—people who were working longer hours than they had to just for the money.

Although the company management information system (MIS) showed $150,000 in overtime pay, the HR director went to the MIS manager with specific instructions for how to calculate overtime. To his surprise, they discovered that the firm actually paid out $850,000 in overtime. The $150,000 overtime figure represented only the one-half time *premium* portion paid to nonexempt staff. Total overtime compensation (at a rate of time and one-half of regular hourly pay) paid to nonexempt staff was calculated to be $450,000, and straight-time overtime paid to exempt staff was $400,000.

The firm's goal was to save money for profit so incentive bonus dollars would be there at year end for distribution to the deserving. One thought was to make key exempt employees share in the risk of the company by not paying them overtime for all hours worked, whether or not the company made profits. Management's concerns with this were threefold:

1. *Losing billable hours*: It didn't make sense to reduce the company's income *and* that of its employees.
2. *Losing valued employees*: Some individuals were earning as much as $10,000 to $15,000 in overtime pay—a big part of their total compensation.
3. *Nonexempt staff earning more than exempt staff*: Many of the firm's hourly people already earned more than some key exempt staff. This problem could be exacerbated by cutting OT for exempt staff.

The company appeared to be in a catch-22 situation. Here are the actions they took to address their problem:

1. They determined exactly how much income they'd lose on cost-plus jobs where people had worked over 40 *billable* hours per week. The total value turned out to be only $20,000.

2. They created three classes of employees: hourly (exempt), hourly-salaried (exempt, but including people like senior technicians and designers), and salaried (exempt professionals). Hourly people would be paid 1.5 OT pay; hourly-salaried, straight OT pay; and salaried, no overtime pay.

3. They prepared a schedule of all salaries, billable percentages, and overtime compensation earned by each person in the company. This allowed management to spot potential abusers easily.

4. They restructured the bonus plan so that salaried people were the only ones eligible to receive more than a token bonus. Hourly and hourly-salaried people were eligible to receive only a token year-end bonus (gift) from the company.

5. They granted a total of $50,000 in raises to employees thought to be most deserving, using market value rather than past overtime earnings as the biggest component to determine adjustment.

6. They retrained all managers in basic supervision and the company performance appraisal process, so that they would be more inclined to give positive feedback to hard-working employees who weren't getting paid for every hour they put in.

7. They communicated the new program—including employee classification, bonus program, and philosophy—to each affected employee both individually and through the company internal newsletter.

As a result of these steps, over the next year the firm realized net savings of $350,000 to $400,000 on overtime for salaried professionals and an increase in the firm's overall billable percentage to close to 70 percent. There was no turnover directly attributed to elimination of overtime compensation. Voluntary turnover was as low as it had ever been for the firm. Overtime compensation paid to hourly and hourly-salaried people fell from $450,000 to $300,000, which could probably be attributed to the fact that professionals were no longer getting paid OT and they were now watching it more closely. Moreover, there were less complaints and morale problems from honest employees who had felt they were being penalized because of overtime abuses by others.

The problems this firm faced are typical of many larger firms that pay overtime compensation to exempt staff. Most principals in design firms will agree that this is not a 40-hour-per-week business. That being the case, it probably isn't a good idea for a firm to be locked into paying overtime in any form to exempt staff. Firms have a hard time monitoring overtime closely, and too many staffers abuse overtime policies. Excessive overtime pay can significantly erode a firm's profits, compromising the firm's ability to use bonuses and raises to reward performance.

9.8 BONUS/INCENTIVE COMPENSATION

Lots of firms in the design business have what they call an "incentive" compensation plan, but most of these plans are really nothing more than discretionary profit distribution plans. That's not to say that they may not serve a valuable purpose, but they don't often conform to the compensation experts' ideas on what an incentive compensation program should be.

What is *incentive compensation*? One definition is that it's compensation for achieving certain goals that is paid to individuals above and beyond their basic compensation. Also present in most definitions of incentive compensation is that the individual who is eligible to receive it should have clearly defined criteria for performance and clearly defined rewards for meeting or exceeding the defined performance criteria.

If this definition of incentive compensation is accepted as valid, then it becomes clear that most design firms' bonus plans don't really qualify as incentive compensation plans. Why is that? There are a number of reasons (see Figure 9.8).

1. The time lapse between the positive behavior and the reward is often too long.
2. The behavior or action that will be rewarded is rarely spelled out clearly.
3. As more firms come up with some variation on the annual bonus plan, it makes any one firm's plan less unique and less of an attraction for new and existing employees.
4. When a company has had a sizeable bonus pool year after year, people start to feel it's an automatic part of their entitlement as employees.
5. Firms don't fund the incentive compensation plan if profits are low; therefore, the employee will only get the reward if the firm achieves certain profit goals.

FIGURE 9.8 Problems with typical incentive compensation plans

To start with, bonus programs aren't necessarily incentive compensation plans. Many are purely discretionary profit distribution vehicles. The people who participate in the plan are often kept in the dark as to how the company or their department or unit is performing. They aren't privy to any performance data. More often than not, there are no performance criteria, and if they do exist they are so nebulous that they have little value. The behavior or action that will be rewarded is rarely spelled out clearly.

Another problem is that the time lapse between the positive behavior and the reward is often too long to be a motivator. For most employees, the thought that something they do in January will result in a bigger bonus at the end of December is not a compelling motivator. Firms that pay out bonuses once a year probably aren't getting the full value from the money they are spending. Some companies increase the frequency of bonus distributions to a monthly schedule in order to allow employees to more readily see the difference from their high performance.

As more firms come up with some variation on the annual bonus plan, it makes any one firm's plan less unique and less of an attraction for new and existing employees. Just about every company in this business has some variation of a bonus plan in place. As a result, they have come to be expected as simply another part of the employee's entitlement. When a company has had a sizeable bonus pool year after year, people start to feel it's automatic. They fail to realize that their individual performance affects the overall company performance. In some states, this interpretation has gone so far as to allow the courts to rule that bonus compensation is in fact part of an employee's entitlement, to the extent of ordering companies to pay a prorated portion to employees who are fired.

Firms sometimes fail to fund the incentive compensation plan because of low profits. In effect, even if the employee achieves his or her goals, he or she will only get the reward if the firm achieves its own profit goals. What does this say to employees who know they themselves have done all that was within their power and who have consistently performed above and beyond expectations while watching others who do not take their goals so seriously drag the firm down? Just about everyone has heard the complaint of a disgruntled design professional who knows all of his or her projects made money or who knows his or her department or branch was profitable, yet didn't receive any bonus compensation because the rest of the firm didn't fare as well. Either they begin seeking employment elsewhere, or their future effort and performance falls closer the lowest common denominator.

Firms that sincerely want to put the incentive back in their incentive compensation plans won't turn a deaf ear to these issues. They may come up with a number of solutions to these problems that fit their unique needs. Be pragmatic. The best solution is the one that works.

One simple plan to consider is to first determine who will be included in the special bonus program—maybe branch managers, department heads, or whoever. Notify them that they are now part of a special program and will be entitled to additional compensation based on company performance and a subjective evaluation of their performance. At bonus time, divide 10 percent of the overall profits among all employees, including those in the special bonus pool. Base distribution on the percentage each employee's salary represents of all salaries and a graduated formula based on profit levels. For example the special bonus program participants could have between 10 and 19 percent of profits divided among them, according to the following schedule:

If firm's profit ≤ 3%, management bonus pool = 0%
If firm's profit > 3% and ≤ 7%, management bonus pool = 10%
If firm's profit > 7% and ≤ 10%, management bonus pool = 15%
If firm's profit > 10% and ≤ 15%, management bonus pool = 17.5%
If firm's profit > 15%, management bonus pool = 19%

Other points for administration of the program: Have the individuals who are part of the special bonus program submit the criteria they want to be evaluated on prior to the beginning of each fiscal year. These must be agreed on by management. Allow new people to be added to the special bonus pool only at the beginning

Incentive Compensation Plan Sample Distributions

Example #1:   Company earns $1,100,000 profit on $6 million in sales

$$\frac{\$1,100K}{\$6,000K} = 18.3\% \text{ profit}$$

1. Management group   19% of $1,100,000 = $209,000
2. All employees   10% of $1,100,000 = $110,000

Example #2:   Company earns $580,000 profit on $6 million in sales

$$\frac{\$580K}{\$6,000K} = 9.7\% \text{ profit}$$

1. Management group   15% of 580K = $86,000
2. All employees   10% of 580K = $58,000

Example #3:   Company earns $750,000 profit on $6 million in sales

$$\frac{\$750K}{\$6,000K} = 12.5\% \text{ profit}$$

1. Management group   17.5% of $750K = $131,250
2. All employees   10.0% of $750K = $75,000

Example #4:   Company earns $190,000 profit on $6 million in sales

$$\frac{\$190K}{\$6,000K} = 3.17\% \text{ profit}$$

1. Management group   10% of $190K = $19,000
2. All employees   10% of $190K = $19,000

FIGURE 9.9   Sample incentive compensation plan distributions

of a new year. Pay out bonus compensation twice per year. Post overall company profits and year-to-date sales each month for all to see. The President/CEO or a bonus committee should divide the special bonus pool among plan participants based on an evaluation of how well they met predetermined criteria (see Figure 9.9). Each person should be informed individually about his or her bonus.

Another idea that is gaining popularity for incentive compensation programs is to pay out the rewards over some extended period of time. One southeastern A/E firm

INTERVIEW

"One Man's View Of Incentive Compensation"

Incentive compensation is a subject that interests just about everyone running a design firm today. Yet, only very few A/E/P firms have plans in place. This month, **A/E Business Review** interviews Mark C. Zweig, Boston-based consultant to the A/E/P industry and former Human Resources Director for two ENR top-500 design firms on the subject of incentive compensation.

A/EBR: "You claim that practically no one in this industry has a "real" incentive compensation plan in place. What does incentive compensation mean to you?"

Zweig: "A lot of firms think that they have incentive compensation plans, and many others have tried to develop one. The problem comes down to what is meant by the term 'incentive.' To me, that means that if an employee achieves or does 'X,' they will get 'Y' reward. The goals to accomplish are well defined in advance of the activity, and the rewards, too, are clearly spelled out for hitting that goal (or goals)."

"All too often, firms use a discretionary bonus plan, paid out subjectively and, to a large extent, arbitrarily. Typically, this bonus is paid out at the end of the fiscal or calendar year, or in some rare instances, twice per year. The driving theory behind these plans is that employees will be motivated to see to it that the firm is profitable, and that this will motivate staffers to insure that projects are profitable."

SEPTEMBER 1989

A/EBR: "So what's wrong with a plan that pays people based on the overall company performance?"

Zweig: "I don't think you can ignore overall profitability in the equation—not too many firms are so well capitalized that they can afford to do otherwise. However, consider how demotivating it is to a department manager, studio head, or project manager who knows that what he is doing is making money for the firm, only to have **his** rewards contingent on the activity of other people whom he has absolutely no control over. There are other weaknesses in these plans. First, since just about every company has a bonus plan, they aren't unique and therefore don't significantly differentiate one firm over another when it comes time for a potential employee to make a job change, or, perhaps even more importantly, when an existing employee contemplates a job change. The other problem is that when a company has paid out good bonuses for a number of years, employees take them for granted and simply consider them part of their regular compensation. When bonuses aren't as high one year, employees get angry, and feel they have been cheated by the firm."

A/EBR: "Well, what do you suggest firms do?"

Zweig: "Firms should design plans that spell out the exact portion of the incentive compensation pool an individual will get for a particular level of performance. The performance rewarded should be that which the individual is in control of. For example,

rewarding project managers on the basis of project profitability when they participate in setting fees for their jobs. Or rewarding on the basis of utilization rates for branch office or department managers. I'd be interested to know if any of your readers know of a branch office manager who is evaluated on the profitability of his office and who feels that his allocation of corporate overhead is fair!"

"Another thing I feel very strongly about is that the portion of the pie should increase as the performance level exceeds the standard. Too many plans I have studied pay a set percentage of profits or cost savings, and don't grant extra rewards for incrementally higher performance."

A/EBR: "What else do you think is important?"

Zweig: "I feel very strongly about the merits of keeping people informed on their progress toward objectives. Performance should be posted conspicuously. People should also get rewards as soon as possible after the activity which merits it. It's simple behaviorism. They see the cause and effect. Quarterly and even monthly performance measurement and reward distribution goes a long way toward reinforcing the incentive plan. And one final point. Don't design an incentive plan and then change it six months later, or each year. Think it through under a wide range of 'what if' scenarios, and stick with it. Otherwise, management's credibility goes down the toilet."

Editor's Note:—Mark C. Zweig can be reached at (506) 651-1559.

FIGURE 9.10   Reprint of article about incentive compensation

has what they refer to as a Deferred Merit Incentive Bonus (D.M.I.B.) Program. This program computes bonuses based on a complex formula that incorporates mutually agreed upon goals for individuals and the overall company's profitability. It then has a long-term payout period, with one-third of the bonus paid in each of the following three years. The strength of this program is that it helps serve as a long-term "golden handcuff," as the future bonus earned is only paid if the employee is still employed by the firm at the time it is due. The weakness is that the payout is pretty far out in time from the performance that merited it.

9.9 CONCLUSION

As the biggest single expense on a design firm's income statement, compensation deserves close scrutiny. Compensation is a necessity of life—some professionals work only for a paycheck, while to others it's a source of personal satisfaction.

People's compensation varies greatly, depending on position, length of tenure, performance, ownership, the market for services in their discipline, and other factors. The amount of compensation the firm can afford to pay is limited by the work it sells, the fees it generates, and how it performs for its clients. The challenge for management is to distribute compensation fairly enough to support and reward all employees. Unfortunately, too often those who complain the most get the lion's share of the rewards.

Design firm management faces an overwhelming array of compensation-related issues. Dealing with these issues requires an understanding of the whole compensation picture. Knowing how to set salaries, make pay adjustments, comply with all laws governing overtime payment, and distribute incentive compensation are all critical for a firm to make the best use of its compensation budget.

10

EMPLOYEE BENEFITS

There must be more to life than having everything.

—Maurice Sendak

10.1 INTRODUCTION

Employee benefits are often referred to as "fringe" benefits to distinguish them from that other more basic benefit of employment—wages or salary. While no design firm can afford to treat fringe benefits as "frills," most would do well to leave them at the fringe where they rightfully belong. For this reason, a minimum of space in this text will be devoted to benefits.

Prior to the Great Depression, employee benefits were a novel idea. Thanks to the efforts of crusaders in organized labor and government, benefits have done much to improve the lot of the average American worker. Some of these benefits, like unemployment insurance and the employer contribution to Social Security taxes, are now part of the law and every employer must provide them. Others, such as vacation, sick leave, and health insurance (legally required in some states), may as well be legally required, for they are almost universally provided and employees consider them part of their entitlement, regardless of where they work. The real cost of these benefits also includes the considerable time and expense of administering them.

Nevertheless, at this point, many HR professionals tend to overemphasize the importance of benefits, while employees have come to take them for granted. Most design firms these days have benefits that are relatively comparable, eliminating any major competitive edge they might give you recruiting in the employment market.

Good benefits may help you get people to join the company. Unusually poor benefits may eventually cause people to leave. Having no benefits will make it hard to hire anyone. But benefits don't *motivate* people to perform any better. Provide

233

what you must and what you can in the way of benefits. Just remember that they are "sticky downward," meaning that it's easy to give people new benefits, but very difficult to take them away.

10.2 PAID AND UNPAID LEAVE

Paid leave consists of time the firm pays employees for, even though they are not at work. This could include everything from lunches to jury duty, but for the most part it means sick leave, vacation, and holidays. There is a distinct, obvious reason and purpose for each of these benefits, and it is not advisable to treat the three interchangeably. Remember that with all paid leave, the firm loses not only the wages it pays with no work in return, but also the opportunity cost and potential fee loss from not having staff members around when they may be needed. With unpaid leave, on the other hand, the firm saves the wage expense, but still must contend with the opportunity cost and potential fee loss from having a temporary vacancy.

Employees should be allowed adequate sick leave to rest and recuperate from routine illnesses and injuries without financial suffering. Five days per year is a conservative figure; some firms provide more. Sick leave should be reserved for the sick. It is not part of an employee's entitlement and there is no reason to let people use up their leftover sick time on "mental health days" or to compensate them for accrued sick time at the end of the year or when they leave the firm. However, there is no harm—and possibly some benefit—in allowing employees to accrue sick time indefinitely, in case of a severe illness or injury.

If abuse of sick time is a widespread problem, it may help to offer some premium for saving sick days—such as exchanging extra sick days (beyond a certain minimum) for legitimate vacation days at a discount of, perhaps, two sick days per vacation day. The problem with this kind of policy is that as most design firms who have tried it will agree, it probably doesn't really serve as a deterrent for those who want to abuse sick leave.

Sick leave is another case where the legal requirements differ for exempt and nonexempt employees. Firms are under no legal obligation to provide sick leave to hourly, nonexempt employees, although most firms choose to do so, both out of concern for employee welfare and because it is the norm. Salaried, exempt employees, on the other hand, must be compensated as usual even though they miss a day or two of work in a particular week. In case of a protracted illness, you may place the employee on unpaid leave after sick leave runs out. Just don't get in a position of docking a salaried employee wages for sick time, regardless of whether he or she has exceeded the normal allowance. You may have to treat that person as nonexempt from then on, paying time and a half for all hours over 40 worked in any week.

If employees abuse sick leave, they should be warned and, if necessary, let go. If employees exceed the sick leave allowance through no fault of their own, you should let them borrow sick days. One small architectural firm docked the pay of a promising new project manager because he missed two days of work while bedridden with the flu. According to company policy, employees could not begin to accrue sick days until they had been with the firm six months. Never mind that the project manager had already worked plenty of unpaid overtime and weekends in his first five months on the job, or that he was not even aware of the policy until he received his paycheck. In fact, if he had wanted to pursue the matter with the Department of Labor, the firm might have ended up in trouble, especially if it were revealed that they had treated other salaried employees in the same manner, and thus owed them time and a half for every overtime hour worked since their pay had been docked.

Although this project manager knew he had been mistreated, he was not a complainer by nature and felt it was unprofessional to haggle over such details. However, about this time he did happen to get a call from one of his former co-workers who had started his own firm. And when the fellow tried to recruit him away, he wasn't of a mind to offer much resistance. Result? The firm saved two days' pay but lost one of its best young project managers.

Vacations are an opportunity for people to refresh and rejuvenate themselves and, theoretically, return as more effective employees. While firms don't have to provide vacation time, the alternative of high turnover, low morale, and recruiting difficulties is generally prohibitive. Once a vacation policy is set, firms may be legally required to observe it. So keep it simple and use good sense.

Two weeks is the norm almost everywhere. It's fine to reward loyalty by allowing more vacation the longer employees stay with the firm. However, that doesn't mean that a newly recruited senior project manager who got three weeks vacation at his previous job should have to go back to only two weeks. Also, employees should be allowed to accumulate vacation time within reason. Most firms compensate employees for unused vacation time, but don't let anyone build up such a stockpile that you might owe them an alarming lump sum if they left the firm.

When employees use their vacation time should be mutually agreed upon with their supervisors. Some firms make a rule against taking vacations at certain busy times of year, or they require that people stagger vacations at the times everyone wants to take off (Christmas and summer). There is nothing wrong with this, as long as it is handled equitably and employees are given fair warning of any restrictions on when they may use their vacation time.

The best policy on holidays is to follow the norm of other firms in your area and to recognize that this norm varies from region to region. Most firms provide somewhere between 6 and 11 holiday days. There is no need to give employees every federal holiday, and not many firms can afford to be so generous. Don't give away more than you have to, but don't require that employees work on a day that everybody in your area has off. To get maximum goodwill effect from holiday time, consider substituting a firm-specific holiday (perhaps a Founder's Day) for one of the marginal federal holidays. Though the total number of holidays remains the same, employees may see this as a unique benefit rather than part of their entitlement. It's a good opportunity to differentiate your firm and enrich its corporate culture.

The same advice goes for other forms of paid leave, such as "personal days," a death in the family, and preparing for or taking registration exams. Jury duty may be required. Be conservative, but do make some allowances in your policies for the inevitable. For the average design professional, these miscellaneous paid leave situations really don't amount to much time taken from the firm, and in the case of salaried professionals, they are usually more than made up in late nights working at crunch time. It is important, however, to have some policy and try to make sure everyone adheres to it. If these issues are handled on a case-by-case, catch-as-catch-can basis, someone is going to end up getting preferential treatment.

Policies on unpaid leave vary widely. In some cases (for example, lengthy illness or educational leave) employees are assured their job will be awaiting when they return. Firms that allow a seriously ill employee to take a leave of absence must also allow pregnant employees the same privilege. Again, state laws vary on pregnancy leave; check with your attorney. In other cases, firms permit an employee to take a sabbatical for personal reasons, but they give no assurance they will be able to bring that person back at the same position, or even at all.

If you do allow a leave of absence, it should probably not include a loss of seniority. This, of course, does not apply to employees who take a "leave of absence" to work for a competitor. At any rate, when formulating a policy and when discussing a leave of absence with an employee, be aware of what you are committing the firm to, because you may be legally bound to make good on an explicit or implicit promise.

10.3 MANDATORY INSURANCE

Nowhere is the two-edged sword of benefits more apparent than with mandatory insurance. On the one hand, firms get no motivational mileage for paying social security taxes and other mandatory employment taxes. And in this case, failing to provide them can do more than demotivate employees; it can get a firm in serious trouble with the law. For this reason, and because they cost firms so much, it is worth reviewing the four kinds of mandatory insurance. These include:

1. *Social Security:* Otherwise known as FICA, which stands for Federal Insurance Contributions Act. Employers withhold half the tax from employees' earnings and make a matching contribution. The current rate (1990) is 7.65 percent on the first $51,300 an employee earns. In other words, the most an employee can pay at this point is $3,924.45 per year. Ostensibly a kind of government-sponsored pension, the Social Security system benefits retired people, widows and orphans, and the disabled.

2. *Worker's Compensation:* Worker's comp is a no-fault insurance program that was created to protect both employer and employees. It protects employers from potential lawsuits from workers who are injured, get sick, or are killed on the job or as a direct result of their work. For employees, it provides 100 percent coverage of medical expenses, support

payments for those who can't work, and lump-sum settlements in case of death or permanent injury. Premiums are paid wholly by the employer and depend on the occupational hazards of the industry you work in and the jobs your employees perform. Firms can realize significant savings in their worker's comp premiums by making sure to assign people in the lowest possible hazard code and reviewing the assignments annually.

3. *Unemployment insurance:* Federal and state unemployment insurance requirements are not a favorite of most employers, who feel some workers abuse the system. Premiums represent a considerable expense to the average firm, depending on the number of people out of work in your state and the number of people filing claims coming from your firm. Firms laying off a significant number of workers will definitely see a corresponding rise in their unemployment insurance premiums. Firms do have a right to challenge an improper claim from an employee who was fired for nonperformance or misconduct. Some firms are reluctant to challenge claims for fear of triggering a wrongful termination suit. However, any firm that is serious about controling costs will sooner or later find itself obliged to challenge a former employee's claim. Just make sure you are on solid ground and have good documentation of why the employee was let go. A consultant or attorney who specializes in employment can be a great asset in this situation. Knowledgeable consultants may also be able to save firms quite a bit of money with a thorough review of recordkeeping, premiums, and tracking of claims.

4. *Statutory disability:* Depending on the state, it may also be mandatory to provide short-term disability insurance for employees who become ill or injured and unable to work for a reason not covered under worker's comp.

In short, mandatory insurance is just another cost of doing business. There really isn't much that design firms can do about it.

10.4 VOLUNTARY INSURANCE

Unlike the mandatory insurance items discussed in Section 10.3, voluntary insurance is, as the name clearly implies, provided at the employer's discretion. Voluntary insurance includes life insurance, health insurance (no longer voluntary in some states), dental insurance, and disability insurance. Of course, for some of these items the term "voluntary" is relative. Almost all firms provide at least some medical and life insurance, and employees expect them to.

Voluntary insurance (as well as some mandatory insurance, such as worker's comp) is available from many providers in many different forms and at many different prices. The degree of choice in the open market affords firms the opportunity to consider carefully what coverage they need and then shop around for the best deal. With the way insurance premiums, particularly for health coverage, have gone up in recent years, firms have been looking *very* closely at their different options. The insurance companies have responded with an even greater proliferation of plans and options. Some firms may want to consider retaining a benefits consultant to sort out the options and pick the best one. At the least, they can deal with a reputable independent broker, knowledgeable in employee benefits, who represents a range of insurers and can make a recommendation with some objectivity. A word of caution: Don't rely on a broker who isn't experienced in health benefits. They won't be able to save you money or fully explain all options that are available to you like one who is experienced.

Life insurance comes in two forms: whole insurance and term insurance. *Whole insurance* is basically a kind of investment. It is significantly more expensive than term insurance, which has no cash value. Firms can buy term insurance at fairly reasonable group rates. No physical exams are usually required and the cost is fairly constant and reasonable, depending principally on the employee's age (for example, approximately $200 per $100,000 of coverage for employees in their 30s). Many employees, especially young, single people, could not care less about life insurance. But it takes on more meaning for employees with families and can be an attractive feature to point out when recruiting these people.

In this day and age, employees take it for granted that employers will provide health insurance. But given the skyrocketing insurance premiums of the last decade, no firm can afford to take insurance expenses for granted. Today, it is a rare design firm that pays 100 percent of employee insurance premiums for family coverage. Most require employees to pay a percentage of the family premium. Some are even requiring employees to pay a portion of their own premiums. Not only does this reduce the firm's immediate expense; it also means that employees will share the burden as premiums mount, rather than the firm alone absorbing the entire impact of the ever more complex, technologically advanced, and expensive system of health care in this country.

There is plenty of good information available on the various aspects of health insurance policies. This is not the place to go into a discussion of deductibles, out-of-pocket maximums, and so on. Nevertheless, it is worth touching on a few key points of interest to design firms.

By now, most everyone is familiar with Health Maintenance Organizations (HMOs), which are able to offer lower premiums by careful cost control, reliance on their own clinics, and negotiation of lower fees with physicians and other health care providers. Some firms are required to offer HMOs to their employees if there is one available in the area, and must pay the same amount toward the HMO premium that they would pay toward their conventional insurance plan. There are also firms that offer only HMOs.

Many employees, however, reject these plans because their family doctor isn't part of the HMO. Often it is the younger, healthier employees who haven't developed a relationship with a particular doctor who opt for the HMO. This in turn robs the conventional insurance group of its healthiest members and drives up rates for the remaining staff.

Preferred Provider Organizations (PPOs) may be an attractive alternative to conventional plans or HMOs. They give employees the option of seeing their regular doctor on the usual 80/20 basis (or whatever it might be) or going to one of the preferred providers—a clinic or a doctor who belongs to the plan—at a lower cost. The result is often the flexibility of traditional insurance at HMO prices. The problem is PPOs are not available everywhere. Look into PPOs in your area.

Although the law has been in effect for several years, many firms are still ignoring or paying insufficient attention to COBRA, (the Consolidated Omnibus Budget Reconciliation Act of 1986). The Act requires that employers of a certain size give employees and their dependents a chance to continue participating in the group insurance plan at their own expense after the employee leaves the firm (except in cases of gross misconduct), after the employee's death, after a divorce, or after a dependent stops being a dependent under the terms of the plan. This applies to all group plans of which any company member has 20 or more employees, which includes most plans. The extended coverage, if elected, must be made available for 36 months in most cases. In certain special cases (for example, termination for gross misconduct) the requirement is 18 months. Employers may add a 2 percent administrative charge to the total cost of continued coverage. Some states, too, have similar laws on the books.

The place where most firms stumble in complying with COBRA is in proper *notification*. Employers must notify employees of their rights under COBRA both at the time coverage begins *and* when the "qualifying event" occurs (for example, the employee leaves the firm). The penalties for failing to notify employees include a $100-per-day fine. Employers who fail to provide continued coverage as required by COBRA may not be able to deduct their insurance payments from taxable income. Make sure to include a notification of COBRA rights in your employee manual for new employees, insert a memo on the law into health insurance information provided to new employees, and make written and verbal notification a standard part of the dehiring procedure, including a signed acknowledgment from the employee in each of these cases.

Dental insurance is gradually becoming part of the employee's entitlement. Many firms now offer dental plans, which usually emphasize *preventive* care and are fairly reasonably priced. As with life insurance, dental plans are more important to workers with families who make a lot more trips to the dentist. Again, look at what your competitors are doing and try not to be too different.

At one time, many firms had mandatory waiting periods for new employees before insurance benefits began. The point was to save a little money in premiums while waiting to see if the new person was going to work out. This policy isn't really fair or practical for employees, who probably cannot afford a lapse in coverage and should not be expected to pay their own premiums while waiting for yours to begin, especially if you've recruited them away from another firm. Any possible savings from such a policy are far outweighed by the difficulties it may cause your recruits or people who want to join the firm, as well as the inevitable resentment that will result if they don't find out about the policy until they've already made the jump.

One final point on voluntary insurance: Firms with less than 10 employees will not be able to buy insurance at group rates on their own. However, small firms can get group insurance rates through professional associations like the American

Institute of Architects (AIA) and American Consulting Engineers Council (ACEC), or through their local chamber of commerce or small business association. For many firms, this is the *only* alternative to paying high premiums or else providing no insurance at all.

10.5 RETIREMENT PLANS

All retirement plans are in one form or another a kind of deferred compensation. Because employees usually don't get their hands on this money until years after it is paid, the motivational effect is very diluted. Nevertheless, retirement plans are an attractive selling point for job candidates (especially the middle-aged), they reward loyalty, and they demonstrate that a firm cares about its people. If nothing else, retirement plans may give firms a means to ease less productive workers out of the system and make room for the advancement of younger workers. To encourage saving for retirement, the federal government allows employers and employees to fund certain retirement plans tax-free, at least until the money is withdrawn from the plan.

Every firm, in effect, contributes toward a retirement plan for its employees through the Social Security System. However, when you get outside this familiar territory, the options grow much more complex. Retirement plans are one area where firm ownership should not learn by trial and error. The best advice is to retain a knowledgeable pension consultant or contact your banking institution's trust department before you do anything. Following are some of the retirement plan alternatives that a good pension consultant will evaluate for a client.

A pension is a fixed amount paid by an employer or its representative at regular intervals to a former employee or the employee's surviving dependents for past services rendered. Pensions are either funded (money is set aside for future payments) or nonfunded (the plan is on a "pay as you go" basis). In a *flat payment method*, the amount of pension payments vary according to a benefit formula, which expresses some relationship between wages and salaries earned while employed and the pension payment. In the case of funded plans, payment may be on an *annuity basis*, where the money set aside is invested in securities, real estate, and so on, and the value of the fund will also have an impact on the size of payments.

Once a pension plan is set up, firms are obligated to pay into the plan year after year. Employers will face legal penalties for failing to meet their pension commitments. Obviously, pension plans are best suited to larger, durable organizations, which are going to be around long enough to keep the plan funded. This leaves out the average design firm.

So-called *defined contribution plans*, (including profit-sharing, Keogh, and the 401(k) offer a lot more flexibility to design firms. They are a lot more widespread in the design industry for good reason. Unlike pensions, they make no promises of what the retirement benefits will be or even what the employer contributions will be except in general terms (5 to 10 percent of salary for example). Firms fund them as they are able and keep track of the value of each employee's account.

A well-designed and administered plan should be qualified by the IRS for tax-deferred status. The firm may deduct all contributions to the plan as a business expense, while participants avoid current taxes on the amount contributed on their behalf. By the same token, violating the rules of the plan may make both employer and employee liable for back taxes and penalties on the amount of the contributions.

The best of these plans, and the most popular among design firms, is probably the 401(k) (so-named for a paragraph in the tax code), otherwise known as the Optional Salary Reduction Plan. A 401(k) plan is part of a conventional profit-sharing plan. Many of these firms have profit-sharing plans that they don't fund; they do, however, fund their 401(k) through some sort of matching provisions. This plan's strength is its simplicity. Employees simply save a portion of their salary that is deducted from their paychecks before taxes. Growth of the fund through interest and/or investment growth isn't taxed, either, until the money is taken out. The plan works much like an Individual Retirement Account (IRA), except that the maximum annual contribution allowed is significantly higher. There are penalties for early withdrawal. Compared to the IRA, the 401(k) also offers certain tax advantages upon withdrawal at retirement.

Whatever retirement plan a firm chooses, federal law requires that it inform employees annually of their benefits. Larger firms (over 100 employees) must complete and distribute ERISA Form 5500 (ERISA is the Employees Retirement Income Security Act of 1974– 75). This is another area where a competent benefits consultant can help firms make sure they are in compliance. Retirement plans are a major investment for firms, and the costs of mishandling them are formidable.

10.6 OTHER BENEFITS

Common practice is that if you work for a restaurant you get free meals, if you work for an airline you get free travel, and so on. Design firms won't find it much of a benefit to offer their employees free design services, but there are many other free "perks"—such as company cars, club memberships, use of a company condo in Florida, and so on—that they can offer to reward employees.

The best approach with perks is to give away as few as possible, but when you do, give something that is really valuable to your people. What people find valuable varies from one firm to another. In a urban area, it may be a parking spot. In the suburbs, it may be a country club membership. Individual preferences also come into play. If you want to hire a key person who happens to live 50 miles from your office, a company car may make the difference. Just remember that once given away, these benefits are hard to take back.

Company cars are probably the single most coveted—and most expensive—special benefit. Some high-end design firms even provide principals and top managers with luxury import cars; in many cases these vehicles are "wet"; that is, gas, oil, and maintenance are also provided at company expense. Like other perks, company cars also create accounting hassles for firms, who must determine the amount they were used for business and then charge employees for the difference or show it as taxable income on their W-2s. A car allowance may be preferable to a company car in some instances. The 7.65 percent employer portion toward FICA on $300/month extra salary income could be avoided by paying a $300/month car allowance instead. Consult your accountant on this one, though.

Principals and top managers generally receive more perks than other employees. Be judicious and discreet in the awarding of special privileges so as not to create a two-class society of "haves" and "have nots." One firm bought new Jaguars for its three principals at the same time they decided not to pay out any annual bonuses to staff. Needless to say, this created some morale problems.

Finally, it should be remembered that "free" perks are hardly ever free to the firm. Look at perks as part of the total compensation package; they have a definite cash value. At one time firms might have been able to provide perks to employees on a pre-tax basis for less than the employees could have procured them on their own. Tax reform has changed much of that. The perquisites of the privileged class in businesses are coming under ever-increasing scrutiny by the IRS.

10.7 CONCLUSION

Benefits are a no-win situation for the average design firm. They rarely help you, but they can create a myriad of problems for you if they are not handled properly. Employees like benefits because most are tax-free. And they probably have a right to expect them in this day and age, but firms are advised to make employees bear some of the burden of potential budget-busters such as health insurance, and to conserve resources for the kinds of benefits that really motivate professionals — salaries and bonuses. Nevertheless, the cost of benefits have gone up twice as fast as pay in the last several decades. Employers have a right to wonder where it will stop.

Benefit administration is usually left to the personnel administrator, personnel manager, or director of finance and administration. Just note that, as with most administrative chores, although they not may be exciting, benefits do need to be handled professionally by someone knowledgeable.

11

POLICIES AND PROCEDURES

Any fool can make a rule.

—Henry David Thoreau

11.1 INTRODUCTION

Just about every design firm with 15 or more staff members has a personnel policy manual or a personnel policy and procedures manual. These manuals typically explain all of the firm's decisions on how to handle recurring personnel questions and issues. They are usually developed in an attempt to introduce consistency and fairness into management decision making with regard to staff.

Policies are official statements of company position or decisions on some specific issues. Procedures are the means by which policies are implemented. They may also include the operating provisions of policies. There are some very good reasons why every design firm should have formal personnel policies and procedures clearly articulated:

1. There are vast differences in how firms deal with staff issues. You can't assume that every staff member knows exactly what the company's policies and procedures are.
2. The policy and procedure manual provides an opportunity for the company to explain what type of behavior is expected from staff members.
3. A properly designed and worded set of policies and procedures can minimize many potential employment-related liability issues. These include the firm's policies on hiring, promotion, termination, benefits, sexual harassment, grievances, and so forth.

243

4. Formalized policies and procedures can also minimize non-employment-related liabilities on issues such as confidentiality of information, conflicts of interest, gifts or special favors, stamping or sealing of all final drawings, and determination of who has contracting authority to commit the firm's resources.

5. Formalized policies and procedures may take the heat off management at times when difficult decisions have to be made.

6. A policy and procedure manual provides one central place where all employee benefits can be summarized and maintained.

11.2 POLICY MANUAL CONSTRUCTION

The form of a design firm's policy manual may be as important as its contents. Policy manuals should be clear and concise, yet comprehensive enough to cover recurring situations and situations that the firm can reasonably anticipate coming up.

Some firms have two documents to cover different or overlapping areas of their personnel policy and procedures. For example, firms may have both a policy manual and some sort of an employee handbook. All too often, they keep the policy manual in the hands of their managers exclusively, yet furnish an employee handbook to everyone in the firm. Generally, firms are best served to have *one* document that is provided to every single employee, both full and part time, regular or temporary.

To illustrate the problems of using two documents, consider the case of the following multidiscipline firm. First, they have a personnel policy and procedure manual, a copy of which is kept by the personnel administrator, the director of finance and administration, and each of their principals. The employees can see it if they make a request, but a copy is not issued to each employee. They also have an employee handbook that contains operational procedures for things such as expense report handling, typing requests, hours of work, and so on. These are distributed to all department secretaries. The result is that *no one* really knows exactly what the firm's policies and procedures are—a bad situation by any standard.

The policy manual should start with a well-organized table of contents that clearly identifies all of the key policy and procedure areas. Figure 11.1 is the table of contents for one real-life design firm's policy and procedures manual; it is a good starting point for a firm that wants to develop a manual or improve the one they currently have.

There are a number of published documents that can be very helpful in pulling a manual together. The American Consulting Engineers Council (ACEC) publishes a complete sample manual. In addition, other materials are available (including manuals on disk for quick customization to meet the firm's specific needs) that, although not specifically designed for A/E/P firms, may be helpful.

TABLE OF CONTENTS

FIGURE 11.1 Sample table of contents for a policies and procedures manual

FIGURE 11.1   *(Continued)*

The way a manual is bound can make a big difference in how easy it is for the firm to update as policies evolve. Rather than reprint the whole manual when policies change, the new policy is usually printed up on an addendum and distributed to employees. If the manual is in a GBC binder, employees will have no convenient way to insert the notification and many will be lost. The result is out-of-date manuals and lack of clarity on the firm's policies.

Policy manuals should be bound in three-ring, loose-leaf binders to facilitate changes. Print each policy on a separate page or pages, and show the date when it takes effect. This makes it easy to replace the old policies with updated ones. Employees simply open the binder, pull out the old page, and insert the new one. Although this practice may make the manual a little thicker than it would be otherwise, the whole thing won't have to be reproduced and redistributed just because one policy changes, and the changes won't be lost. Binders can be customized with the company name and logo, and they are relatively inexpensive if purchased in quantity.

Each individual manual should be numbered. Numbered policy manuals should be provided to all staff members. Each staff member, including all full- and part-time, regular and temporary employees should sign a receipt (see Figure 11.2) acknowledging that they have received copy [number] of the *XYZ Associates Company Policy and Procedures Manual,* and that they agree to read the manual and abide by all of the policies it contains.

Having the employee acknowledge receipt of the policy manual accomplishes three things:

1. It serves as an internal control procedure to help the company make sure that *every* employee has received a copy of the manual and that no one person was excluded inadvertently.

2. It ensures that no employee can claim ignorance of the company's policies as a defense against some disciplinary action taken on his or her behalf by the company.

3. Upon an employee's termination, the company should collect the policy manual issued to the employee. Having the copy numbered will help make sure that the company does in fact get back the manual they issued to that individual and not one given to someone else.

What could have been a major liability potential for one firm in the Southeast was averted because they had paid attention to policies and procedures. The firm was forced to terminate a senior project manager who was accused of and admitted to sexual harassment of another employee. The only thing that could have made this situation stickier would have been a wrongful termination suit. Fortunately, they were completely prepared to defend a lawsuit from the discharged employee because they had done their homework on the company policy manual they revised the previous year.

The steps this firm took in developing and distributing their policy manual included:

1. They published a complete policy manual that was reviewed by two outside experts: a human resources consultant and a competent labor attorney.

2. They distributed the policy manual to all employees and got an acknowledgement from each (similar to the receipt in Figure 11.2) to read and abide by the policies in the manual.

3. They established a clearly worded policy prohibiting sexual harassment and spelled out that disciplinary action for any offending employees could include termination of their employment with the firm.

4. They clearly spelled out their right to terminate any employee for any reason they deemed necessary as a result of actions that could be construed by management as potentially harmful to the company.

POLICY MANUAL RECEIPT

I, _____, acknowledge that I received copy #_____ of the Lowe & Granger, Inc. "Personnel Policies and Procedures Manual." I agree to read that manual, ask questions on any matters it contains that I do not understand, and follow the policies and procedures as described in the manual unless I have appropriate authorization (as noted in the manual) for an exception.

Employee Signature:_____ Date Signed: _____

FIGURE 11.2   Sample policy manual receipt acknowledgement

This company saved themselves from hours of headaches and potentially hundreds of thousands of dollars from a wrongful termination lawsuit by spending no more than a few thousand dollars on their personnel policy manual. They also protected themselves from a sexual harassment lawsuit through taking swift and decisive action in accordance with their published harassment policy.

11.3   POLICIES TO INCLUDE

Whatever else a design firm chooses to include in its policy manual, there are a number of important ingredients that should always be there. Some of these ingredients and the reasons for their importance are:

1. A description of the firm, including information on the company's history, growth, mission, goals, and overall organization chart. This is important information with which to familiarize new employees with the company and its management philosophy.

2. A statement of what the company policy manual is, including a description of the process for distributing the manual, an explanation of how changes will be made and revisions published, and a disclaimer that the manual does not represent an employment contract in any form. There should also be a statement to the effect that the company reserves the right to change its policies at any time and that any changes will supercede and replace previous policies. This information is extremely critical in minimizing the likelihood of an employee lawsuit based on changes in benefits or other policies.

3. An explanation of the various employee classifications, including the differences between exempt and nonexempt employees, regular and temporary employees, and full- and part-time employees. This is important information for all employees to understand because it will affect how they get paid, what their benefits are, and what kind of employment obligation the firm has made to them.

4. A description of the firm's policies regarding equal employment opportunity and affirmative action, as well as an indication of when and where the plans and the firm's progress toward stated goals can be reviewed. All employees should understand the company's commitment is to affirmative action and equal employment opportunity.

5. A statement on management's policy against hiring illegal aliens in accordance with the Immigration Reform and Control Act of 1986.

6. A statement of the company's policy prohibiting sexual harassment, as well as the process employees may follow who feel they have been subject to harassment. This is to ensure that the firm does not tolerate violations of Section 703 of Title VII of the Civil Rights Act of 1964. This kind of

policy, when supported and enforced, minimizes the firm's likelihood of losing a sexual harassment suit.

7. A statement of the company's policy on hours of operation and the number of hours of work expected for full and part-time employees.

8. A statement of how people will be paid, including time-sheet submittal, frequency and schedule for paychecks, paycheck distribution procedures, overtime, lunch hours, holidays, and all other issues related to pay. This policy must be in accordance with all laws related to payment of employees, and it will ensure that company employees have no misunderstandings related to their pay.

9. A statement of the company's policies and practices on salary and wage adjustments. This should include a statement of how often and on what schedule base pay is reviewed and how raise requests are processed. This section should also include a statement to the effect that there are no guaranteed raises for any employees at any time, unless the company has a policy of granting automatic pay increases based on cost-of-living changes, promotion, or for achieving professional registration. (Automatic pay increases, by the way, are not advised because of potential extenuating circumstances surrounding those events.)

10. A description of the company's policy on conducting performance appraisals. This should include the purpose of the appraisals, what the appraisal means, what areas are covered in the performance appraisal, and how the final appraisal forms or notes will be distributed.

11. The company's policies on all types of leaves of absence, including sick leave, vacation, medical, maternity/paternity, military, jury duty, educational or other personal leaves of absence. This should include an accrual schedule for sick and vacation leave, payment practices for employees under other types of leave, and information on how this leave affects benefits and seniority status. This is extremely critical, particularly as to how the company deals with maternity/paternity leave. Federal laws require that maternity leave be treated the same as any other illness, but some state statutes add a requirement that the firm *must* hire back an employee to their same job within a certain period of time after starting leave. Companies violating federal and state statutes on maternity leave are open to significant lawsuits from employees not treated in accordance with the law.

12. A description of how the company maintains its personnel records, including how the confidentiality of records is protected and how the employee can view what is in his or her personnel file.

13. A grievance procedure for employees to follow should they feel mistreated in any way. This will include a step-by-step process for the aggrieved employee to follow, and can help the company protect itself from employee lawsuits where the employee or employees have not followed the firm's established grievance procedure.

14. The company's policy prohibiting moonlighting. This is extremely important to minimize potential professional liability suits resulting from company employees performing unauthorized work on or off company premises.

15. A statement of the company's policy prohibiting conflicts of interest or potential conflicts of interest. This section should also include a statement prohibiting offering or receiving gifts or favors to or from those outside the organization. The purpose of this policy is to minimize potential conflict-of-interest problems with clients and government or regulatory officials.

16. A complete explanation of the company's policy on terminations and resignations. This is a particularly important policy and should establish both the company's and employee's rights in the event of either voluntary or involuntary termination due to lack of work, termination for cause, or termination for poor job performance. It should spell out the complete process for termination, including the employee's right to continue insurance under COBRA or other applicable state statutes. It should also state the company's policy on severance pay (if any), payment of all other accrued pay, as well as provisions for the employee to pay debts to the company.

17. A statement of the company's policy regarding safety and employee injury or illness on the job. This should spell out the fact that the company as well as all employees will comply with all OSHA (Occupational Health and Safety Administration) requirements as well as other safety requirements while performing work. It should also address the requirements for filing worker's compensation claims in accordance with state and federal worker's compensation laws in all offices the firm operates.

18. A statement of the company's policy prohibiting theft of company or client property and all disciplinary actions that could be taken against an employee who violates the policy. This policy may also contain a statement prohibiting duplication of company-owned or -developed computer software.

19. A description of the company's policy on providing references or other confidential personnel information to those outside the firm. The best policy: In general, don't do much more than confirm dates of employment, title upon departure, and last compensation, providing this information was already given to the former employee's potential new employer by the employee.

20. A description of the company's policy regarding stamping or sealing of drawings to conform to various state statutes and the requirements of the firm's professional liability carrier.

21. A description of the firm's policy regarding smoking while at work, to address the needs of both smokers and nonsmokers in the office.

22. A statement of the company's policy (if one exists) on any pre-employment tests required, including physical examinations. This, too, should be written in accordance with all applicable state and federal laws regarding pre-employment testing.

23. A section describing various operational issues, such as purchasing, parking, mail processing, reference library usage, use of company vehicles, use of company telephones for both business and nonbusiness purposes, soliciting for charity solicitations in the office, contracting authority, and so on. This catch-all section should deal with the typical day-to-day questions of a new or existing employee as they pertain to the company's operations.

24. A statement of the firm's procedures for processing employee expense reports, including how they are to be prepared, what the limits are, how they are submitted, and when they will be paid.

25. A statement of how the firm handles travel on company business, including making flight or other travel arrangements, meals and hotel expenses and limits, rental cars (including insurance on them), and other travel-related matters, including how to charge travel time.

26. A statement of the company's policy with respect to bad weather closings or inability to work due to bad weather. Again, certain statutes have to be considered that pertain to payment of an hourly worker who was sent home after he or she has reported to work.

27. A statement of how the firm handles incoming inquiries from the media to make sure no public relations damage is done to the firm or its clients. This should clearly spell out who these inquiries are to be directed to and what that person should and can say.

28. A complete section on professional development, including the firm's general policy toward training and its policy on tuition reimbursement and time off for educational purposes. This section should also include a clear statement of the firm's policy regarding payment for the costs of professional licenses and licensing examinations and for time off to take the exams.

29. A complete, detailed section on all mandatory and voluntary employee benefits, including conversion rights and requirements in each area where they exist. This section of the policy manual should address medical, life, dental, disability, worker's compensation, and unemployment insurance coverage as it relates to availability, eligibility, employee's share of costs, coverages, and applicability to differing types of employees. It should describe any profit-sharing, pension, 401(k), or other retirement plans the firm has in place. It should also include information on other benefits, such as special employee loans through the company's banking institution, wholesale club or other special discount purchasing memberships, credit union memberships, and other unique voluntary benefits the company offers.

Any firm that is updating or designing a company policy manual should submit their draft to a qualified local attorney knowledgeable in employment law for review *prior* to putting a copy in the hands of each of their employees.

11.4 COMPANY-POLICY–RELATED PROBLEMS

In spite of all a well-designed company policy manual can do for employees and for the firm that publishes and* distributes it, it can also backfire. Some of the typical problems with firms' policies include:

1. The lack of, or widespread unavailability of published policies and procedures can lead to resulting inconsistent management decision making and consequent employee confusion and morale problems.

2. Improperly worded maternity leave policies may require an employee to be back at work by a certain specified period of time regardless of what their doctor says. (This doesn't mean that in all states the company must give the exact same job back to the employee who takes a leave and returns to work by a certain date. Check with a local attorney knowledgeable in employment law.)

3. Ambiguous statements on a host of policy issues allow different people to have widely varied interpretations of what the policy says or means. Design firms often sacrifice clarity in an effort to maintain a maximum degree of flexibility, but it usually backfires.

4. No provisions, or poorly worded provisions about who can authorize exceptions to company policies can result in inconsistent treatment of employees, a potentially dangerous situation for the company when protected job groups (minorities, women, or older workers) are involved.

5. Multiple violations of the laws governing payment of overtime, including flex-time policies for nonexempt employees may allow the firm to avoid payment of overtime. Also, too rarely seen in design firms' policies is any explanation of what it means for an employee to be classified as exempt or non-exempt.

6. Lack of clear standards on how part-time and full-time employees are treated in the areas of benefits, vacation and sick leave accrual rates, and other matters could increase liability.

7. Lack of a defined vehicle and means for disseminating changes to the company's policies and procedures may result in employees not being informed of policy changes that directly affect them.

8. The use of the term "permanent" employee instead of "regular" employee has been construed in some states as a lifetime employment agreement in court cases involving wrongful termination.

9. Mandatory pre-employment testing for personality, intelligence, or skills and aptitudes that cannot be proved to accurately predict on-the-job performance, but that is actually used as input to the process of making hiring or promotion decisions can be extremely dangerous. Court cases have awarded significant damage settlements to plaintiffs who were kept out of a job or a company on this basis. The only exceptions to this are tests for typing speed

and accuracy or tests that evidence other specific skills required on the job. Again, check with competent labor counsel on any questions concerning pre-employment testing.

11.5   EXCEPTIONS TO COMPANY POLICIES

Whether a firm should make exceptions to company policies is a matter for individual discretion. What *is* important is that the firm clearly spell out how exceptions are made and who has the authority to make them in any specific case.

It is a rare firm that hasn't made an exception to its published policies and procedures at one time or another. The danger comes in two areas. One sort of problem arises when lots of different people are authorized to make exceptions and not all of them have the same philosophy, perspective, or understanding of the big picture for the firm. For example, some firms state that any *principal* is authorized to make exceptions, and they have 16 principals. Second, when certain individuals or groups of individuals end up being treated differently than others because of the way exceptions are made, inequities can do more than cause hard feelings—they can result in lawsuits when women, minorities, or other protected groups are involved.

One firm got sued by a clerk, who happened to be both a protected minority and a woman, when her request for an employee loan was denied. It turned out the company had a long-established practice of granting loans to white males, and didn't really have a good reason for turning down this woman's request.

Another firm got in trouble because of an inconsistent policy prohibiting nepotism. After two employees got married, only the female employee was told she would need to find a job elsewhere because of the company's policy prohibiting nepotism. To top it off, shortly after the woman found another job, one of the principals hired his son to be an errand boy in the office for the summer. The result was both morale *and* turnover problems for the firm.

The moral of the story is to keep exceptions to a minimum by designing fair, legal policies in the first place. The person or entity that can authorize exceptions should be clearly spelled out. And, when exceptions are made, considerations as to their effect on morale and protected employee classes should be given proper scrutiny. Finally, full documentation should be kept as to how and why the exception was made.

11.6   CONCLUSION

There's no excuse for a design firm not having a company personnel policy manual or a policy and procedures manual. Manuals serve multiple purposes and are usually designed to make management decision making with regard to personnel and operational issues consistent and fair. It can't be assumed that every staff member knows exactly what the firm's policies, procedures, and benefits are. The policy manual helps the company communicate the behavior that is expected from staff. Employment-related liability issues can be minimized by having a properly worded set of policies and procedures, as can other liability issues, such as conflicts of interest and sealing of drawings. Finally, policies and procedures may help management at times when potentially controversial decisions have to be made.

How a firm's policy manual is organized and distributed can be as important as what it contains. Policies and procedures should be clearly stated. All exceptions to company policies should be cleared through one person or decision body. And *always* get qualified outside legal help to review a policy manual prior to distributing it to staff members.

SPECIAL TOPICS

If you have a job without aggravations, you don't have a job.
—Malcolm Forbes (1919-1990)

12.1 INTRODUCTION

This chapter addresses 11 important topics that didn't fit neatly into any of the preceding chapters. Some of these topics are obvious parts of the well-accepted definition of HR management—things like equal employment opportunity/affirmative action, job descriptions, firing (currently, "dehiring"), contract employees and job shoppers, internal communication processes, and the future of human resources management for design firms.

Other topics in this section *don't* necessarily enter into traditional notions of what HR management is. Topics such as quality control, the conflict between designers and managers, issues of ownership, and organization are nevertheless addressed here because, as a little reflection will show, they have profound impact on other aspects of HR management in a design firm.

12.2 EEO/AFFIRMATIVE ACTION

Equal employment opportunity (EEO) is the legally established right of all persons to work and advance on the basis of merit, ability, and potential, free from discrimination because of race, color, religion, sex, national origin, handicap, or Vietnam-era veteran status.

The requirements for equal employment opportunity and affirmative action are unquestionably established in U.S. law. Their legal basis springs from the laws surrounding Title VII of the Civil Rights Act of 1964, as amended by the Equal Employment Opportunity Act of 1972 and the Pregnancy Discrimination Act of 1978. Supporting legal acts are the Equal Pay Act of 1963, the Age Discrimination in Employment Act of 1967 and its 1978 amendments, the Vocational Rehabilitation Act of 1973, and Presidential Executive Order 11246 (as amended). The latter requires that firms prepare two affirmative action plans (AAPs): one dealing with minorities and women, and the other dealing with handicapped workers, disabled veterans, and Vietnam-era veterans. Instructions for how to prepare these plans are available from various government contracting agencies as well as the Office of Federal Contract Compliance Programs (OFCCP), Equal Employment Opportunity Commission (EEOC), and the U.S. Dept. of Labor (DOL).

No design firm, least of all those that handle government contracts, can afford to ignore the issue of EEO/affirmative action. Many state and local government agencies may require that firms have an AAP for minorities and women during the selection process. Federal government design contractors with 50 employees and $50,000 per year in design contracts are required to have up-to-date affirmative action plans. Companies with design contracts worth over $1 million go through an EEO audit as part of an overall series of audits conducted by the OFCCP. State requirements for AAPs are not necessarily the same as federal requirements, and vice versa.

Still, the whole idea of EEO/affirmative action hasn't been taken seriously enough by most design firms. Firms that do go to the trouble to prepare affirmative action plans probably do so more out of necessity than out of commitment to furthering the causes of minorities and women. That's not to say that there aren't socially conscious design firm CEOs who feel strongly about the cause, but they are definitely in the minority. What drives most firms to attempt to comply is their desire to avoid problems with the government agencies who select them for design service contracts.

The procedure followed in an AA program is, first, to determine the percentage of the local population made up of protected groups (minorities, women, for example), the relative availability of the types of workers the firm employs, and the percentage of employees from protected groups in each job category. If these figures indicate any imbalance (which they often will in a typical design firm) the firm draws up policies, goals, and timetables to demonstrate an effort in good faith to remedy the situation. All affirmative action programs should include the following:

1. *Availability analysis* to determine the availability of workers in particular job classifications and geographical areas.
2. *Utilization analysis.* Underutilization means having fewer workers from protected categories in a job classification than would reasonably be expected based on their availability.
3. *Goals and timetables* to eliminate the underutilization of personnel that exists in any job classification.

4. *Equal employment opportunity policies* to govern the firm's personnel actions in hiring, training, transferring and promoting employees, along with all associated recordkeeping.

5. *Formal internal and external dissemination processes* for the firm's equal opportunity employment policy.

6. *Establishment of responsibility for the implementation of the affirmative action programs* of the firm.

7. *Plans to actively support community action and education programs* aimed at improving employment opportunities of workers in protected categories.

8. *Internal audit and reporting systems* to measure the progress toward the goals of the AAP.

Any firm (or office) with at least 50 employees should file an annual EEOC *Equal Employment Opportunity Employer Information Report (EEO-1)*. Forms are available from the EEOC or OFCCP. Once a firm completes an *EEO-1* form (or forms), a new form(s) will be sent to the company annually thereafter.

Design firms may at times be contacted by an agency representative for an audit or to follow up on an employee complaint. Frequently, audits come out of employee complaints on discrimination or as a result of a disgruntled worker who doesn't think he or she was compensated in accordance with the law. One question that frequently comes up is how to deal with the EEOC, OFCCP, or state or federal DOL representative when he or she calls. Here are three suggestions:

1. *Be prepared*. If you haven't done your homework, stall the representative for a few days or a week. Always be ready for a desk audit of your EEO/AA plans and support documentation. Get outside help from competent labor counsel, a consultant, or both if you need it.

2. *Cooperate*. Give the representative everything he or she needs. Don't act like you are hiding anything. Ask what you can do to help.

3. *Be nice*. Remember, these people are only doing their jobs. Treat them like you would want to be treated. Offer a cup of coffee or soft drink when meeting with them. Don't keep them waiting in the lobby. Don't ever be hostile or antagonistic—it will probably result in your coming under intensified scrutiny.

12.3 JOB DESCRIPTIONS

Developing job descriptions is usually one of the first tasks assigned to someone who is developing an HR management program in a design firm. As anyone who has ever done it can attest, it can be a painfully slow and drawn-out process. Just about every text on personnel and human resources management advocates the development of formal job descriptions for everyone in the firm. They are useful for personnel administration, for hiring, and for clearly defining responsibilities.

But as important as they can be, they are not one of the most critical parts of HR management. There are many design firms that have no formal job descriptions, yet are significantly more progressive in their overall human resources management orientation than others that do have them.

What keeps many firms from creating formal job descriptions is a feeling on the part of top management that employees will use them to fight doing what needs to be done. In a typical design firm environment, nothing could be further from the truth.

Preparing job descriptions for even a small firm can be a major undertaking. Job descriptions shouldn't be pulled from a book. They should instead be customized to meet the specific needs of the company they will be used in. Good job descriptions share four characteristics:

1. *They are based on functional responsibilities*—not on ownership, title, or years of experience.
2. *They are developed only after significant research.* This research isn't limited to outside sources; it should include input by supervisors, subordinates, and (most importantly) people functioning in each job to be defined.
3. *They are consistent in format.* If the job descriptions are all formatted differently, the distinctions between one position and another may not be clear.
4. *They are actually useful.* They clearly delineate responsibilities within the organization structure, and each is clearly identifiable on the company organization chart.

A process based on review and input from many people is really critical to developing good job descriptions. A good way to start the process is to sit down with the firm's key managers to decide what functional positions are required in the firm. Once this list is established, make some preliminary assignments of who would fit into each of the positions identified. Next, representatives from each of the company's job classifications should be asked to write down exactly what it is that they do. This can form the basis for the descriptions.

These lists of duties and responsibilities by position should be refined and added to by whoever is in charge of developing the job descriptions, and the person in charge should also include things such as the education, registration, and experience requirements for the job. The first drafts should then be sent to the supervisors for their comments. Then send the refined description for each position back to the individuals who occupy those positions for more comments and changes. Finally, top management should review and approve the descriptions before they are formally adopted (see Figure 12.1).

Each position should be classified as exempt or nonexempt for salary administration purposes. The *EEO-1* category (see Section 12.2 for explanation) should be noted on the job description so as to facilitate preparation of the required *EEO-1* reports mentioned earlier. It's also important to define each position's purchasing and contracting authority and to put this right on the job description. Too many

Job Description Format

(Title)

Reports to: _____

Status: _____ Job Group No: _____ EEO-1: _____

I. General Description and Examples of Work Performed:

_____

_____

_____

_____

_____

_____

II. Qualification Requirements:

A. Experience: _____

_____

B. Education: _____

_____

C. Registration: _____

_____

D. Knowledge, Skills, Abilities, and Attributes: _____

_____

_____

_____

III. Degree of Decision Making Latitude:

A. Purchasing Authority: _____

B. Contracting Authority: _____

C. Other Authority: _____

FIGURE 12.1   Sample job description format

times these things are ignored in job descriptions, and as a result they aren't widely known throughout the company.

Job descriptions shouldn't be so rigid that exceptions can't be made. Anyone who is currently functioning in a role should be "grandfathered" even if he or she doesn't have the exact background the company will require in any future individuals assigned to that particular role. Also, rigid salary structures based on a particular job description are not advised (see chapter 9). Exceptions will eventually have to be made at the high or low end of the spectrum.

Too many design firms, especially those that do lots of government projects, use billing classifications for the basis of salary administration and job classification. This is not recommended, as it can cause problems when delineating functional responsibilities in the organization. For example, there may be a need for four classes of design architects when working for a particular client on an hourly billing rate or cost-plus basis, yet internally there may not really be a need for four classifications to assign the various duties and responsibilities on job descriptions.

Generally speaking, the less internal position categories a firm has, the fewer HR management problems it will encounter on issues of pay, title, and who is responsible for what. There is a definite trend in the design industry to move away from vertical structures with lots of different positions in the hierarchy toward flatter structures with fewer levels of staff. Flatter structures tend to have less problems with communication, and they allow the firm to adapt more quickly to a rapidly changing environment.

12.4 CONTRACT EMPLOYEES/JOB SHOPPERS

Contract employees, or "job shoppers" as they are known in some circles, have been around a long time, but they haven't really been used to any great extent by any but the giant design and design/construction firms. In cases where design firms use independent contractors, it would be safe to say that many are on shaky legal ground.

Contract employees are people who function as independent contractors. They are technically self-employed. They are usually hired for some limited duration of time to achieve a particular result.

The determination of whether someone can be considered self-employed and therefore not subject to employee tax withholding requirements falls under the jurisdiction of the Internal Revenue Service (IRS). The IRS uses 20 factors or elements to test whether sufficient control exists to identify an employer-employee relationship. These were developed from an examination of cases and rulings to determine whether an individual is an employee. They are:

1. *Instructions.* A worker who is required to comply with other person's instructions about when, where, and how he or she works is ordinarily considered an employee.
2. *Training.* Training a worker by requiring an experienced employee to work
   with the worker, by corresponding with the worker, by requiring the worker

to attend meetings, or by other methods indicates that the persons for whom the services are performed want them performed in a particular method or manner.

3. *Integration.* Integration of the worker's services into the business operations generally shows that the worker is subject to direction and control. When the success or continuation of a business depends to an appreciable degree upon the performance of certain services, the workers who perform those services must be considered employees.

4. *Services rendered personally.* If the services must be rendered personally, presumably the person or persons for whom the services are performed are interested in the methods used to accomplish the work as well as the results.

5. *Hiring, supervising, and paying assistants.* If the persons or persons for whom the services are performed hire, supervise, and pay assistants, that factor generally shows control over workers on the job. However, if one worker hires, supervises, and pays the other assistants pursuant to a contract under which the worker agrees to provide materials and labor and under which the worker is only responsible for the attainment of a result, this factor indicates independent contractor status.

6. *Continuing relationship.* A continuing relationship between the worker and the person or persons for whom the services are performed indicates that an employer-employee relationship exists. A continuing relationship may even exist in cases where work is performed at frequently recurring though irregular intervals.

7. *Set hours of work.* The establishment of set hours of work by the person or persons for whom the services are performed is a factor indicating control, hence an employer-employee relationship exists.

8. *Full-time hours required.* If the worker must devote substantially full-time hours to the business of the person or persons for whom the services are performed, such person or persons have control over the amount of time the worker spends working and therefore restrict the worker from performing other gainful work. An independent contractor, on the other hand, is free to work when and for whom he or she chooses.

9. *Doing the work on an employer's premises.* If the work is performed on the premises of the person or persons for whom the services are performed, that factor suggests control over the worker, especially if the work could be done elsewhere. Work done off the premises indicates some freedom from control. However, this fact by itself does not mean that the person is not an employee. The importance of this factor depends on the nature of the service involved and the extent to which an employer generally would require that employees perform such services on the premises of the employer.

10. *Order or sequence set.* If a worker must perform services in the order or sequence set by the person or persons for whom the services are performed, that factor shows that the worker is not free to follow the worker's own pat-

tern of work but instead must follow the established routines and schedules of the person for whom the services are performed.

11. *Oral or written reports.* A requirement that the worker submit regular oral or written reports to the person or persons for whom the services are performed indicates a degree of control.

12. *Payment by hour, week, or month.* Payment by the hour, week, or month generally points to an employer-employee relationship, provided that this method of payment is not just a convenient way of paying a lump sum agreed upon as the cost of a job. Payment made by the job or on a straight commission generally indicates that the worker is an independent contractor.

13. *Payment of business or traveling expenses.* If the person or persons for whom the services are performed ordinarily pay the worker's business or traveling expenses, the worker is ordinarily an employee. To be able to control expenses, an employer generally retains the right to regulate and direct the worker's business activities.

14. *Furnishing of tools and materials.* The fact that the person or persons for whom the services are performed furnish significant tools, materials, and other equipment tends to show the existence of an employer-employee relationship.

15. *Significant investment.* If the worker invests in facilities that are used by the worker in performing services and are not typically maintained by employees (such as an office rented at fair market value from an unrelated party), that factor tends to indicate that the worker is an independent contractor. On the other hand, lack of investment in facilities indicates dependence on the person or persons for whom the services are performed for such facilities and, accordingly, the existence of an employer-employee relationship.

16. *Realization of profit or loss.* A worker who can realize a profit or suffer losses as a result of the worker's services (in addition to the profit or loss ordinarily realized by employees) is generally an independent contractor, but the worker who cannot is an employee. For example, if the worker is subject to a real risk of economic loss due to significant investments or a bona fide liability for expenses, such as salary payments to unrelated employees, that factor indicates the worker is an independent contractor. The risk that a worker will not receive payment for his or her services, however, is common to both independent contractors and employees and thus does not constitute a sufficient economic risk to support treatment as an independent contractor.

17. *Working for more than one firm at a time.* If a worker performs services for a multiple number of unrelated persons or firms at the same time, that factor generally indicates that the worker is an independent contractor. However, a worker who performs services for more than one person may be an employee of each, especially where such persons are part of the same service arrangement.

18. *Making service available to the general public.* The fact that a worker makes his or her services available to the general public on a regular and consistent basis indicates an independent contractor relationship.
19. *Right to discharge.* The right to discharge a worker is a factor indicating that the worker is an employee and the person possessing the right an employer. An employer exercises control through threat of dismissal, which causes the worker to obey the employer's instructions. An independent contractor, on the other hand, cannot be fired as long as he or she produces a result that meets the contract specifications.
20. *Right to terminate.* If the worker has the right to end his or her relationship with the person for whom the services are performed at any time he or she wishes without incurring liability, that factor indicates an employer-employee relationship.

Firms who treat employees as independent contractors expose themselves to significant liabilities. Some of these include:

1. Back taxes and penalties for failure to make payroll deductions for unemployment compensation insurance under the Federal Unemployment Tax Act and various state unemployment laws.
2. Back taxes and penalties under the Federal Insurance Contribution Act.
3. Liability to the IRS pursuant to subchapter C (Collection of Income Tax at Source of Wages) of the Internal Revenue Code.
4. Full tort liability to employees injured on the job, due to failure to maintain worker's compensation coverage on punitive independent contractors.
5. Fair Labor Standards Act liability for overtime pay, including liquidated damages.
6. Liability under the Employee Retirement Security Act for denial of fringe benefits.
7. Unintended coverage under state and federal anti-discrimination laws, labor relations laws, and other laws governing the employer-employee relationship.

Agreements that allow the firm to treat individuals as independent contractors when they really function as employees according to the IRS definition are not valid. If in any doubt, firms are probably better off treating the individual as a temporary employee under all of the terms and provisions of that classification within the context of their personnel policies.

Although contract employees offer the advantages of limited commitment and simplified payment and recordkeeping on the part of design firms using them, they can pose some problems. For example, project managers may see a benefit in using contract employees *before* borrowing an underutilized staff member from elsewhere in the organization, because the same markup or multiplier is not applied to the contract employee that is to the regular employee. Hence, internal transfer-pricing policies and procedures should be developed that encourage internal labor swapping *before* contract help is brought in.

Firms that prefer not to get involved in the potential hassles associated with contract employees have three options:

1. Hire these people through an outside agency that supplies temporary talent or contract labor. That way, the agency, not you, will be responsible for recruiting them in the first place and for withholding taxes and paying other mandated benefits.
2. Treat the person as a temporary employee. Create this classification with restricted benefits.
3. Move all existing independent contractors to the payroll of a legitimate contract or temporary labor firm. Pay the firm a reduced markup (15 to 25 percent) on those services over what they would normally earn (30 to 50 percent) because you recruited the person in the first place.

12.5 QUALITY CONTROL FROM AN HR PERSPECTIVE

High quality service is the outcome of effective human resources management in a design firm. Quality (or a lack thereof), is typically evidenced by four areas. They are:

1. The amount of repeat business a firm has with the same clients.
2. The appearance of a firm's plans, specifications, and report documents.
3. The characteristics of the designs the firm produces. Do projects win awards? Are the end users satisfied? Are all project goals for function and budget achieved?
4. The number of problems that crop up in the field on the firm's projects.

Quality control experts tend to concentrate on developing standard processes for design, production, and plan review, most of which break down sooner or later because of time or budget constraints or just plain lack of commitment on the part of management to enforce them.

The two really significant ways a design firm can affect quality over the long haul are by doing the following:

1. Select the best possible people for every position in the firm, train them, and do what's necessary to keep them. High staff turnover almost always leads to quality problems.
2. Ensure that the firm has clearly articulated values and standards for quality that are communicated to every employee in the firm. Do this through effective management training in supervision, through rewarding high quality, and by penalizing or sanctioning individuals who don't produce quality ac-

cording to the firm's definition. This is an important part of a firm's culture (see Chapter 5 for more on corporate culture for design firms).

These two tasks fall squarely on the shoulders of the HR manager, who needs to be involved heavily in recruitment, development, and retention of personnel and in molding the firm's culture.

12.6 DESIGNERS VERSUS MANAGERS

Ever since design firms began to resemble businesses, architects and engineers who *design* and architects and engineers who *manage* have gone their separate ways, mistrusting and misunderstanding each other. This wreaks havoc on a firm's human resources management. Why, ask the head-in-the-clouds designers, do *we* do all the work while *they* get all the rewards? What, ask the hard-headed managers, do *they* know about running a business?

Who comes out on top in this conflict? It's no news to anyone who has spent much time around a medium- or large-size design firm: design professionals who want just to design don't often advance. It's manage or perish. The question is, why do the best designers so seldom rise to the top of their organizations? The answer lies in the contrasting characters and skills of designers and managers.

A designer is someone dedicated to the arrangement of elements or details in a building, site, or other facility (in effect, a *thing*). In general, designers:

1. Are perfectionists and seek to optimize (find the single best solution).
2. Believe that profits are incidental to doing good design work.
3. Are more interested in objects and things than in people.
4. Believe design is an art and a science, while anyone can be a manager.

A manager, by contrast, is someone dedicated to the planning, organization, leadership, and control of people and resources in a firm. In general, managers:

1. Are pragmatists and seek to *satisfice* (find a reasonable solution under the conditions).
2. Believe that good design is incidental to making a profit.
3. Are more interested in people and their problems than in things.
4. Believe that management is an art and a science, while anyone can design.

What the best designers and the best managers have in common is a powerful urge to control. When things go well, the designer controls the project and the managers run the firm. But when their compulsion to be in charge draws designers or managers out of their respective dominions, conflict results.

The day-to-day pressures of managing a profit-making enterprise favor rational and skeptical thought processes over creative powers. The longer managers live with these pressures, the less interested they become in what seems to them the trivialities of a project's design and the less sensitive they are to the opinions of pure designers. Sometimes this leads to trouble. Managers tend to promise the sky to clients and expect the designers to make it happen. Management may then ignore designers' warnings of potential problems or liabilities in the project. If this happens too often, the firm suffers. The successful design firm is a mosaic of many successful projects, and it is chiefly the designers who are responsible for producing these projects.

Most designers are perfectionists who need to constantly evaluate, critique, and rearrange their own and others' designs. They become either mad or discouraged when their opinions on management or production are dismissed by the managers. In their zeal to command more time and resources for projects, designers often lose sight of the overall goals of the firm, which in the long run are more important than any single project. This is perpetually a point of friction between managers and designers, because each group thinks it knows where the true priorities lie.

There are those who argue that each member of the organization must be allowed to participate in the decision-making process, and it's true that all points of view should be consulted in decisions at the *strategic level*. Unfortunately, attempts at the implementation level to get managers involved in design and designers involved in management are usually disastrous, since it is rare to find a single individual who does both especially well. Every design professional in a firm has been trained as a designer. So it's not completely without reason that technical skills are sometimes taken for granted. On the other hand, good managers don't decide to become design professionals so they can manage A/E/P firms. They happen into it. And when firms spot management skills, they reward them because they are so rare. It's a matter of supply and demand. Naturally, this impedes the career progress of designers in design firms, in spite of the fact that the firm's line of business is to provide design services! But let's face it; unless a firm is turning out a truly unique product, it is good management and effective selling that make a profit and ultimately keep the firm going.

So how do successful firms manage the communication and conflict between designers and managers while at the same time respecting role specialization?

1. They find out what people do best and what they like to do. They then make every effort to see that they get to do it.
2. They constantly work at getting each group to respect the other, because neither designer or manager can survive without the other.
3. They solicit all points of view to determine mission and strategy, but once the course is set, they leave the steering to the pilots.
4. They know that designers who don't make good managers may make great business developers. Winning projects for the firm gets designers out of the "drone" pigeonhole.

There is a good reason that responsibilities for management and design have been divided, and a corresponding divergance of career paths evolved, in design firms. A certain amount of conflict between design and management will always exist. It's even healthy to the extent that it gets different perspectives into the open before a radical change is considered. The danger is in allowing conflict to tear apart the company through too much focus on internal issues and too little attention to working on projects and servicing clients.

12.7   THE IMPORTANCE OF OWNERSHIP

For most design professionals, owning a practice or being part owner of a larger practice is the ultimate goal. One of the strengths of the professional design service industry is that most firms are privately held and can deliver highly personalized services through professionals who bear a considerable degree of risk for the success of what they do. Ownership, or the potential for ownership, has long been used as a carrot in this industry to attract and keep the best professionals.

In spite of this fact, design firms of all types and sizes have problems dealing with this issue. When should someone be allowed to buy stock? Should the company give the stock away? Should the firm finance the purchase of stock? Should the firm have a wide base of ownership, or a small, tightly controlled group of owners? What are the requirements for stock ownership? What are the benefits and privileges associated with ownership? Should all of the firm's top management positions be staffed with owners? Should professionals who are not design professionals be allowed to purchase stock? Should there be performance standards for owners as there are for all other employees? Can or should owners be fired if they aren't carrying their weight?

To answer these questions adequately would require another complete book. The point is (from a HR management perspective), all of these issues should be thoroughly discussed and the resulting decisions should be communicated to all of the company's staff members. To ignore these issues and let things happen in a haphazard and unplanned manner can create major problems.

First, firms not addressing the issues surrounding stock ownership will undoubtedly lose some of their best staff to self-employment or competitor firms. Second, the whole issue of what it means to be an owner and how to deal with principals who aren't performing must be addressed unless the firm wants to be dragged down by a cadre of highly paid but unproductive people. And third, if all management positions in the firm *must* be held by owners, the firm better be taking steps to ensure that these individuals are competent in their roles.

12.8   DEHIRING/TERMINATION

Dehiring is the nouveau management term for the process of terminating, firing, or otherwise letting people go. Anyone who has had to tell someone they no longer have a job will attest that this is at best an unpleasant task.

Unfortunately, because of the cyclical nature of the design and construction industry, for most firms layoffs are inevitable at some point along the way. Also, because the whole process of employee selection is an inexact science and because so many firms don't even practice the basics of effective hiring, employees may not always work out. In these cases, they have to be dehired.

Firms dehiring people because of a decline in workload should consider the following:

1. Try to assess staff workload on a regularly scheduled, ongoing basis so as to minimize the short and quick swings between aggressive recruiting and massive layoffs. Some firms in this industry have actually been advertising for people at the same time they are laying off others in the same positions, just because the right hand doesn't know what the left is doing. Smart firms lay off because of an anticipated problem. Less well-managed firms do it after the problem has already been around for a while.

2. In the case of layoffs, make all decisions on who goes and who stays on the basis of merit. Don't let people go on a seniority basis only.

3. For firms laying off, assess how many people have to go in each area and make the cuts all at once. Firms dragging this process out over weeks and months demoralize all staff, even those the firms would probably never let go. Dragging out the layoff process often occurs because of management's tendency to procrastinate on dealing with the inevitable.

4. Make the cuts at the end the day on the last day of the week if at all possible. This suggestion applies to *all* dehiring situations. Letting people go the first thing in the morning, or at the beginning of the week always kills productivity. Friday afternoon at three or four o'clock is probably the best time to do it. It gives the affected employees and the rest of the staff time to cool off over the weekend. On the other hand, be considerate enough not to let people go the day before a major holiday or on their last day before taking a vacation. One firm was so anxious to let a senior architect go that they called the man at home on the first day of his vacation and asked him to come to the office. He went inside the office to get fired while his entire family waited in the car to leave for their trip.

5. After a layoff, call the remaining employees together and assure them the mass exodus is over and they are secure in their positions. This is a critical step in rebuilding morale.

6. Make sure that all decisions as to who stays and who goes are well-documented and justifiable, should you get involved in a wrongful-termination lawsuit from one or more of the dehired employees. Check the employee's personnel file for his or her original offer letter to ensure no long-term employment commitments had inadvertently been made. Consult competent labor counsel whenever there is the potential for a lawsuit.

7. Don't just lay off those at the lowest level in the firm. When cuts are required due to lack of work, they will probably be required at all levels. Too many firms just go after clerks, drafters, and secretaries, and never even consider cutting middle- and upper-level managers.

8. For firms having multiple departments or offices, an effort should always be made to see if any of those targeted for layoff could be transferred to another area in need of staff. Often, one office may be hiring while another is letting go.

9. Don't use lack of work as an excuse to fire a nonperformer. Too many firms simply don't have the guts to tell people the real reason they are going. Be honest with your staff.

10. Try to find laid-off staffers new employment. It's always in your best interests to do this, from both a public relations standpoint and from the standpoint of holding down your costs for unemployment insurance. The other benefit is that firms have no way of knowing who will end up being their client some day. One firm that laid off a senior engineer in their HVAC department and then went all out to find him a new position was well rewarded when the engineer went on to become one of their biggest clients after getting a job in a major government agency.

11. In cases where someone is being let go for nonperformance, be sure all documentation exists to justify it. If all of the performance appraisals suggest otherwise, and the person has a consistent record of receiving raises and bonuses, you may be putting yourself in a difficult position to defend. This is critical for all performance-related terminations, but particularly so when dealing with any member of a protected job class.

12. Use a termination checklist to be sure that all required steps are taken. Give the employee a chance to sign up for insurance continuation (as per COBRA—The Consolidated Omnibus Budget Reconciliation Act— requirements), collect all company credit cards and building keys, and so on. Figure 12.2 is one example of a termination checklist.

Terminated employees often feel rejected, scared, and betrayed— and sometimes even relieved. Termination ranks right up there with death of a loved one, moving, and divorce in terms of the stress-induced trauma it creates. Although the reaction of terminated employees varies greatly, almost all feel some grief over it. Anger is the emotion most managers who have to let someone go anticipate. Anger from terminated employees leads to bad-mouthing the firm, and, in some cases, stealing or sabotage. Often, threats are made by terminated employees—even design professionals.

Considering the traumatic nature of terminations for all concerned, the termination process should be planned carefully. Managers who anticipate the wide range of responses are apt to deal with the situation more effectively. Some hints for making termination meetings go as smoothly as possible:

1. Always talk with the employee who is being terminated privately. Do it in your own office, if it's private. Never send a memo or FAX to inform someone that he or she is being let go.

2. Bring along someone else, just in case problems erupt that would require a

Name/Title of Employee: _____

Office: _____ Department: _____ Last Date Worked: _____

Checklist Completed By: _____

_____ Insurance cancelled/converted per COBRA requirements. All insurance documents signed as required by employee.

_____ Termination report completed and filed in personnel file.

_____ Company car turned in, if required.

_____ Company credit cards turned in, if required.

_____ Company building keys turned in, if required.

_____ Company alarm system code changed, if required.

_____ Letter of resignation or termination memo entered to personnel file.

_____ Exit interview completed, notes prepared, routed, and entered to personnel file.

_____ Telephone number and forwarding address entered to personnel file.

_____ Expense account reconciled and final check cut, if required.

_____ Drafting, computer, and office equipment turned in.

_____ All library books returned.

_____ All project files returned.

_____ Marketing department notified of departure.

_____ All outstanding debts to company repaid (for example relocation expenses per agreement, signing bonus per agreement, loans, credit card charges, IOUs, and the like.)

_____ Final paycheck produced, including all accumulated vacation pay, severance (if required) pay, and compensation for time worked but not yet paid.

_____ Personnel file moved from active section to inactive section.

FIGURE 12.2   Sample termination checklist

witness. Write up notes on what happened in any termination meeting that develops into a volatile situation.

3. Be considerate and caring in your approach. Realize that the termination, for whatever reason, is going to be taken personally by the employee. Show that you are concerned for his or her well-being by offering to help in any way that you can.

4. Don't give two weeks' notice of being terminated. After it's over, help the employee get his personal belongings or have someone else go with the employee back to his or her work area to get their things so they can leave. Or, make arrangements to come back over the weekend or in the evening for the employee to clean out his or her office or work area. In any case, you don't want employees continuing to work after being notified that they are being let go. All they will do is stir up negative feelings in other employees or ill will in clients.

Letting one or more people go can be the worst experience any manager will ever have in his career. One design firm human resources director who, in one day, had to either sit in or personally notify over 20 employees that they were being let go, recalls that day as the worst day in his entire working career. It took him months to recover from the experience.

12.9 OUTPLACEMENT

Realizing that terminations are sometimes inevitable, what else can a design firm do to make it easier on the employee as well as on their own individual and collective consciences? The answer is to offer real help to the dehired employees in the form of outplacement assistance. The firm can either do it itself or use an outplacement consultant.

The advantages to outplacement include:

1. It minimizes public relations damage and avoids creating an image that the firm doesn't care about its people.
2. It controls unemployment insurance rates. One firm, after laying off over 10 percent of its staff in one year, got socked with a 3 percent increase in its unemployment tax rates. This means that on top of everything else going wrong with this company, their payroll expense went up 3 percent.
3. It can help the employee make his or her transition into another gainful employment situation faster and easier.
4. Occasionally, former employees end up working for clients. In those situations, the firm that has made every effort to help the employee who was let go can actually strengthen its relationship with the client.

The kind of assistance provided during outplacement largely depends on whether an outside consultant is used. Consultants who specialize in outplacement charge fees ranging from $3000 to $10,000 or more per person they take on. Their services usually involve providing counseling to the terminated employee, running him or her through an extensive battery of psychological, aptitude, and ability tests, preparing a resume, helping set up interviews, and coaching assistance throughout the interviewing/hiring process. High-end outplacement consultants may even provide offices for the outplaced employee, including unlimited telephone use and secretarial support. These kinds of consultants are rarely used in the design industry. When they are used, it is almost always for executive employees.

Do-it-yourself outplacement assistance that design firms can and should try to offer to their displaced staff members includes assistance in preparing and copying resumes, making contacts to competitors and friends in the industry to see if they have any need for someone with the dehired employee's specific background, and providing some coaching assistance in how to interview properly. These "stripped-down" outplacement assistance services are also available in some areas through outside consultants, often for fees as low as $400 or $500 a head. In any case, it is always a good idea to try to help the dehired employee find a new job, and it should be a regular practice to offer and provide whatever assistance the company can reasonably afford.

12.10 EXIT INTERVIEWS

Exit interviews allow you to probe the reasons people are leaving your company voluntarily, which gives the firm a chance to deal with these issues before losing more people. Regardless of the circumstances surrounding an employee's departure, an exit interview is usually a good idea. People are often more truthful in their "swan songs" than at any other time.

The exit interview should be conducted by someone skilled in the art of listening and note taking. Many of the suggestions given in Chapter 8 for career development meetings apply just as well to exit interviews. In order to find out someone's real reason for leaving, you need to use good interviewing techniques. In other words, ask probing questions and do a lot of listening.

Exit interviewers should find out what the person who is leaving liked and disliked about his or her job and the company. They should find out where the person is going, and whether he or she will have an increase in compensation. They should find out what the person's responsibilities will be in his or her new job. They should be able to get to the bottom of what is motivating the person to take a position elsewhere.

A good exit interview will take anywhere from 30 to 90 minutes. The notes should be prepared by a trusted secretary and confidentially routed to everyone from the CEO to the person's immediate supervisor. They should also be filed in the employee's confidential personnel file.

Some firms have found it useful to wait until a week or two after the employee has left to conduct the exit interview. That way, the person will have calmed down. A more objective interview could be the result of waiting until after the person is gone. Some experimentation may be required to determine what works best for you.

In any case, it makes good sense to conduct exit interviews. They are one of the best ways to shed light on a firm's human resources problems and, if the problems can be corrected, to aid in the retention of people you have spent money on to recruit and develop. But don't wait until it's too late—deal with your HR problems now.

Figure 12.3 is an example of a real-life exit interview report. This is typical of the feedback a firm can get through a well-conducted exit interview. The names, dates, and places have been changed to protect the individual's identity.

Sally Wu is a 32-year-old HVAC and plumbing designer who has worked for a mid-sized A/E firm for about three and one-half years. She is joining a small engineering firm that was founded by two former employees of her present company. A number of other veteran employees have already gone there.

Exit Interview Report
Name of Employee: Sally C. Wu
Interviewer: Mark C. Zweig
Termination Date: 1/29/87

FIGURE 12.3 Sample exit interview report

Zweig talked with Sally Wu for approximately 35 minutes. Following are the notes from that discussion:

Sally is going to work at Mechelec-Plumb Associates, the MEP company formed with Tsongas/Dobbs/Hilson's ex-mechanical and electrical engineering department managers. Her position will be that of HVAC designer, and she is going to work for a lower hourly rate than what she is currently earning at Tsongas/Dobbs/Hilson. She stated that she was not actively looking to make a job change, but felt the move was the best thing in the long run for her future.

Sally said that she came to Tsongas/Dobbs/Hilson from Benjamin Bassani & Partners in Mesquite, and that she felt Tsongas/Dobbs/Hilson was the best firm she had ever worked for. She did point out several potential problems, however, including:

1. Sally said that she didn't like having to work so much overtime. She averaged 48.3 hours per week last year, and had only two Saturdays off. That was a major problem for her, although she said not everyone feels it is a problem.

2. Sally wants to work on the kinds of projects she is accustomed to. She was assigned a refueling station project and said she just didn't feel comfortable with it.

3. Sally said she frequently needs information that she can't get. She said that although Dan Dillinger is an outstanding individual and engineer, he won't delegate any authority, which creates bottlenecks. She said Dan makes all decisions run through him, and yet is never available for consultation. Sally added that Barry Sims and Rob Richards were completely overloaded, too.

4. Sally said that she still needs guidance and, although she considers herself very competent in her field, she doesn't feel that she has good technical resource personnel in the MEP group whom she can count on for assistance when she needs it.

5. Although Sally participated in the company CADD training, she never touched the CADD the whole time she was with the firm.

6. Sally said that we set deadlines that just aren't realistic, and that they rarely met a deadline on any job she worked on. She summarized by saying that for the most part, deadlines just don't mean anything.

7. Sally feels that our building is a problem, and it's not that people don't have enough space. She said the problem is that people just don't know if we'll be moving to new quarters or not.

8. Sally said lack of leadership is a problem in her department. She said to put someone in the MEP department manager's position probably won't work, because as far as she can see, Dan won't let loose of the reins. She added that Dan is plenty smart and works hard but is almost overly concerned about quality.

9. Sally said that she is tired of working in a department that doesn't make any money. All she ever hears is that all MEP jobs are losers and that Dan, Rob and Barry all put out lots of negative vibes. She didn't know if it was that we didn't negotiate good fees, or if it was that we have such high overhead we can't be competitive.

10. Sally said she and most of the others in her department feel that MEP is a forgotten stepchild to the other disciplines in the firm.

11. Sally feels that we are taking on too many small projects in MEP that we should probably be walking by, especially considering the other in-house work.

12. Sally's final comments were that she felt she was appreciated at Tsongas/Dobbs/Hilson, and in the whole, was treated quite well by the company while she was here.

FIGURE 12.3 *(Continued)*

MCZ/slc

Copies to: Harvey Tsongas
               Jeffrey Almerici
               Deborah Hilson
               Dan Dillinger
               Ken Parkinson
               Sally Wu's personnel file

FIGURE 12.3 *(Continued)*

12.11 COMMUNICATION PROCESSES

It should be clear by now that communication is one of the most important keys to any human resources management program. Firms must keep open the channels for both one-way and two-way communication. Information should flow easily from firm management to employees *and* from employees to management. Even small firms constantly make the mistake of needlessly keeping staff in the dark on important management concerns that directly affect them and, by the same token, insulating principals from the concerns of staff until, in many cases, it is too late to do anything about them.

Good communication can be as simple as an informal discussion between two managers in a hallway, but it probably isn't a good idea to rely on the "grapevine" to collect or disseminate important information. That's why most organizations, including design firms, have created formal communication vehicles. These include:

1. Employee newsletters.
2. CEO presentations or talks with all or a group of employees.
3. Bulletin board postings or internal memo distribution of firm or organizational unit performance data.
4. Conducting attitude surveys and publishing the results.
5. Employee suggestion box programs.
6. Career development interviews (as described in chapter 8).

Employee newsletters (see Figures 12.4 and 12.5) range in cost and complexity from one-page documents done on a typewriter to four-color printed magazine pieces. But the form of a newsletter isn't nearly as important as the content. The employee newsletter offers top management a chance to communicate to staff its vision for the firm and confidence in the future. It's a great place to include news on company successes, such as new work, design awards, or satisfied clients. It's also a good place to put news on what's happening with employees both at work and home. Employees like a regular newsletter; it may help create the impression that the firm cares enough about its people to keep them informed. It may also help initiate new employees into the corporate culture.

Carter & Burgess Inkling

May/June 1987

PRESIDENT'S
MESSAGE

All of us have dreams and
aspirations for the future.
If we are to realize these
dreams, we must have a
Standard of Excellence to
help us succeed.

I would like to suggest some
things to consider in setting
a Standard of Excellence for yourself:

1. Develop a desire to do your best. Only you
   know when you have done your best at
   whatever you do.

2. Make decisions. Be decisive in what you say
   and do.

3. Do things with determination. Persevere in
   what you set out to do.

4. Develop your skills. If you are to be
   successful, you must continue to improve
   your abilities and skills.

5. Detach yourself from any bad environment.
   Get away from negative thoughts and negative
   actions.

6. Discipline yourself. Control your emotions
   and moods. And - a very important point -
   discipline your tongue in what you have to
   say.

7. Develop priorities. Each of us has only so
   much energy to expend. If we are to succeed
   in the things that we set out to do, we must
   develop priorities for our activities and
   then follow through on them.

8. Last, but certainly not least, ask for some
   divine guidance for what you are doing and
   for your life.

None of us will ever reach perfection in any of
these areas. However, if we work at improving
ourselves in each of them, we will stand a
better chance of fulfilling our dreams for the
future.

CARTER & BURGESS PROJECT JUDGED AS OUTSTANDING

A New Orleans project designed by Carter &
Burgess has been selected as one of Texas's
outstanding engineering projects of the year by
the Consulting Engineers Council of Texas. The
company was honored at CEC-T's 28th annual
conference in Austin on May 3-4.

We provided the civil, mechanical, and
electrical engineering, plumbing design, and
landscape architecture for the new headquarters
building housing the U.S. Army Corps of
Engineers for the New Orleans district.

This project is being used as a successful model
for future design/build and privatization
projects to be undertaken by the Corps.

NEW LOGO AND COLORS ADOPTED

A slightly modified version of the C&B logo and
script, including the words "Engineers-Planners-
Surveyors" has been adopted, along with new blue
and grey colors. All existing stock will be
used from now until September 1, at which point
new stationery, business cards, and
marketing-related materials bearing the logo and
script will be put in place.

This change was made to improve the appearance
of consistency between all three offices as well
as within each office; to better express what
services the firm does provide through the
addition of "surveying;" to reduce waste in
printing costs associated with the production of
incompatible materials; and to help project a
more contemporary image to our clients and the
public at large.

PROFIT SHARING AND 401(k) FUND PERFORMANCE

Following are the investment returns for the
quarter ended March 31, 1987, for the Carter &
Burgess, Inc. Profit Sharing Plan and three
401(k) contribution accounts:

Profit Sharing Plan	8.87%
Bond Fund	2.46%
Stock Fund	12.63%
Money Market Fund	1.59%

FIRM SELECTED FOR MAJOR PROJECT

Carter & Burgess was recently selected to
provide engineering services for a new $35
million Tarrant County Municipal Courts
Facility. The architect for the project will be
John Firestone of Fort Worth.

TECHNICAL TERMINOLOGY TEST

Recently spotted in The Chicago Tribune was a
"techno-speak trivia test," appropriate for all
engineers, planners, surveyors and technicians.
Test your skills by translating the following
(answers will appear in the next Inkling):

1. Avian species of identical plumage
   congregate.

FIGURE 12.4   Sample internal newsletter (Carter & Burgess)

The problem with employee newsletters is that some firms use them as the *only*
formal communication channel between management and employees. Newsletters
can be effective, but don't expect them to do too much. They are rather impersonal
and are not a substitute for old-fashioned interpersonal communication, especially
when it comes to communicating bad news. One other pointer: distribute the com-

2. Freedom from incrustations of noxious substances is contiguous with conformity to divine prescription.

3. Pulchritude possesses solely cutaneous profundity.

4. A superannuated canine is immune to indoctrination in innovative maneuvers.

5. Ululate not over precipitated lactal secretion.

6. All that coruscates with resplendence will not assay auriferous.

7. The existence of visible vapors from ignited carbonaceous materials confirms conflagration.

8. Mendicants are interdicted from elective recipiency.

9. Probity gratifies reflexively.

10. Male cadavers are unyielding of testimony.

11. Inhabitants of vitreous edifices ill-advisedly catapult petrous projectiles.

12. Ergonomia exclusive of diversion renders John a hebetudinous progeny.

13. He who cachinnates ultimately, cachinnates optimally.

FORT WORTH/DALLAS C&B PICNIC TIME AND PLACE ANNOUNCED

The annual company picnic for the Fort Worth and Dallas offices will be held on Saturday, July 11, at 2:00 p.m. The spot will be the Austin Patio Ranch, the same place we've used over the last couple of years.

All employees are encouraged to attend and to join in the festivities. Sign up sheets are going around now in the Dallas and Fort Worth offices. Don't miss out on this annual event!

NAMES IN THE NEWS

NEW EMPLOYEES - "Welcome Aboard!"

Steve Adams - Marketing Coordinator, Fort Worth
Richard Harrison - Lead Designer, Fort Worth
David Silva - Designer, Dallas
Barry Gilbreath - Maintenance Person, Fort Worth
Sonia Contreras - Mail Clerk, Fort Worth

PROMOTIONS - "Congratulations!"

Thad Brundrett - Associate, Fort Worth
Ed Oram - Associate, Fort Worth
Jeff Peterman - Associate, Fort Worth
Mark Zweig - Associate, Fort Worth
Robert Paul - Survey Technician, Dallas

TRANSFERS - "Good Luck in Your New Assignments!"

Tom Moore from Fort Worth, Civil to Dallas, Civil

MARRIAGES - "We Hope You Have Happy Lives Together"

Jerry Allen (Fort Worth, Principal) married Paula Ware on April 17, 1987.

Suana Schoen (Dallas, Civil) married Mark Jiminez on May 15, 1987.

BIRTHS - "Break Out the Cigars!"

Rick and Sue Lewis are the proud parents of a 7 lb., 13 oz. baby boy Jonathan James, born Thursday, May 14, 1987. Jonathan is their fourth child!

CORRECTION

In the last issue of the Inkling under "Names in the News," Ronald Smith who was promoted to Survey Technician in Dallas was incorrectly listed as Ronald Snider. Sorry for the error!

Ed.

Happy Father's Day, Dads! June 21, 1987

FIGURE 12.4 *(Continued)*

pany newsletter at the end of the work day. All too often, staffers will drop whatever they are doing to read the newsletter the minute it hits their in-boxes!

CEO talks are another communication technique used successfully in design firms. These may occur on a regularly scheduled basis, or they may take place whenever the CEO feels they are necessary. Some CEOs prefer to deal with small groups. Others like to address the whole company or office at the same time.

President's Newsletter

Vanasse Hangen Brustlin, Inc.   February 1989

*One of the most important benefit programs existing at Vanasse Hangen Brustlin, Inc. is our Profes-
sional Development Program. All of us at VHB are recipients of the benefits derived from this program,
either directly or indirectly. Directly, nearly 170 individuals at VHB actively participated in some form
of professional development in 1988--conferences, training seminars, professional society memberships
and meetings, and courses at local universities. Indirectly, all of us benefit from this program because
well-trained personnel are innovative in problem-solving and create a satisfying work environment.*

Our goal for professional development at VHB is simple and straightforward--yet requires planning and follow-up to assure its effectiveness. This goal can be stated as follows:

*Provide training and education
to all employees to enable them
to grow professionally
and to perform their duties in a
technically sound and
cost-effective manner.*

To achieve this objective, VHB invested nearly $250 thousand in 1988 in the following manner:

Conferences and Seminars:	
Registration and Consulting Fees	$ 64,000
Travel and Subsistence	$ 23,500
Professional Dues/Licenses	$ 33,500
Books and Periodicals	$ 20,000
Tuition Reimbursement	$ 20,000
Salaries of Participants	$ 83,500

Although the investment was significant, so were the accomplishments in 1988. Specific accomplishments were:

Public Speaking Course. Thirteen individuals from Traffic Operations were taught by an outside consultant for ten weeks and learned stress-free public speaking techniques. VHB employees are often called upon to make presentations to the general public. This course enhanced the firm's ability to communicate effectively.

Quality Manual. Developed by the Highway Department, this is VHB's first formal quality control process designed to reduce errors in the production of highway design drawings, specifications, and estimates. As a result of this effort, procedures are being implemented to plan for quality in the production process. The underlying message of this manual is "do it right the first time."

AutoCAD Training. Sixteen employees have been trained to use VHB's first CAD system. Individual work stations are located in Site/Civil, Highway, and Survey departments with plans to network these stations in the future.

Department Procedures Manual. Developed in the Site/Civil Department, this two-volume set establishes guidelines for producing high quality products. Volume 1 details office procedures for documenting work efforts, filing systems, and project management from a general overview of the project manager's role to the invoicing process. Volume 2 contains design guidelines and review procedures, technical summary papers developed within the department, and quality control checklists.

FIGURE 12.5   Sample internal newsletter (Vanasee Hangen Brustlin, Inc.)

Technical Papers. Several technical papers were written, presented, and ultimately published. These papers involved Transportation Planning in the private development sector and were presented at three national conventions of the Institute of Transportation Engineers:

Traffic Congestion '88 - Tampa, FL .
Annual Meeting - Vancouver, Canada
N.E. Conference on Congestion - Boston, MA

A Pavement Management Paper was also presented at a Technology Transfer Seminar sponsored by FHWA and the University of New Hampshire.

Professional Society Meetings. Many individuals attended meetings and conferences at both local and national professional societies. VHB has many people who actively participate as officers in local societies. Professional societies offer learning opportunities, keep you abreast of new techniques and advances in your field, and provide professional camaraderie. We encourage you to become an active participant in the society of your choice.

Seminars. During 1988, VHB staff attended several seminars on a variety of topics--both presented by employees and by outside agencies:

■ At 230 Western Avenue, luncheon seminars were held every two weeks covering a wide range of topics varying from specific technical issues such as advances in aerial photography to inviting a client to speak on "An Outsider's Perspective of Service from VHB."

■ In the Transportation Department, monthly luncheon seminars were held to inform staff about unique projects underway, use of AutoCAD in preparation of Traffic Signal Design, etc.

■ Attendance at seminars conducted by outside agencies included discussions on Project Management, Financial Planning & Accounting for the Design Firm, use of DBase III and SPSS standard computer packages, etc.

As we enter 1989, each of our technical areas and branch offices is preparing or has prepared Professional Development Programs to continue VHB's tradition of improving the quality of our work and providing technical training to all our staff. Specific plans for 1989 include:

■ The highly successful "Stress-Free Public Speaking Course" will continue with four 10-week sessions scheduled in Winter/Spring and Fall/Winter.

■ Additional support will be provided for technical paper preparation, luncheon seminar series, and outside seminar attendance in several technical areas.

■ Tuition reimbursement will be increased to a maximum of $2,500 per employee per year in recognition of rising college education costs.

We appreciate the input many of you have given in continually upgrading VHB's Professional Development Program and look forward to another successful year.

FIGURE 12.5 *(Continued)*

Whatever the size of the group addressed or the schedule of the meetings, these sessions can be great for morale. They let the CEO, who is often the most charismatic leader in a firm, personally sell staffers on management's plans for the future. Interested staffers can get questions answered straight from the horse's mouth (although smaller meetings tend to encourage this more than larger ones). These meetings can and will backfire if the company has a bland CEO who doesn't project confidence in the firm's ability to survive and prosper in a hostile environment. When the groups are addressed in shifts, problems can also crop up from false rumors circulating in between meetings.

Just about every firm posts memos on company bulletin boards or distributes them individually. Memos have their place, but just as with newsletters, problems remain if no personal communication is used to reinforce the message and allow for feedback. No one likes to first learn of something that significantly affects them through a memo. All too often, memos are sent because managers don't have the guts to deliver what could be perceived as negative news face to face.

There is a great motivational value to keeping design professionals informed of the profitability or productivity of their group and the company. People want a barometer of how they are doing. It gives employees a greater sense of control over their environment. It also makes the actions of management—which is usually reacting to performance data—more understandable.

Although some principals have a real reluctance to reveal financial performance information to staff, the benefits of doing so far outweigh the drawbacks associated with it. As long as the proper explanation is given with this kind of data, it can be an effective motivator to the staff. One firm posts a thermometer poster (similar to those used by the United Way during its fund drives) in the company lunch room. The thermometer shows where the firm stands in terms of actual billings and collections compared to goals. All employees know exactly how well they are doing, which is important because they also have their incentive compensation tied to the firm's overall performance.

Good news is always welcome. Management cannot send too many memos congratulating staff members for a job well done. One old-line company in the southwest regularly posts any letters praising the performance of the firm and its staff with a big gold star pasted on them. Another firm sends thank-you letters to spouses during periods of peak workload. These rituals really help boost morale in times of heavy workload and long work weeks.

Many design firms have at one time or another conducted an attitude survey. Most have found that while they can be interesting nothing really comes of them. They are usually some sort of questionnaire, the results of which are compiled merely to sit on the CEO's bookshelf for no one else to see. The problem with these kinds of surveys is that the guaranteed anonymity makes it all too easy for management to discard the feedback as not being representative of the opinions of those in the company they really care about. The other problem is that surveys tend to be one-shot exercises— the firm is not surveyed on some consistent and ongoing basis to see if things are getting worse or better over time. Repeating the same survey on a regularly scheduled basis and then having the guts to publish the results for all to see makes the process much more worthwhile as a bottom-up communication vehicle.

Employee suggestion boxes have been used by design firms with widely vary-ing degrees of success. Firms that encourage use of the suggestion box and then regularly monitor *and react* to the suggestions may find a suggestion box valuable. Firms that put in a suggestion box only to check it infrequently and then never do anything with the input will likely find a suggestion box useless. If nothing else though, perhaps it may at least provide a harmless means for employees to vent their hostility.

Last but not least is the career development interview process described in Chapter 8. This is probably the most costly of the communication vehicles described, in terms of the man-hours it requires to institute. It is, however, one of the best vehicles for two-way communication that you can put in place.

12.12   THE FUTURE OF HR MANAGEMENT IN THE DESIGN PROFESSION

What lies ahead for HR management in the coming decade? Considering the difficulty design firms are having in all aspects of human resources management—recruitment, development, retention, and minimizing employment-related liability exposure—and considering the fact that design firms provide professional services sold and delivered by *people*, it's not hard to imagine that HR management's prominence must increase as time goes on.

In spite of the increasing pressures on principals of all but the largest firms, to stay job-chargeable, the HR director's role will eventually become a principal one in the company. The function is just too critical for it not to be. It's already on equal par with the top finance and accounting positions, as well as the top marketing person, in some of the more progressive companies in the industry. The next decade will certainly see less HR professionals reporting to a finance or administration director, and more reporting directly to the firm CEO. It will also see recruiters rivaling business developers in terms of the rewards they receive for their work.

Employment-related liability exposure is an area of specialized knowledge that is a must for human resources professionals, and potential legal problems will require firms to pay more attention than ever before to human resources.

The exponential growth of technology in the design and construction industries means that staff members' skills will become obsolete at a faster rate than they did in the past. This, coupled with a declining supply of raw talent at the graduate level in many discipline areas will require a significantly increased investment in the areas of training and development than was ever seen before.

A greater portion of design professionals' compensation in the future will come in the form of incentives. There will be strengthened bonus programs with extended payout terms acting as "golden handcuffs" for key people. There will be a larger percentage of design professionals who own stock in their firms, although the share of ownership typically held by a principal will probably decline. Despite these things, there will probably be more job hopping than ever before. It's just the cyclical, regional nature of the design and construction industry; plus, the workers of the baby boomer generation are just not as loyal as their parents were.

CADD-skilled professionals, designers and technicians are rapidly replacing conventional drafters. Drafters will probably never go the way of the varitypist, but they will become far less common than they are today. In the next five years, computer skills will be a prerequisite for practically anyone in any position of responsibility in a design firm. With terminals much more widely available and more professionals versed in word processing and desktop publishing, design firms will probably have less secretarial support than they do now.

There will be less mid-sized, generalist firms, and more megafirms and small boutique-type single-discipline companies. All firms' organization structures will likely become flatter, with less levels of decision making and faster channels of communication. This will streamline decision making and allow firms to adapt more quickly to changing needs in the marketplace. More firms will adopt studio or permanently assigned team organization structures. Matrix project management organizations continue to function poorly in all but the biggest firms working on major long-term projects.

The technology for employee screening and monitoring is rapidly becoming more sophisticated. Big brother already has a foothold in the management of data entry and telemarketing workers, allowing supervisors to count the typists' keystrokes or randomly monitor workers' phone conversations. Many businesses retain outside security consultants to conduct polygraphs (which are illegal in many states), drug tests, or psychological tests of workers. Don't be taken in by any of these futuristic panaceas; these technologies may not have any place in a professional services firm. Professionals need and deserve to be treated as professionals. Nine out of 10 are as honest as the people that hire them. Managers who cannot trust their staffs are probably either too paranoid to be working in this industry or have done an abysmal job of recruiting their people.

The biggest change in the way design firms manage their human resources in the next decade will come from the new awareness that is developing in CEOs. The industry leaders have a new, expanded view of the human resources management function, once perceived to be the domain of pencil-pushing clerks who were at best a necessary evil. It is becoming increasingly evident to those at the top that the problems faced by professional services firms can only be solved by a highly capable and motivated staff of professionals. Dealing *strategically* with the human resources management issues of recruitment, development, retention, and minimization of employment-related liability exposure is quickly moving to the top of the CEO's agenda.

INDEX